Practical JBoss® Seam Projects

Jim Farley

Apress®

Practical JBoss® Seam Projects

Copyright © 2007 by Jim Farley

ISBN-13 (pbk): 978-1-59059-863-4

ISBN-10 (pbk): 1-59059-863-6

Printed and bound in the United States of America 9 8 7 6 5 4 3 2 1

Trademarked names may appear in this book. Rather than use a trademark symbol with every occurrence of a trademarked name, we use the names only in an editorial fashion and to the benefit of the trademark owner, with no intention of infringement of the trademark.

Lead Editor: Steve Anglin
Technical Reviewer: Floyd Carver
Editorial Board: Steve Anglin, Ewan Buckingham, Gary Cornell, Jonathan Gennick, Jason Gilmore, Jonathan Hassell, Chris Mills, Matthew Moodie, Jeffrey Pepper, Ben Renow-Clarke, Dominic Shakeshaft, Matt Wade, Tom Welsh
Project Manager: Kylie Johnston
Copy Edit Manager: Nicole Flores
Copy Editor: Ami Knox
Assistant Production Director: Kari Brooks-Copony
Production Editor: Elizabeth Berry
Compositor: Gina Rexrode
Proofreader: Nancy Riddiough
Indexer: Julie Grady
Artist: April Milne
Cover Designer: Kurt Krames
Author Cover Photo: Sandra Mallalieu
Manufacturing Director: Tom Debolski

Distributed to the book trade worldwide by Springer-Verlag New York, Inc., 233 Spring Street, 6th Floor, New York, NY 10013. Phone 1-800-SPRINGER, fax 201-348-4505, e-mail orders-ny@springer-sbm.com, or visit http://www.springeronline.com.

For information on translations, please contact Apress directly at 2855 Telegraph Avenue, Suite 600, Berkeley, CA 94705. Phone 510-549-5930, fax 510-549-5939, e-mail info@apress.com, or visit http://www.apress.com.

The source code for this book is available to readers at http://www.apress.com in the Source Code/ Download section.

This book is dedicated to Madeline. The world is better for her time in it.

Contents at a Glance

Contents

About the Author

■**JIM FARLEY** is a technology architect, strategist, writer, and manager. His career has touched a wide array of domains, from commercial to nonprofit, finance to higher education. Jim is currently a program manager at Pearson PLC and teaches enterprise development at Harvard's Extension School. Jim is the author of *Java Distributed Computing* and coauthor of three editions of *Java Enterprise in a Nutshell,* and contributes articles and commentary to various online and print publications.

About the Technical Reviewer

 **FLOYD CARVER** has been building software systems for over 20 years. During this time, he has performed in many roles, from developer to architect. Floyd's work has crossed several industries and continents. He has worked in the scientific, chemical, telecommunications, and retail industries for various-size companies, including Fortune 50 companies. He is currently providing consultant services as an applications architect. When not consulting, Floyd enjoys traveling, playing sports, and coaching for his community youth athletic association.

Acknowledgments

I'd first like to thank Gary Cornell, whose encouragement (bordering on nagging) started the efforts that eventually led to this book.

I'd also like to acknowledge the impressive editing and production team at Apress for their work on this book. In order of appearance, Steve Anglin, Kylie Johnston, Ami Knox, Elizabeth Berry, and a cast of others whose names are unknown to me shepherded this work and its author from the beginning, lending their talents and professionalism to it all along the way.

Finally, I have to thank my wife, Sandra Mallalieu, and my family, for tolerating yet another writing project and the preoccupation that it inevitably becomes.

Introduction

This book is a practical guide to JBoss Seam, a framework aimed at enhancing the development of Java EE applications. The goal of the book is to get you up to speed with Seam as quickly as possible by introducing the core Seam framework and key additional features, following a practical, projects-oriented approach.

Who This Book Is For

This book was written with enterprise Java developers in mind, especially enterprise Java developers who are hungry for a framework that will make their work easier. JBoss Seam is aimed squarely at this audience, and this book, as a guide to Seam, inherits its target demographic.

I wrote this book assuming that the reader is already proficient in Java programming, has done some web application programming (using Java or other environments), and is familiar (to some degree) with some of the key Java EE tools and APIs, such as JavaServer Faces (JSF), Enterprise JavaBeans (EJB) 3.0, and so forth. If you don't already know Java, you'll find it very difficult (but not impossible) to follow the material here. If you know Java but haven't tried your hand at web application development, you should be able to follow along, but some of the motivations for the Seam contextual component model, and for the various Seam services, may not be very apparent to you. If you're not familiar with JSF, EJB 3.0, and the other Java EE tools, you should be able to follow the material with just a few bumps in terms of specific technical details related to these tools.

How This Book Is Structured

The book is structured around the incremental development of a sample application (the "Gadget Catalog"). As we walk through the fundamentals of Seam and the framework services that it provides, we gradually integrate new capabilities into the Gadget Catalog using these Seam features. This provides you with a view of the practical issues involved in using Seam, as you watch a realistic web application unfold from chapter to chapter. Alternatively, if you decide to jump around and read about specific services of interest to you, the discussion in each chapter highlights the specific parts of the application that are affected by the integration of the specific service. So whether you decide to read the book in sequence or go "nonlinear," you should find that the material and the examples serve as an effective guide.

The first four chapters of the book cover the fundamentals of JBoss Seam, and really should be read whether you plan to use any of the other Seam services (security, pageflow, etc.) or not. The first chapter is an introduction to the overall framework and the model that Seam uses as the backdrop for all of its runtime services. The second chapter is a primer on installing and configuring Seam in your application and application server. The third chapter discusses the unified component model that Seam provides, bridging JavaBeans, JSF managed beans, and EJB 3.0 components. The fourth chapter discusses the runtime contextual model that Seam supports, especially the powerful concept of *conversations* that Seam introduces to web programming.

The last four chapters discuss a set of key services that are provided in the Seam framework. These services are pageflow support, security, business process management, and rich web client (i.e., AJAX) support. This is not an exhaustive coverage of the services included in Seam—there are several others that are not discussed here, such as e-mail support, PDF generation, and so on. I wanted to keep this book short and focused, so these four areas of the Seam framework were included because they are likely to be interesting to many readers, and they serve well as a backdrop (along with the first four chapters) for studying the remaining Seam services if you find them useful.

Prerequisites

The examples in this book were developed using JBoss Seam 1.2.1, the latest released version at the time of this writing. Certain configuration and code details will not work correctly in earlier versions of Seam, so please be sure you are using version 1.2.1 before trying out any of the examples. The examples were deployed to JBoss Application Server 4.0.5, with the exception of the "vanilla" Java EE example in Chapter 1, which was deployed to the Glassfish 1.0 application server. In theory, the examples should be deployable to other J2EE 1.4 or Java EE 5.0 application servers (as discussed in Chapter 2), but the example code has not been tested in any other environments.

In order to build and run the examples in the book, you will need a Java 5.0 (or later) environment and Apache Ant 1.6.5 (or later) to use the build scripts.

Downloading and Running the Code

All of the example code for the book can be found on the Apress web site, at http://www.apress.com in the Source Code/Downloads section. The code is arranged into separate directories for each chapter. Each chapter's code directory contains its own version of the Gadget Catalog application, with an Ant build script that you can use to deploy the application to your application server.

In most cases, you should be able to deploy the code by simply setting the `jboss.home` and `lib.dir` properties in `build.properties`, and running the `deploy-app` target in the build script.

Contacting the Author

You can contact Jim Farley at `jim@jimfarley.org`.

CHAPTER 1

■ ■ ■

Introducing Seam

The first thing to understand about Seam is that it's a framework. Actually, it's a framework that sits on top of another framework (Java EE), and that framework sits on top of another one (Java). But don't get distracted by that just yet.

That word "framework" is a broad one, adopting many meanings depending on how it's used (and who is using it). In this case, I mean "framework" in a typical software technology sense: Seam knits together a set of APIs and services into an environment that makes it easy (or easier) to write Java EE web applications.

A framework typically "makes it easier" to do something by simplifying common tasks and providing built-in utilities that you'd otherwise have to write yourself. Seam is no different. Seam is based on Java EE, so it satisfies its framework duties in two fundamental ways:

- *Seam **simplifies** Java EE*: Seam provides a number of shortcuts and simplifications to the standard Java EE framework, making it even easier to effectively use Java EE web and business components.

- *Seam **extends** Java EE*: Seam integrates a number of new concepts and tools into the Java EE framework. These extensions bring new functionality within the Java EE framework.

You'll get familiar with Seam in this chapter by briefly examining each of these aspects. In the rest of this chapter, I'll list for you the various services and utilities that Seam provides. In the chapters that follow, you'll see these services in action directly, applied in application development cases.

Seam Simplifies Java EE

The standard Java EE environment consists of the Java Standard Edition (Java SE) with all of its APIs (JDBC for database access, JAXP for XML processing, etc.) supporting all of the enterprise-level capabilities of Java EE (JSF/JSP/servlets for web components, JAX-WS for web services, etc.). Your application components are then built directly on top of this overall framework, as depicted in Figure 1-1.

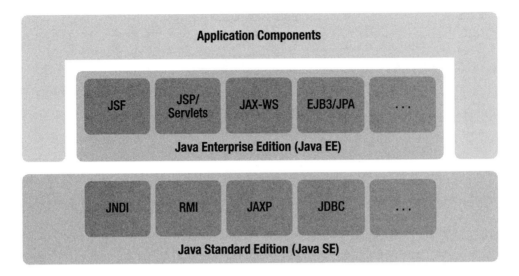

Figure 1-1. *Standard Java EE framework*

In addition to the APIs and component types depicted in Figure 1-1, Java EE also provides the deployment services, runtime security, and other services you need to create effective applications. And Java EE provides a number of improvements over its predecessor framework, J2EE, for example:

- Java 5.0 annotations are integrated liberally throughout the APIs in Java EE, giving you the option of using either externalized XML deployment data or embedded code annotations.

- The JavaServer Faces (JSF) 1.2, Java API for XML-based Web Services (JAX-WS) 2.0, and Enterprise JavaBeans (EJB) 3.0 APIs offer easier programming models than their J2EE predecessors, allowing you to implement most web, web service, and business components using simple JavaBeans.

- EJB 3.0 eliminates the need for many of the interfaces and other artifacts required in earlier versions of EJB, in most situations.

Even with the improvements delivered with Java EE, the JBoss Seam team saw room for simplifying things even further. Figure 1-2 depicts the Seam framework layered between your application code and the Java EE framework.

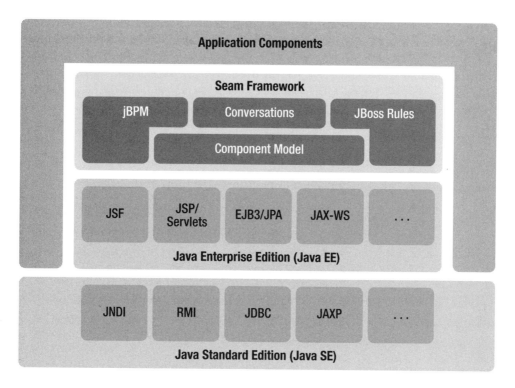

Figure 1-2. *Seam-enhanced Java EE framework*

The Seam Component Model

The simplifications provided by Seam stem mostly from the Seam component model—this component model can be considered, in essence, as an extension of the component model used for JSF managed beans. But it can be used for more than just web tier components, as you'll see in later chapters.

A key benefit provided by Seam's component model is the direct use of EJB components as backing beans for JSF pages. JSF's standard model allows for regular JavaBeans to be used as managed beans, configured in the JSF `faces-config.xml` file. EJB components can be invoked from the managed bean's callback methods, serving as a façade for the EJB component. Seam provides a direct bridge between JSF's component model and the EJB component model, allowing you to use an EJB directly as a JSF managed bean. This eliminates the need for extraneous façade beans when all you require is a single EJB.

Another simplification provided by Seam is the ability to use code annotations to directly bind beans to JSF component names, rather than writing `managed-bean` entries in the `faces-config.xml` file. The Seam component model includes annotations that can be used to link an instance of a bean directly to a JSF managed bean name. When the name is used in a JSF (one of its properties is used as the value of an HTML input field, for example), the bean instance will automatically be initialized, if necessary, and used as the backing bean for the JSF. There's no need to connect the bean to the JSF managed bean name using `faces-config.xml`.

The Seam component model also supports a more general version of dependency injection, called *bijection*. Standard dependency injection involves a one-time initialization of a bean reference within a component, typically done by some kind of container or other runtime service. Seam bijection extends this to support the following:

- *Two-way propagation of references*: A component can have a reference injected by the container, and a component can also "outject" a reference to the enclosing context as well.

- *Dynamic updates*: Instead of doing one-time injection of references, bijection is done on each invocation of the component. This is key in the Seam component model, since components can be stateful, and therefore they and their dependent beans can evolve across invocations.

- *Multiple contexts*: Dependencies (incoming and outgoing) can be established across multiple Seam contexts, rather than being forced to exist within a single context. So a session-scoped component can inject request-scoped beans and outject application-scoped beans, for example.

This may all sound a bit esoteric at this point, but the value of these features in the Seam component model will be clear once I show you some example code.

Running Example: A Gadget Catalog

The example we're going to use for much of the book is an online catalog of high-tech gadgets (mobile phones, laptops, digital media players, etc.). In coming chapters, we'll build up this application from the simple data entry tool described here into something a bit more interesting, and we'll also build solutions to other real-world cases, using the various capabilities of the Seam framework. But for now, we'll start with a very simple application that can only do two things:

- Display a list of gadgets contained in the catalog.

- Allow the user to enter a new gadget into the catalog.

At this point, our model for the application will be painfully simple: a gadget will only consist of a description (e.g., "Acme Powertop X1 Laptop") and a type (e.g., "laptop"). The data about these gadgets will be stored and managed in a relational database. The page-flow for the user interface will be equally simplistic: a main page will display the list of gadgets in the database and offer a single option to add a new gadget to the database. This option will bring the user to an entry form that prompts for the necessary attributes, and on submission the new gadget will be stored in the database, and the updated list of gadgets will be displayed again.

We can represent the "solution design" at this point with a pageflow diagram and a relational database diagram. The pageflow for the first iteration of the Gadget Catalog is shown in Figure 1-3, and the database structure (such as it is) is shown in Figure 1-4.

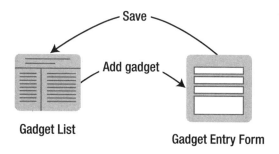

Figure 1-3. *Gadget Catalog pageflow*

GADGET	
TYPE	CHAR(3)
DESCR	VARCHAR(100)

Figure 1-4. *Gadget Catalog database*

Now all we have to do is build it. As a point of reference, let's first see what the Gadget Catalog looks like in the vanilla Java EE framework.

The Gadget Catalog Without Seam

The code for this example can be found in the code bundle for this book, under the `intro-JavaEE` subdirectory. In the Java EE framework, without JBoss Seam, the customary approach to implement the Gadget Catalog is to use JSF for the UI in conjunction with EJBs for the backing business logic and persistence.

To start, we'll implement an EJB 3.0 entity bean to represent the gadgets to be stored in the GADGET table. Listing 1-1 shows the Gadget bean. This is a simple EJB 3.0 entity bean that is mapped to the GADGET table using the EJB @Table annotation. The bean has two per-sistent properties: the description property is mapped to the DESCR column, and the type property is mapped to the TYPE column.

Listing 1-1. Gadget *Entity EJB*

```
@Entity
@Table(name="GADGET")
public class GadgetBean implements Serializable {
    private String mDescription = "";
    private String mType = "";

    public GadgetBean() { }

    @Id
    @Column(name="DESCR")
    public String getDescription() {
        return mDescription;
    }

    public void setDescription(String desc) {
        mDescription = desc;
    }

    @Id
    @Column(name="TYPE")
    public String getType() {
        return mType;
    }

    public void setType(String t) {
        mType = t;
    }
}
```

■**Practical Tip** Be careful about SQL reserved words used as EJB entity bean class or property names. Persistence engines may try to map them directly to auto-generated columns/tables, resulting in unexpected SQLExceptions. Notice that we called our GadgetBean property "description", rather than "desc". This is longer to type, but "desc" is reserved in some databases. If you decided to auto-generate the schema, a property called "desc" could be mapped into a column named "DESC", and problems could ensue. We're being extra careful here by using explicit @Column EJB3 annotations to map the properties to columns in our database model, so even if we auto-generated the schema (as we do in the sample code provided in the book's code bundle), we're sure not to run into issues.

In order to implement the functionality we've laid out for our Gadget Catalog, we'll need to be able to get a list of all gadgets currently in the database, and we'll need to be able to add a new Gadget to the database. Using a fairly typical "session façade" pattern for EJBs, we create a GadgetAdminBean session EJB to provide these functions. The code for this is shown in Listing 1-2.

Listing 1-2. GadgetAdminBean *Session EJB*

```
@Stateless
public class GadgetAdminBean implements IGadgetAdminBean {
    @PersistenceContext(unitName="gadgetDatabase")
    private EntityManager mEntityManager;

    /** Retrieve all gadgets from the catalog, ordered by description */
    public List<GadgetBean> getAllGadgets() {
        List<GadgetBean> gadgets = new ArrayList<GadgetBean>();
        try {
            Query q =
                mEntityManager.createQuery("select g from GadgetBean " +
                                           "g order by g.description");
            List gList = q.getResultList();
            Iterator i = gList.iterator();
            while (i.hasNext()) {
                gadgets.add((GadgetBean)i.next());
            }
        }
```

```
            catch (Exception e) {
                e.printStackTrace();
            }
            return gadgets;
        }

    /** Insert a new gadget into the catalog */
    public void newGadget(GadgetBean g) {
        try {
            mEntityManager.persist(g);
        }
        catch (Exception e) {
            e.printStackTrace();
        }
    }
}
```

This session EJB uses standard EJB 3.0 and Java Persistence API (JPA) calls to implement the required functions. We've marked this as a stateless session bean using the EJB 3.0 @Stateless annotation on the class declaration. We're also using the JPA @Persistence-Context annotation to inject a JPA EntityManager into this session bean, allowing us to perform the persistence operations necessary to query and insert into the gadget database. We're referencing a persistence unit named "gadgetDatabase", so we'll need to define a persistence unit with this name in the persistence.xml deployment file when we package up these EJBs.

The getAllGadgets() method loads the entire Gadget Catalog using a JPA query created from the EntityManager. The newGadget() method persists a new gadget (in the form of a GadgetBean) using the EntityManager.

These two EJBs seem to take care of our current needs in terms of persistence operations, so now we can turn our attention to the UI. To implement the UI we specified in the pageflow design earlier, we create two JSF pages, one for each of the pages we specified. The first JSF page displays the list of gadgets in the database along with a link to create a new gadget. In building these pages, let's assume we can access the persistence functionality we built earlier through a JSF managed bean named "gadgetAdmin". Our gadget list JSF is shown in Listing 1-3. It simply uses a JSF data table component to iterate through the gadgets returned from the getAllGadgets() operation on the gadgetAdmin bean, displaying each gadget as a row in a table. Then, at the bottom of the table, we generate a link that invokes a JSF action named "addGadget".

Listing 1-3. *Gadget List JSF Page*

```
<%@ taglib uri="http://java.sun.com/jsf/html" prefix="h"%>
<%@ taglib uri="http://java.sun.com/jsf/core" prefix="f"%>

<html>
<head>
    <title>Gadget List</title>
</head>

<body>
    <f:view>
        <h:messages/>
        <!--  Show the current gadget catalog -->
        <h:dataTable value="#{gadgetAdmin.allGadgets}" var="g">
            <h:column>
                <f:facet name="header">
                    <h:outputText value="Type" />
                </f:facet>
                <h:outputText value="#{g.type}" />
            </h:column>
            <h:column>
                <f:facet name="header">
                    <h:outputText value="Description" />
                </f:facet>
                <h:outputText value="#{g.description}" />
            </h:column>
        </h:dataTable>
        <h:form>
            <!-- Link to add a new gadget -->
            <h:commandLink action="addGadget">
                <h:outputText value="Add a new gadget" />
            </h:commandLink>
        </h:form>
    </f:view>
</body>
</html>
```

The addGadget action is supposed to bring us to the second page in our pageflow, the gadget entry form. The JSF page that implements this, addGadget.jsp, is shown in Listing 1-4.

Listing 1-4. *Gadget Entry JSF Page*

```
<%@ taglib uri="http://java.sun.com/jsf/html" prefix="h"%>
<%@ taglib uri="http://java.sun.com/jsf/core" prefix="f"%>

<html>
<head>
    <title>Add a Gadget</title>
</head>

<body>
    <f:view>
        <h:form>
            <table border="0">
                <tr>
                    <td>Description:</td>
                    <td>
                        <h:inputText value="#{gadget.description}"
                                     required="true" />
                    </td>
                </tr>
                <tr>
                    <td>Type:</td>
                    <td>
                        <h:selectOneMenu value="#{gadget.type}"
                                         required="true">
                            <f:selectItems value="#{gadgetAdmin.gadgetTypes}" />
                        </h:selectOneMenu>
                    </td>
                </tr>
            </table>
            <h:commandButton type="submit" value="Create"
                             action="#{gadgetAdmin.newGadget}" />
        </h:form>
    </f:view>
</body>
</html>
```

This page generates a simple entry form that prompts the user for a type and description for a new gadget for the catalog. The description field is a simple text entry field, while the type is a drop-down menu populated with allowed values from the GadgetTypes enumeration. Both fields are bound to properties on a new managed bean named "gadget". At the end of the form is a submit button that invokes the newGadget() operation on the gadgetAdmin managed bean.

At this point, as with any JSF application, we need to wire the JSF managed beans to classes in our model. We could try to associate the gadgetAdmin bean with an instance of our GadgetAdminBean session EJB and the gadget bean to our GadgetBean entity EJB, using entries in our faces-config.xml like this:

```
<faces-config>
    <managed-bean>
        <managed-bean-name>gadget</managed-bean-name>
        <managed-bean-class>GadgetBean</managed-bean-class>
        <managed-bean-scope>session</managed-bean-scope>
    </managed-bean>

    <managed-bean>
        <managed-bean-name>gadgetAdmin</managed-bean-name>
        <managed-bean-class>GadgetAdminBean</managed-bean-class>
        <managed-bean-scope>session</managed-bean-scope>
    </managed-bean>
</faces-config>
```

But what you'll find is that this won't work, at least not the way you'd expect. In JSF, managed beans are expected to be simple JavaBeans, and they'll be managed that way at runtime by the JSF container. When the gadget or gadgetAdmin beans are created and used at runtime, the JSF container won't follow the rules for EJB components when handling them. It won't, for example, use the EJB container to obtain an instance of the GadgetAdminBean, as you should for any session bean. Instead, it will try to construct instances of GadgetAdminBean directly, outside of the EJB container and all of its services. This obviously isn't what we want—we defined GadgetBean and GadgetAdminBean as EJB components because we wanted them to use the persistence and transaction management services of the EJB container.

In order to integrate our EJB components into our JSF pages, we need to create JavaBean wrappers that the JSF components can use directly. These JavaBean wrappers will then interact with the EJB components to get the gadget persistence done.

First, we'll have to write a simple JavaBean version of our GadgetBean entity EJB that can be used as the gadget managed bean. This JavaBean class, Gadget, is shown in Listing 1-5.

Listing 1-5. *Simple JavaBean for Gadget Values*

```java
public class Gadget {
    private String mDescription;
    private GadgetType mType;

    public String getDescription() { return mDescription; }
    public void setDescription(String desc) { mDescription = desc; }

    public String getType() { return (mType != null ? mType.name() : null); }
    public void setType(String t) { mType = GadgetType.valueOf(t); }
}
```

This JavaBean just carries the value of the gadget's properties between the JSF in the UI and the GadgetBean in the EJB container. It has the same two properties as our GadgetBean entity EJB, naturally.

Now, we need a JavaBean façade for our GadgetAdminBean session EJB. We'll be using this bean to implement JSF actions, so we call it "GadgetAdminAction". The code for this wrapper is shown in Listing 1-6.

Listing 1-6. *Action Wrapper for* GadgetAdminBean

```java
public class GadgetAdminAction {
    @EJB
    private IGadgetAdminBean mGadgetAdmin;

    // Managed property for our JSF action, populated with the
    // Gadget being operated in the current request (added/deleted/edited)
    private Gadget mGadget;
    public Gadget getGadget() { return mGadget; }
    public void setGadget(Gadget g) { mGadget = g; }

    /** Facade to the newGadget operation on the GadgetAdminBean */
    public String newGadget() {
        // Convert the Gadget into a GadgetBean and persist it
        GadgetBean bean = gadgetToBean(mGadget);
        mGadgetAdmin.newGadget(bean);
        return "success";
    }

    /** Facade to the getAllGadgets operation on the GadgetAdminBean */
    public List<Gadget> getAllGadgets() {
```

```
        List<Gadget> gadgets = new ArrayList<Gadget>();
        List<GadgetBean> beans = mGadgetAdmin.getAllGadgets();
        Iterator i = beans.iterator();
        while (i.hasNext()) {
            Gadget g = beanToGadget((GadgetBean)i.next());
            gadgets.add(g);
        }
        return gadgets;
    }


    public Map<String,String> getGadgetTypes() {
        Map<String,String> types = new HashMap<String,String>();
        for (GadgetType value : GadgetType.values()) {
            types.put(value.label(), value.name());
        }
        return types;
    }


    /** Convert a Gadget JavaBean to a GadgetBean EJB */
    private GadgetBean gadgetToBean(Gadget g) {
        GadgetBean bean = new GadgetBean();
        bean.setDescription(g.getDescription());
        bean.setType(g.getType());
        return bean;
    }


    /** Convert a GadgetBean EJB to a Gadget JavaBean */
    private Gadget beanToGadget(GadgetBean g) {
        Gadget ig = new Gadget();
        ig.setDescription(g.getDescription());
        ig.setType(g.getType());
        return ig;
    }
}
```

The GadgetAdminAction wrapper bean does two things: it converts GadgetBean entity
EJBs into Gadget JavaBeans for the JSF components with the beanToGadget() utility
method and also converts Gadget beans from the JSF beans back into GadgetBean EJBs to
persist them with the gadgetToBean() utility method. It also has a method for each operation on the GadgetAdminBean that we want to invoke as actions. The getAllGadgets()
method invokes the GadgetAdminBean.getAllGadgets() method and converts the list of
GadgetBean references into Gadget instances. The newGadget() method takes the managed

Gadget property and converts it into a new GadgetBean, and then passes it to the GadgetAdminBean.newGadget() method to be persisted.

Finally, we can wire these JavaBean wrappers into the JSF UI as managed beans, using the faces-config.xml file shown in Listing 1-7.

Listing 1-7. *JSF* faces-config.xml *for Java EE Gadget Catalog*

```
<faces-config>
    <managed-bean>
        <managed-bean-name>gadget</managed-bean-name>
        <managed-bean-class>Gadget</managed-bean-class>
        <managed-bean-scope>session</managed-bean-scope>
    </managed-bean>
    <managed-bean>
        <managed-bean-name>gadgetAdmin</managed-bean-name>
        <managed-bean-class>GadgetAdminAction</managed-bean-class>
        <managed-bean-scope>session</managed-bean-scope>
        <managed-property>
            <property-name>gadget</property-name>
            <value>#{gadget}</value>
        </managed-property>
    </managed-bean>

    <navigation-rule>
        <navigation-case>
            <from-outcome>success</from-outcome>
            <to-view-id>/listGadgets.jsf</to-view-id>
        </navigation-case>
        <navigation-case>
            <from-action>addGadget</from-action>
            <to-view-id>/addGadget.jsf</to-view-id>
        </navigation-case>
    </navigation-rule>
</faces-config>
```

Notice that, in addition to using the Gadget JavaBean as the gadget managed bean and GadgetAdminAction as the gadgetAdmin managed bean, we've also defined the pageflow in a navigation-rule section. Any "success" outcome should take the user back to the gadget list page, and the addGadget action we referenced in the link on the listGadget.jsp page should take the user to the addGadget.jsp JSF page.

The Gadget Catalog with JBoss Seam

The last few steps that we were forced to carry out in creating the plain Java EE version of the Gadget Catalog provide some of the motivation for the simplifications introduced in JBoss Seam. If you look back at the previous section, you'll notice that we had all the required persistence and UI functionality for the Gadget Catalog defined as of Listing 1-4. Everything that follows in the section is just overhead that's needed in order to bridge from the JSF components to the EJB components, and to configure everything. This "overhead" includes the following:

- The `Gadget` and `GadgetAdminAction` JavaBean wrapper classes

- The managed bean declarations in the `faces-config.xml`

The JBoss Seam project team saw these steps as wasted effort to be eliminated. Creating the JavaBean wrappers to integrate the JSF and EJB component models doesn't add anything to the functionality of the Gadget Catalog; it's just an implementation detail required because Java EE doesn't provide its own bridge between these two component models. And their philosophy on the `managed-bean` entries in the `faces-config.xml` file is that these represent missing code annotations in the JSF model. In EJB, virtually all of the details in the `ejb-jar.xml` deployment descriptors can (optionally) be replaced with code annotations in EJB 3. Why not give JSF programmers the same option with all those `faces-config.xml` options?

JBoss Seam eliminates both of these issues, making our Gadget Catalog simpler to implement when we use a Java EE server enhanced with Seam. First off, we can use our `GadgetBean` and `GadgetAdminBean` EJB components directly as managed beans within JSF pages. We no longer need the JavaBean wrapper classes, because Seam provides a bridge between the JSF and EJB component models.

Second, Seam provides a `@Name` annotation that can be inserted into our EJBs to specify their JSF managed bean names. Our updated `GadgetBean` EJB is shown in Listing 1-8.

Listing 1-8. *Seam-Enhanced GadgetBean Entity EJB*

```
@Entity
@Table(name="GADGET")
@Name("gadget")
public class GadgetBean implements Serializable {
    private String mDescription = "";
    private String mType = "";

    public GadgetBean() { }

    @Id
```

```
@Column(name="DESCR")
public String getDescription() { return mDescription; }
public void setDescription(String desc) {mDescription = desc; }

@Id
@Column(name="TYPE")
public String getType() { return mType; }
public void setType(String t) { mType = t;}
}
```

The only difference in the Seam-enabled version is the @Name("gadget") annotation at the start of the class. This annotation is equivalent to the "gadget" managed-bean entry in the faces-config.xml file shown in Listing 1-7. We can eliminate the "gadgetAdmin" entry as well if we put a corresponding @Name annotation on the GadgetAdminBean EJB class.

In summary, Seam has helped us to significantly simplify the implementation of our little application. There are fewer objects in our model, and the relationship between the UI views and the objects in the model makes more sense. You'll experience this again in Chapter 3, where we use an expanded version of our Gadget Catalog to examine the component model in JBoss Seam. There, I compare the object models with and without Seam, and show you direct evidence of the benefits of linking the EJB and JSF component models. That chapter also examines a number of other features of the Seam component model and the benefits that they bring.

Seam Extends Java EE

The previous section gave you a sense for the ways that JBoss Seam simplifies Java EE development, especially when it comes to applications using JSF and EJB components. This section quickly surveys the various extended capabilities that Seam provides in its framework. These capabilities are pretty compelling in their own right, even if the programming simplifications described earlier don't interest you.

Seam Component Services

I mentioned the Seam component model in the previous section because it serves as the basis for the JSF/EJB simplifications provided by Seam. The Seam component model also provides a number of powerful extended services on top of the Java EE framework.

All of the Seam component services discussed next will be explored in more detail in Chapter 3.

Seam Component Contexts

As with most Java EE component models, Seam components support various runtime contexts or scopes. Seam components support the typical contexts found in web components (request, page, session, and application scopes). But the model adds several additional contexts that can be useful in enterprise applications.

Seam components support an explicit representation of a stateless context, for example. This context isn't usually represented explicitly, because components with stateless context really don't have any context (context refers to the scope of the component state, and stateless components by definition have no state).

In addition, Seam components also have contexts for conversation scope and business process scope. The conversation context is a critical piece of Seam's overall web application model, so I discuss it next in its own section. I also devote Chapter 4 to the conversation model in Seam because of its importance in Seam and the many practical benefits it can bring to your application development.

The business process context represents state for a (possibly long-running) business process. Since business processes can run much longer than the lifetime of a request, a session, or even the application server itself, the business process context uses persistence services for its state data. Business processes also involve multiple users, potentially, so the context supports concurrent access as well.

Seam Conversations

Seam conversations are a very interesting and potentially powerful concept provided by the framework. One way to describe Seam's conversation concept is that it is a truly user-oriented transaction. Persistence transactions (like those managed in a JTA context) are typically defined around data consistency concerns, and business process transactions typically are defined around task dependencies and process structural consistency. Seam conversations provide another dimension of transactions, defined by what a user needs/wants to do within an application.

Another, less formal but more palatable, way to describe conversations is that they provide another layer between request scope and session scope in web applications. A conversation can group together data across multiple web requests, and it can track multiple groupings like this within a single user session.

Seam Events

JSF provides an event model in its component model, but Seam introduces two new types of events that can be utilized within Seam applications: *page actions* and *component-driven* events.

Seam page actions are events that you can have triggered after a user makes a web request, but before the requested web component or page is rendered. You can specify page actions that are to be invoked on request to specific views, or use wildcards to cover groups of views. Page actions are implemented by component operations (JSF managed bean methods and/or Seam component methods).

Seam component-driven events provide a general event notification scheme for Seam components. A set of named events can be defined, and component methods can be registered as "callbacks" on these events. Any component can trigger an event anywhere in its business code, and any component operations on the notification list will be invoked.

Integrated Pageflow with jPDL

Seam integrates jBPM into the framework in two ways. First, it's used to implement a rich pageflow capability. The jBPM Process Definition Language (jPDL) supports more complex and robust pageflows than JSF navigation rules can provide. jPDL pageflows are stateful, in the sense that the flow is defined as transitions between explicit, named states. jPDL pageflows are much more structured than JSF navigation rules—they define starting states, transitions, intermediate state nodes, and end states. And jPDL pageflows can be more explicit and externalized than JSF pageflows—transitions are defined around component actions and their outcomes, state transitions can themselves trigger state changes by invoking component methods, and so on.

You'll learn more about the pageflow capabilities provided by Seam and jPDL in Chapter 5.

Integrated Business Processes with jBPM and JBoss Rules

jBPM is also used in Seam to provide support for business process management in Seam applications. Business processes merge pageflow, transactions, task definitions, and rules to provide a way to define structured task flows. A business process defines what needs to be done and in what order, who needs to perform specific tasks or task types, and the rules under which all this happens.

In addition to jBPM, Seam also integrates the JBoss Rules framework into its business process services. These two capabilities work hand-in-hand to allow you to define and implement business processes in your Seam application.

You'll explore Seam's business process and rules engine support in Chapter 7.

Rich Internet Applications (aka Web 2.0)

You may have noticed the "Web 2.0" buzz word in the title of this book. I didn't add that just to sell books—Seam provides some powerful facilities for integrating rich Internet UIs into your Seam component model, providing interesting ways to plug your business logic directly into your client-side UI.

Seam supports rich Internet applications built using Asynchronous JavaScript and XML (AJAX) in two fundamental ways. First, it supplies a remoting capability for Seam components (mentioned earlier in this chapter) that allows JavaScript code to invoke your components directly from the client side of the web UI. Second, Seam supplies a set of JavaScript "shim" code that makes it easy for you to make use of this component remoting capability in AJAX contexts.

You'll explore this aspect of Seam in Chapter 8.

Read On

I largely mapped out the bulk of the book in the previous sections of this chapter. Chapter 3 provides a basic, practical overview of the core capabilities of Seam and its component model by creating an extended version of our Gadget Catalog application. Chapter 4 looks at Seam's conversation concept in depth, and how it can be used to more easily manage complex user interactions and easily support multiple concurrent "workspaces" for users. Chapters 5 through 8 explore specific extended capabilities that Seam provides within its framework (specifically, pageflow with jPDL, security services, business processes with jBPM and Rules, and rich Internet UIs with component remoting and AJAX).

But first, in Chapter 2, I discuss another practical issue related to any framework, including Seam. That is the installation, configuration, and debugging of Seam applications. These topics are a necessary evil that comes with developing applications using a framework. If you'd prefer to blissfully ignore these topics for now and jump right into the "fun stuff," you can safely proceed to Chapter 3 and get your teeth into the Seam component model right away. You should read Chapters 3 and 4 before proceeding on to the rest of the book, however, because the Seam component and conversation models provide the backdrop for all of the other capabilities integrated into the framework. And like it or not, if you do start using Seam "for real," you'll find yourself returning to Chapter 2 for assistance with the administrative details of Seam.

Summary

In this chapter, you've had a brief (but hopefully motivating) introduction to the capabilities JBoss Seam brings to the table when building Java EE applications. You saw how Seam simplifies Java EE by bridging its EJB and JSF component models, and how Seam extends Java EE with a number of additional capabilities, like structured pageflow, business process management, and rich web application support. You were also introduced to the Gadget Catalog application, which I'll use throughout the rest of the book to demonstrate all of these areas of Seam.

■■■■

CHAPTER 2

Seam Configuration and Administration

The title of this chapter isn't very compelling, but that's for a reason: this chapter discusses the dull but critical details related to the configuration of Seam applications. Before you can jump in and start writing applications with Seam, you need to set up your application deployment package with the necessary Seam libraries and configure your application code to "plug in" the Seam capabilities.

Much as you might want to ignore these issues, they are essential to actually working with Seam. A book with the title *Practical JBoss™ Seam Projects* would be remiss if it didn't cover these topics, and you'd be negligent if you didn't get familiar with them to some degree. Luckily, I've figured out a lot of the hiccups in installing, configuring, and debugging Seam applications for you, so read on to avoid learning these lessons all over again.

Preparing the Application Server

Seam expects certain standard APIs and services to be available in the application server where a Seam application is going to run. Depending on the type and version of application server you plan to use, the task of preparing the application server to run a Seam application can be more or less involved.

In this section, I'll first describe some basic requirements of Seam, and then discuss some specific environments and issues specific to getting Seam applications to run in these environments.

Java 5.0 Required

Regardless of the particular server you plan to use, Seam requires a Java 5.0 runtime, at a minimum. You can't use any of the annotations provided by JBoss Seam, or by EJB 3.0, in a Java 1.4 environment. If your application server does not operate in a Java 5.0 environment or isn't "certified" in that environment, you might want to reconsider using Seam, or switch to a different application server to run your Seam applications.

Before you do any of the installation I describe in the upcoming text, make sure you have a current Java 5.0 runtime installed on your system, and ensure that your application server is configured to use the Java 5.0 runtime. Java 5.0 for Linux, Windows, and Solaris can be found on the Sun Java site (http://java.sun.com). Apple provides their own Java runtime implementations for Mac OS X, and they are available through the Software Update tool on OS X.

JavaServer Faces

Seam integrates many of its core services (contextual components, web controls, etc.) into the JSF runtime environment. At the time of this writing, Seam is compatible with both JSF 1.1 and 1.2. A compliant Java EE 5.0 environment requires a JSF 1.2 implementation, but several "pre-Java EE" environments, such as JBoss 4, have either JSF 1.1 or 1.2 implementations bundled into their configurations. The JBoss 4.0.x releases, for example, use Apache MyFaces as their JSF implementation, and MyFaces is only compliant with JSF 1.1. But Sun has released a full reference implementation of JSF 1.2 that can be integrated into your application server if needed, and the Seam facilities are compatible with it.

Enterprise JavaBeans 3.0

Technically, it is possible to run JBoss Seam without an EJB 3.0 container. You'll be eliminating some of the interesting features of Seam, such as the use of session beans as JSF managed beans, but you can still make use of Seam's contextual component services, and many of the other Seam integrated features, such as jBPM and pageflow.

If your application server includes an EJB 3.0 container, you shouldn't have to do anything special to configure it for use with Seam. If your server doesn't have an EJB 3.0 container, you have a few choices, as explained next.

Running Seam with the JBoss Embedded EJB 3.0 Container

You can use the JBoss embedded EJB 3.0 container with Seam in your application. The embedded EJB 3.0 container can be embedded directly into your application (hence the name), allowing you to run EJB 3.0 components regardless of the application server capabilities. The advantage of this is that you don't need to alter any application server configuration details, which could be an issue in some situations. You may be running multiple applications on your server, for example, some of which need an EJB 2.1 environment. You could also be running in an environment where an operations group tightly controls the application server configuration (for very good reasons), and significant changes like this are difficult to implement globally.

Seam ships with the JBoss EJB 3.0 container, allowing you to embed it into your applications where needed. Integrating the embedded container into your Seam application involves the following steps:

Add the Embedded EJB 3.0 Configuration Files

All of the configuration files found in the `embedded-ejb/conf` directory in the Seam distribution (with the possible exception of `jndi.properties`) need to be available on your application's classpath. The `jndi.properties` file included in the `embedded-ejb/conf` with Seam is specialized for use with the JBoss application server. If you are running your Seam application in JBoss, you can use this `jndi.properties` file. If you are using another application server, you should not include this `jndi.properties` file, because it could cause your application to fail to connect to the application server's JNDI services to access runtime resources.

If your application is deployed as an enterprise archive (EAR) file, put these configuration files into the root of the EAR to ensure that all modules can "see" them on the classpath. If your application is deployed as a web archive (WAR) file, put these configuration files into the `WEB-INF/lib` directory of the WAR.

Install the Embedded EJB 3.0 Libraries

As of this writing, all of the libraries required for the embedded EJB container are located in the `lib` directory of the Seam distribution.

The specific libraries required are as follows:

- The `hibernate-all.jar` library, which includes all of the Hibernate classes that the embedded container uses for its JPA implementation

- The `thirdparty-all.jar` library, which includes several extra utilities used by the container

- The `jboss-ejb3-all.jar` library, which includes all of the classes that implement the EJB 3.0 container itself

Again, these libraries can be included in the root of your EAR file or in the `WEB-INF/lib` directory of your WAR file, depending on how you are packaging your application for deployment.

Configure the Seam EJB 3.0 Component

The EJB 3.0 embedded container ships with a Seam component, `org.jboss.seam.core.ejb`, that initializes the EJB container when the Seam application starts and shuts it down when the Seam application is undeployed. To install the component, you need to add the following to the Seam components.xml configuration file in your application:

```
<core:ejb/>
```

I'll discuss more details about the components.xml file in its own section later in this chapter.

Configure a Default DataSource

The embedded EJB 3.0 container is configured to use a default DataSource for its persistence operations. This default DataSource is configured to use an embedded Hypersonic Java database that the embedded EJB container initializes for you at startup. If you want to use this default DataSource with your EJB components, you'll need to reference it in your JPA persistence.xml file using the JNDI name "java:/DefaultDS". If you want/need to have your data persisted to a different database, you'll need to define your own DataSource for the EJB container to use. This is done by creating a jboss-beans.xml configuration file with the appropriate settings and placing it into the classpath of your application.

An example DataSource configuration is shown here:

```xml
<?xml version="1.0" encoding="UTF-8"?>
<deployment xmlns:xsi="http://www.w3.org/2001/XMLSchema-instance"
          xsi:schemaLocation="urn:jboss:bean-deployer bean-deployer_1_0.xsd"
          xmlns="urn:jboss:bean-deployer">
    <bean name="GadgetDSBootstrap"
          class="org.jboss.resource.adapter.jdbc.local.LocalTxDataSource">
        <property name="driverClass">
            <value>org.hsqldb.jdbcDriver</value>
        </property>
        <property name="connectionURL"><value>jdbc:hsqldb:.</value></property>
        <property name="userName"><value>sa</value></property>
        <property name="jndiName"><value>java:/GadgetDS</value></property>
        <property name="minSize"><value>0</value></property>
        <property name="maxSize"><value>10</value></property>
        <property name="blockingTimeout"><value>1000</value></property>
        <property name="idleTimeout"><value>50000</value></property>
        <property name="transactionManager">
            <inject bean="TransactionManager"/>
        </property>
        <property name="cachedConnectionManager">
            <inject bean="CachedConnectionManager"/>
        </property>
        <property name="initialContextProperties">
```

```
        <inject bean="InitialContextProperties"/>
    </property>
</bean>

<bean name="GadgetDS" class="java.lang.Object">
    <constructor factoryMethod="getDatasource">
        <factory bean="GadgetDSBootstrap"/>
    </constructor>
</bean>
</deployment>
```

The properties and attributes that you will likely have to change to suit your database are highlighted in bold in the preceding listing. The first bean entry in the file, with its name set to "GadgetDSBootstrap", defines a bootstrap service that will initialize the DataSource at runtime. The second bean, with its name set to "GadgetDS", actually puts the entry into the JNDI runtime services of the application server. The name of the boot-strap bean ("GadgetDSBootstrap" in the preceding example) needs to match the name of the bean referenced in the constructor factory element of the second bean. Also, the name of the second bean ("GadgetDS" in this example) needs to match the JNDI name you give to the DataSource in the bootstrap configuration. This is set in the "jndiName" property ("java:/GadgetDS" in this example).

Running Seam Without EJB 3.0

If you need to run your Seam application in a J2EE 1.4 environment, and you can't use the embedded EJB 3.0 container, you'll simply need to do without the use of EJB-based Seam components. You'll see the power of these components in Chapter 3, which explores the core component services in Seam. Without an EJB 3.0 container, Seam only allows you to use JavaBeans as Seam components. These are still very useful in them-selves, of course. But other advantages of the EJB integration, such as the ability to use EJB session beans directly as JSF managed beans, are no longer available, and you'll need to resort to JavaBean façades around your EJB components to integrate them into the JSF tier of your applications.

Configuring JBoss 4

The JBoss team developed Seam, so of course it integrates easiest with the JBoss applica-tion server. The JBoss 4 server, however, is a J2EE 1.4 server, which means some special measures have to be taken to enable the Java EE services that Seam expects.

The standard JBoss 4 download does not include the JBoss EJB 3.0 container. JBoss 4 is a J2EE 1.4–compliant server, and EJB 3 comes into the picture in Java EE 5.0. You can, of course, embed the EJB 3.0 container into each of your applications, as described in the previous section. It's much more convenient, however, to enable the EJB 3.0 container within the JBoss application server itself, so that all of your applications can make use of it.

It is possible to install the JBoss EJB 3.0 container into an existing vanilla JBoss 4 server—JBoss provides full details in the documentation for the embedded EJB 3.0 package. But thankfully the JBoss team has provided a much easier option—the JEMS installer. This is a smart installer for the overall JBoss Enterprise Middleware Suite (JEMS) and can automatically install various optional packages (including the EJB 3.0 container) into a new JBoss application server when you create it.

If you need to use Seam in an existing JBoss 4 server, and it does not have the EJB 3.0 container installed, download the embedded EJB 3.0 container from JBoss and run through the instructions to install it. If you can start from scratch with a new JBoss 4 server, get the JEMS installer from the JBoss, site and choose the EJB 3.0 option when going through the installer wizard.

Installation in a Generic Java EE 5.0 Environment

Since a Java EE 5.0 environment includes an EJB 3.0 container by definition, as well as JSF 1.2, there's nothing you need to add to a Java EE application server to make it ready for Seam.

One potential issue that you will encounter in a Java EE 5.0 environment is stricter validation of deployment descriptors and deployment archives in general. Java EE tightened up some of the rules concerning deployment details, and if an application server is truly compliant, you might find that some of your configuration details that have worked fine in other, less strict application servers will not deploy correctly in a fully compliant Java EE server.

One commonly encountered issue in this category when dealing with Seam applications is the specification of EJB interceptors. When using Seam with EJB 3.0 components, you need to include Seam's EJB interceptor in your EJB deployment descriptor, so that Seam can interject itself into EJB life-cycle events (see the section "EJB Component Configuration" later in this chapter). Some application servers (most notably JBoss) will allow you to include an interceptor in the `assembly-descriptor` section of the `ejb-jar.xml` file, without having a corresponding entry in the `interceptors` section of the deployment descriptor. Here's a typical `ejb-jar.xml` file for a Seam application:

```
<ejb-jar xmlns=http://java.sun.com/xml/ns/javaee
         xmlns:xsi="http://www.w3.org/2001/XMLSchema-instance"
         xsi:schemaLocation="http://java.sun.com/xml/ns/javaee
                             http://java.sun.com/xml/ns/javaee/ejb-jar_3_0.xsd"
         version="3.0">
    <assembly-descriptor>
        <interceptor-binding>
```

```
        <ejb-name>*</ejb-name>
        <interceptor-class>
            org.jboss.seam.ejb.SeamInterceptor
        </interceptor-class>
    </interceptor-binding>
    </assembly-descriptor>
</ejb-jar>
```

■Practical Tip It's a good idea to specify the XML schema that you are using in your XML files, especially with Java EE deployment descriptors. This is good XML practice, since it allows for development-time or runtime validation, but it's also a clear statement to the container about what level of the specification you are using. Some servers (JBoss and Glassfish are known offenders) will use the schema reference as a shortcut to see whether to enable various container services. Glassfish 1.0, for example, won't parse JPA annotations in web components if you don't use the servlet 2.5 schema in your web.xml.

Having said that, however, I'm going to omit the schemas from the XML examples for the remainder of this chapter, and the book. I do this for the sake of brevity only, and because the schema location isn't usually relevant to the example at hand. The code examples included with this book include XML configuration files with schemas referenced whenever possible. If you're curious about which schema to import and how, you can refer to the example code directly.

In a Java EE–compliant server like Glassfish, you may need to include the corresponding interceptors entry in order for your archive to deploy properly:

```
<ejb-jar>
    <interceptors>
        <interceptor>
            <interceptor-class>
                org.jboss.seam.ejb.SeamInterceptor
            </interceptor-class>
        </interceptor>
    </interceptors>
    <assembly-descriptor>
        <interceptor-binding>
            <ejb-name>*</ejb-name>
            <interceptor-class>
                org.jboss.seam.ejb.SeamInterceptor
            </interceptor-class>
        </interceptor-binding>
    </assembly-descriptor>
</ejb-jar>
```

This is a good habit to follow whether you are using a Java EE server or not, since it makes your application more "server-proof" in general, especially if you make heavy use of EJB interceptors.

Installation in a Generic J2EE 1.4 Environment

If you want to deploy a Seam application to a J2EE 1.4 environment, you'll need to consider each of the technical components mentioned earlier, since none of them are guaranteed to be present in a J2EE 1.4 application server.

- *Java 5.0*: Verify that the application server can run in a Java 5.0 virtual machine. J2EE 1.4 only requires support up to Java 1.4, so you may find compatibility issues with your particular server. If you simply cannot run your server in Java 5.0, you cannot run a Seam application on that server.

- *JSF*: JSF is not a required element of J2EE 1.4 servers, so unless your application server bundles it as an extra feature, you will need to install the Apache MyFaces or Sun reference implementation of JSF 1.1 or 1.2. You either install the required libraries directly into the application server or add the libraries to your Seam application(s) directly, as described earlier in the section "JavaServer Faces." If you want to install JSF in the server itself, consult the administration documentation for your application server for the details on how this is done.

- *EJB 3.0*: J2EE 1.4 requires an EJB 2.1 container. As mentioned previously, you can opt to run a Seam application without using Seam's EJB support and stick to basic JavaBeans for Seam components. If you do want to enable Seam's EJB support, your best bet is to use the JBoss embedded EJB 3.0 container, following the steps outlined earlier in the section "Running Seam with the JBoss Embedded EJB 3.0 Container."

Configuring a Seam Application

Once the application server environment is ready, you can turn to "Seam-enabling" your application. The basics of enabling Seam are fairly simple to start. The configuration of your Seam application becomes more complex as you start to use more of the optional services provided in the framework.

In this section, I'll cover the most common configuration needs for a Seam application. I'll start with the libraries and configuration details that you must provide in order for the core Seam services to function. Along the way, I'll also point out some common-but-optional configuration steps that you should be aware of when starting your Seam application.

Specifics on configuring the various optional services in Seam (pageflow, security, BPM, etc.) will be covered in their respective chapters. The material here provides an essential backdrop for those details, however, since I describe the general purpose of the various Seam configuration files within the framework. Once you understand their general purpose, the details in the later chapters are just a matter of understanding specific options you can include in these configuration files.

Install Seam Core Libraries

Like any software, Seam needs code to run. At the bare minimum, any Seam application must include the core Seam library, jboss-seam.jar, in its classpath. If you are deploying your application as an EAR file, the most convenient (and portable) way to include the library is to put it in your EAR file and add it as a java module in the application.xml file. This ensures that any web or EJB modules in your application also have the Seam library available. If you put the jboss-seam.jar file in the root of the EAR file, for example, you would reference it in the application.xml file like so:

```
<application>
    <display-name>Practical Seam: Configuration</display-name>
    <module>
        <web>
            <web-uri>myWebStuff.war</web-uri>
            <context-root>/myApp</context-root>
        </web>
    </module>
    <module>
        <ejb>myEJBs.jar</ejb>
    </module>
    <module>
        <java>jboss-seam.jar</java>
    </module>
</application>
```

If you are deploying your application as a WAR file, you would just drop the jboss-seam.jar file into the WEB-INF/lib directory of the archive.

There are numerous support libraries included with Seam that you may or may not need to include in your application archive, depending on how you are using Seam. Most of these will be covered in later chapters, when I discuss the various optional services available in Seam.

Configure Facelets

One general "service" that you will likely want to use with your Seam applications at some point is Facelets. Facelets is not tied in any deep way to Seam—it is a separate open source project, operated within Sun's java.net community, that provides an XML-based alternative to using JSPs for page views in a JSF-based application. If for no other reason, you might want to use Facelets because nearly all of the Seam sample applications use it for their views, and Seam ships with a tool that generates application shells, including template Facelets pages. Also, several of the more recent Seam features, such as its PDF and e-mail facilities, actually require Facelets. But Facelets does provide some interesting advantages over JSP that might lead you to use it independent of these other concerns.

Because of its use of Facelets, Seam ships with all of the required Facelets libraries. As of the 1.2 release of Seam, these libraries reside in the `lib` directory of the Seam distri-bution.[1] You'll need to include the following libraries in your application's classpath in order to enable Facelets in your application:

- jsf-facelets.jar

- el-api.jar

- el-ri.jar

Like the Seam library, you can include these as `java` modules in your `application.xml` descriptor, or just place them in the `WEB-INF/lib` directory of your web archive(s). Before including these in your application archive, though, make sure your application server does not bundle them in the server classpath by default, since having them in both the server classpath and your application classpath can cause class loading issues in some situations.

In order for Facelets-based pages to be parsed correctly, you also need to install the Facelets view handler into the JSF runtime environment. This is done by adding the following to your `faces-config.xml` file:

```
<faces-config>
    . . .
    <application>
        . . .
        <view-handler>
            com.sun.facelets.FaceletViewHandler
        </view-handler>
        . . .
    </application>
    . . .
</faces-config>
```

---

1. Like other JBoss projects, the Seam distributions tend to change in significant ways, even in "minor" point releases. So the precise location of these libraries in your version of Seam might vary.

Some of Seam's services provide enhanced JSF Expression Language (EL) syntax features. Seam's security features, for example, allow you to optionally make use of extended EL functions in your configuration files and JSF pages, in order to drive your application's security aspects. In these cases, to enable the extended EL functions, you'll need to use Seam's specialized Facelet view handler:

```
<view-handler>
    org.jboss.seam.ui.facelet.SeamFaceletViewHandler
</view-handler>
```

Web Component Configuration

Each Seam application must configure some core Seam *plug-ins* in their deployment descriptors. These plug-ins inject themselves into the standard processing cycle of JSF and EJB components, and implement the core component and contextual capabilities of Seam. I'll discuss the nature and benefits of these services in Chapters 3 and 4, but for now, suffice it to say that these various plug-ins are necessary for Seam to function properly.

Seam JSF Phase Listener

At the heart of Seam's component and context services is the Seam JSF phase listener. It receives events from the JSF runtime during request processing, allowing Seam to keep its various contexts in their proper state, among other things.

The Seam phase listener is installed in your `faces-config.xml` file:

```
<faces-config>
    . . .
    <lifecycle>
        <phase-listener>org.jboss.seam.jsf.SeamPhaseListener</phase-listener>
    </lifecycle>
    . . .
</faces-config>
```

Seam Servlet Listener

In order to initialize the Seam core services and to correctly manage some Seam contexts that are in common with standard web container contexts, you have to install the Seam servlet listener in your `web.xml` deployment descriptor:

```
<web-app>
    . . .
    <listener>
        <listener-class>org.jboss.seam.servlet.SeamListener</listener-class>
    </listener>
    . . .
</web-app>
```

Optional Seam Web Features

There are several basic but optional web features that Seam provides, with some simple configuration requirements of their own.

Seam ships with a number of servlet filters that can be individually enabled in the Seam components.xml file (described in the next section). Each of these filters provides some basic functionality in the context of a web application, such as more flexible exception handling, or easier handling of multipart form submissions. In order to use any of these filters in your Seam application, you first have to configure the primary Seam filter in your web.xml deployment descriptor:

```
<web-app>
    . . .
    <filter>
        <filter-name>Seam Filter</filter-name>
        <filter-class>org.jboss.seam.web.SeamFilter</filter-class>
    </filter>
    <filter-mapping>
        <filter-name>Seam Filter</filter-name>
        <url-pattern>/*</url-pattern>
    </filter-mapping>
    . . .
</web-app>
```

Once the base Seam filter is in place, you can add any of the other optional Seam web filters to your application as well, with additional filter entries in your web.xml.

In addition to these back-end web filters, Seam also provides several very useful JSF controls that you can use in your JSF pages for things like validation of JSF form submissions and automatic data conversion. In order to use these JSF controls, you must include the Seam UI library, jboss-seam-ui.jar, in the classpath of your web archive. Again, this is done by placing the library into the WEB-INF/lib directory of the WAR file.

EJB Component Configuration

If you plan to use Seam with EJB components, you need to install the Seam EJB interceptor in your EJB deployment descriptor:

```
<ejb-jar>
    . . .
    <assembly-descriptor>
        <interceptors>
            <interceptor>
                <interceptor-class>
                    org.jboss.seam.ejb.SeamInterceptor
                </interceptor-class>
            </interceptor>
        </interceptors>

        <interceptor-binding>
            <ejb-name>*</ejb-name>
            <interceptor-class>
                org.jboss.seam.ejb.SeamInterceptor
            </interceptor-class>
        </interceptor-binding>
    </assembly-descriptor>
    . . .
</ejb-jar>
```

This entry will apply the Seam interceptor to all EJB components that you deploy as part of your application. The Seam interceptor allows EJB components to be used as Seam components, by "plugging" them into the Seam component life cycle when you annotate your EJBs with the Seam @Name annotation.

In addition, you need to tell Seam how to find EJB components in your application server's JNDI services. This is done with an entry in the components.xml file. See the next section, "Seam Configuration Files," for details.

Seam Configuration Files

The first part of this chapter discussed how to configure the application server features that Seam requires at runtime, and you've seen the required configuration entries that you need to include in the web and EJB deployment descriptors, and the faces-config.xml file, of your Seam application.

Now, I'll discuss the configuration files specific to the Seam framework. At this stage, I'll introduce the basic purpose of each configuration file, so that it's clear what role each one plays in general. The remaining chapters will constantly be revisiting these configuration files, since virtually every Seam service makes use of one or more of these to configure its runtime behavior.

seam.properties

Let's start with the most important Seam configuration file, `seam.properties`. This configuration file is the most important, not because you need to configure a lot of things in it, but because Seam's core component services won't operate correctly if this file is absent from your deployment archives. Seam will not scan an archive for component definitions unless it has a `seam.properties` file sitting in the root or the `META-INF` directory of the archive.

It's possible to use `seam.properties` to specify properties for Seam components, but it's more typical to do this in the `components.xml` file discussed in the next section. Components are "installed" into your Seam application in `components.xml`, so keeping all of the component configuration in this one file makes things cleaner overall.

components.xml

The `components.xml` file is used to configure Seam components. The `components.xml` file normally sits in the `WEB-INF` directory of your WAR file. But it can also be placed in the `META-INF` directory of any of your application jar files, or in any directory of an archive that has at least one component annotated with an `@Name` annotation. If you are deploying a WAR file, however, it's probably best to put the `components.xml` file in its `WEB-INF` directory, so that it's easy to locate.

The `components.xml` file is typically used to configure Seam's core components, enabling support for the various Seam runtime services (jBPM, pageflow, security, etc.). You can also use `components.xml` to declare and configure your own application components, if you'd like. But typically your application components will be declared and named using an `@Name` annotation in the code for the component.

An entry in `components.xml` typically looks like the following:

```
<components>
    . . .
    <component name="com.myorg.mycomponentimpl">
        <property name="myproperty1">someValue</property>
        <property name="myproperty2">someOtherValue</property>
    </component>
    . . .
</components>
```

Some services, however, can use their own XML formats for the configuration details in `components.xml`. The Seam security services, for example, have their own schema for the configuration details, which you would reference in the root element of the `configuration.xml` file. In the following example, we're including the schema references in the file, so that we can see how the security service schema is referenced and used in the configuration:

```
<components xmlns="http://jboss.com/products/seam/components"
            xmlns:security="http://jboss.com/products/seam/security"
            xmlns:xsi="http://www.w3.org/2001/XMLSchema-instance"
            xsi:schemaLocation=
                "http://jboss.com/products/seam/security
                http://jboss.com/products/seam/security-1.2.xsd">
    . . .
    <!-- Setup the Seam security component -->
    <security:identity authenticate-method="#{login.login}"/>
    . . .
</components>
```

It is possible to deploy a Seam application with little or nothing in the `components.xml` file. This won't be the case in a typical application, because any Seam service you use will probably involve some kind of configuration data to operate the way you require. If you are using any EJB 3.0 components as Seam components, you do need to provide a minimal `components.xml` file in your application. In order for Seam to interoperate with the EJB container, you need to include an entry for Seam's core initialization component, and this entry needs to include a setting for the JNDI pattern that Seam should use to find your application's EJB components in the JNDI services of the application server. The following example shows how this setting is provided for the JBoss application server:

```
<components>
    <component name="org.jboss.seam.core.init">
        <property name="jndiPattern">myApplication/#{ejbName}/local</property>
    </component>
</components>
```

In this example, the "myApplication" portion of the JNDI pattern represents the context root of the application, and the "#{ejbName}" portion is an EL expression that refers to the name of the EJB, as specified either in its `@Entity`, `@Stateless`, or `@Stateful` annotation, or in its `ejb-jar.xml` entry.

pages.xml

As the name implies, the `pages.xml` configuration file is used in Seam to specify various properties for page views within your application. The `pages.xml` file is placed in the `WEB-INF` directory in your WAR file. A `pages.xml` configuration file doesn't make any sense unless there are web pages involved, so a WAR file is the only place where you can provide a `pages.xml` file.

A number of useful Seam features can be applied to your pages in `pages.xml`, including the following:

- *Page actions*: You can specify actions on components that should be invoked before a page is invoked.

- *Page navigation*: The same navigation rules that you define in your `faces-config.xml` file can optionally be placed in pages.xml. These describe how users should be taken from one page to the next, depending on the outcome of actions they trigger in the pages.

- *Error handling*: You can specify what should be done (redirect to a page, generate a JSF message, end the current conversation, all of the above) when errors occur on your pages.

- *Conversation management*: A page can be configured to automatically start or end a conversation context when it is rendered.

- *Security*: Using Seam's security services, you can specify declarative security constraints on your pages, saying what pages require authenticated users, who can access them, and what roles they require.

I'll discuss the specifics of how most of these are configured in `pages.xml` when I cover the related services in later chapters of the book.

Some Seam applications may have no need to use a `pages.xml` configuration file at all. The application may not need to use page actions or the other features specified previously, or these features might be configured in other ways (e.g., the navigation rules are placed in `faces-config.xml`). But most Seam applications will make use of a `pages.xml` file, since there are often page-specific settings that you want to provide, and this is the logical way to do that in Seam.

Summary

This chapter provided a summary of the configuration and administration requirements for a Seam application. You started with a look at how the application server is configured to properly run Seam applications. You saw how the JBoss server can be configured to use Seam, and then explored the general issues with running Seam in a generic Java EE 5.0 application server and in a J2EE 1.4 application server.

Next, you learned how a Seam application itself is configured, in terms of the libraries and configuration files that need to be present to "Seam-enable" an application. The various entries required in the standard Java EE deployment descriptors were described, along with the various Seam configuration files and how/why they are used.

Once you've read through this chapter, you should have an understanding of what it takes to get a working Seam environment and a basic Seam-enabled application configured. In the rest of the book, you'll study the capabilities that Seam provides, and how these various configuration areas are used to control how these capabilities work at runtime.

CHAPTER 3

▪▪▪

Component Fundamentals

In this chapter, we're going to explore the core capabilities of Seam's component model, which is at the heart of all of the services provided by the framework. We'll do this in a practical way (of course), by building out a (slightly) more complete version of the Gadget Catalog application that I introduced in Chapter 1. As you move along in the chapter, you'll see me demonstrate the key capabilities of the Seam component model by adding these extensions to the Gadget Catalog application.

■Caution Java EE combined with Seam is different from just plain Java EE. As you move along through this chapter and the ones that follow, I'll try to highlight the important differences between life in standard Java EE versus life in Java EE plus Seam. There will be times when this may seem a bit daunting, especially if you're not completely versant in Java EE. Stick with it and walk through the sample code I provide in the book's code bundle as you read this chapter. You won't be disappointed in the richer development framework that Seam provides once you master its various services and capabilities. It's a satisfying experience to master any framework that helps you do good things faster.

Seam Component Types

Seam provides a broader component model for Java EE, one that subsumes, in a sense, both the JSF and EJB component models. Note that Seam doesn't replace these other component models. Instead, it tries to unify them into a single component model that can be used (almost) interchangeably between JSF and EJB contexts.

If you put the various types of EJB components together with Plain Old Java Objects (POJOs) and JavaBeans supported by JSF, you have five options for implementing Seam components:

- JavaBeans/POJOs

- Stateless session EJBs

- Stateful session EJBs

- Entity EJBs

- Message-driven EJBs

It's important to understand from the outset that, while Seam makes it possible to use all of these component types in general, there are specific cases where the different types can be used and cases where they can't and/or shouldn't be used. Rather than describe each of these situations in an analytical fashion, I'll take a more practical approach (naturally). Let's look at some common development contexts in web applications and the types of Seam components that can be applied to them. The first two, form backing beans and action listeners, are directly supported by JSF, but native JSF only supports the use of regular JavaBeans for these, and the use of EJB components in these contexts is more complicated than you might like. The last context, browser-accessible components, is not supported directly by JSF at all. So here again, we're seeing how Seam both simplifies and extends Java EE.

Form Backing Beans

Backing beans are a common pattern used in Java web frameworks, including JSF and Struts. In JSF, backing beans are the targets of JSF forms and are also used to inject data into JSF pages. Standard JSF supports the use of JavaBeans/POJOs as form backing beans. The Seam component model extends this to allow EJB 3.0 components to serve as backing beans within JSF web applications as well.

If you think about the EJB component model for a minute, you'll realize that the best fit for backing beans are stateful session EJBs or entity EJBs. These types of EJB 3.0 components are meant to represent client state data, which aligns very well with their use as backing beans. If you really don't need the container services offered by EJB components, however, such as life-cycle management and instance pooling, plus persistence management in the case of entity EJBs, you'll probably want to stick to regular JavaBeans or POJOs for your backing beans.

You shouldn't use stateless session EJBs as backing beans, because their component models just don't make sense for this purpose. This isn't a limitation imposed by Seam or JSF, it's simply the nature of how stateless session EJBs are managed by their container. Stateless session beans are considered "shared property" among the clients hitting the application, with no association to any particular client. Backing beans, however, need to have an association with a single client session in order to be consistent with the transactions that the client is carrying out.

Message-driven EJBs are ruled out as backing beans for the same reason (the EJB container manages message-driven beans much like stateless session beans), but also because their purpose is to handle incoming JMS messages from clients. This isn't really relevant when dealing with backing beans in a web context—the client is interacting directly with the beans through their web requests. If any asynchronous and/or remote messaging is necessary behind the scenes, the backing beans can act as clients to the JMS destinations served by the message-driven beans. But having message-driven beans act directly as backing beans for JSF views isn't useful in general.

Action Listeners

Action listeners are used as the target of form submissions and command links in web applications. They act as part of the controller in the MVC design pattern supported by frameworks like JSF and Struts. Action listeners perform whatever business logic is necessary to handle the data provided by users in their requests. This might include making perisistence calls to store the information, changing the state of the user interface, or whatever else is required to satisfy a user's request.

As with backing beans, standard JSF supports the use of JavaBeans or POJOs as action listeners, but Seam extends this to also support the use of some types of EJB components as action listeners. The natural choice for an action listener is a stateful session EJB, since its component model matches nicely with the life of an action listener—the bean can hold state on behalf of a client (good for accepting data as part of a form submission), and the container can provide instance pooling for them (which helps in terms of scaling up to support many web requests). Stateless session beans can also serve as action listeners, but they are limited in the sense that they cannot carry any state (hence the name). If you find yourself in a situation where the action listener really doesn't need any state, stateless EJBs can provide some performance/scaling benefits (since they can be freely pooled and reused by incoming clients). But you'll probably find that in most cases the action listener needs to keep some state for the client, making a stateful session EJB the best fit.

It's technically possible to use entity EJBs as action listeners in Seam, but this isn't usually the appropriate design choice. Action listeners typically implement business logic, not just simple persistence operations. It often makes more sense to use a session bean for the action listener, and then have the session bean implement any needed persistence using internal calls to entity EJBs. But if you find yourself in a situation where an entity EJB would really be handy as an action listener, Seam supports this.

Of course, if none of the EJB component services are useful for your situation, you can still use a POJO as an action listener and still make use of the other Seam component services this chapter will describe.

Browser-Accessible Components

There are times when you need to access your server-side components remotely, either from another server-side process (potentially on a different server) or from a client. EJB

3.0 supports remote access (via RMI or CORBA) to session beans, and message-driven beans are inherently remote-capable, since a JMS destination can typically be accessed from distributed messaging clients.

The Seam component model introduces another form of remote access—direct component calls from client-side JavaScript. As you can imagine, this capability was built into Seam components primarily to support AJAX applications, where web user interfaces need to make server-side updates out-of-band of the regular HTTP request protocol of the browser.

You can make just about any Seam component accessible in this remote fashion, although accessing message-driven beans directly through an AJAX call doesn't usually make much sense. As we mentioned earlier about using them as backing beans, message-driven beans are created to support JMS messaging clients. Invoking them directly in addition to having the JMS "interface" usually means you are giving too much responsibility to a single object. It's likely a better idea to define a separate session or entity EJB (or a simple POJO or JavaBean), and have both the browser JavaScript and the message-driven bean invoke this separate bean to do the "heavy lifting."

Full details on remoting components in Seam will be discussed in Chapter 8.

Extending the Gadget Catalog: Managing Types

To demonstrate the various types of Seam components and their runtime services, we'll create an extended version of the Gadget Catalog application introduced in Chapter 1. In that version, the user was simply able to add new gadgets to the catalog by providing a short description and choosing from a canned list of gadget types. These gadget types were hardcoded into the system, in the form of the GadgetTypes enumeration. This isn't a very practical solution, of course, since the types of gadgets we might want to manage will change over time. Changing the source code to keep up with the dynamic electronics market is a losing battle, as any self-respecting gadgeteer will tell you.

So, we're going to extend our data model, as shown in Figure 3-1, to add a new GADGET_TYPE table to store a type code and description for each gadget type. Our UI page flow will also be extended, as shown in Figure 3-2, to add a new branch that allows users to create new gadget types. The gadget entry page will also be changed, to pull the type list from the GADGET_TYPE table rather than a fixed enumeration.

GADGET	
GADGET_ID	LONG
TYPE_ID	LONG
DESCR	VARCHAR(100)

GADGET_TYPE	
TYPE_ID	LONG
LABEL	VARCHAR(20)
DESCR	VARCHAR(500)

Figure 3-1. *Updated Gadget Catalog data model*

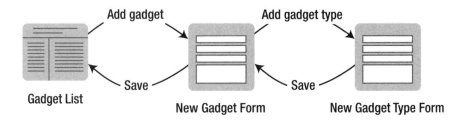

Figure 3-2. *Updated Gadget Catalog page flow*

Of course, we'll have to make the code match up with these design changes, and we'll use these enhancements to demonstrate the Seam component services discussed in the rest of this chapter.

Component Services

Now that you've been introduced to the types of Seam components and the general situations where they can be applied, we're going to look in detail at the specific runtime services that Seam's component model brings to the table for application development. We'll do this by integrating these capabilities directly into the extended version of our Gadget Catalog sample application.

Component Name Binding

Standard JSF components (backing beans or action handlers) are bound to names using entries in the `faces-config.xml`. You saw an example of this in our "vanilla" Java EE version of the Gadget Catalog, as shown in Listing 3-1.

Listing 3-1. *Standard JSF Component Binding in* `faces-config.xml`

```
<faces-config>
    <managed-bean>
        <managed-bean-name>gadget</managed-bean-name>
        <managed-bean-class>Gadget</managed-bean-class>
        <managed-bean-scope>session</managed-bean-scope>
    </managed-bean>
    <managed-bean>
        <managed-bean-name>gadgetAdmin</managed-bean-name>
        <managed-bean-class>GadgetAdminAction</managed-bean-class>
```

```
        <managed-bean-scope>session</managed-bean-scope>
        <managed-property>
            <property-name>gadget</property-name>
            <value>#{gadget}</value>
        </managed-property>
    </managed-bean>
    . . .
</faces-config>
```

In this case, we're binding two beans to JSF component names. Our Gadget bean is bound to the component name "gadget", and our GadgetAdminAction bean is bound to the name "gadgetAdmin". We can then refer to these components in our JSF pages. In our addGadget.jsp page, for example, we use the Gadget bean as the backing bean for our form:

```
    . . .
    <h:form>
        <table border="0">
            <tr>
                <td>Description:</td>
                <td>
                    <h:inputText value="#{gadget.description}"
                                required="true" />
                </td>
            </tr>
    . . .
```

Seam extends and simplifies the configuration of components. It extends it to support the broader array of component types supported by Seam, as discussed earlier in this chapter. Seam components can be POJOs, JavaBeans, or EJBs, and they can be used in JSF and non-JSF contexts, so naturally Seam can't rely strictly on JSF configuration files to configure its components. Also, Seam simplifies component configurations by giving you the option to specify these component name bindings using code annotations rather than as entries in an XML configuration file. Seam also provides its own XML configuration file, components.xml, for its components. But in most cases the preferred approach is to use code annotations, so I'll spend the bulk of this section discussing that approach, and then at the end I'll give some details on the components.xml file.

Seam's primary code annotation for binding components is the @Name annotation. Using the @Name annotation on a class will automatically bind an instance of that class to a JSF component name. You've already seen this in action in our Gadget Catalog. We bound our GadgetBean entity EJB to the "gadget" component name by annotating the class as shown in Listing 3-2.

Listing 3-2. *Binding a Component Using an* @Name *Annotation*

```
. . .
import org.jboss.seam.annotations.Name;
. . .
@Entity
@Table(name="GADGET")
@Name("gadget")
public class GadgetBean implements Serializable { . . . }
```

We did the same for our GadgetAdminBean class, binding an instance of it to the component name "gadgetAdmin".[1] This eliminated the need for the managed-bean entries in our faces-config.xml. This may seem like a trivial convenience, but in applications where you have a very large number of named components, it can be very convenient indeed to avoid having to keep your faces-config.xml file synchronized with all of your code. Of course, having the @Name annotations distributed throughout your code makes it tougher to track down the class that's bound to a particular name, but thankfully Seam prints out a log of all the name annotations that it finds, including the component name and the fully qualified class name. And if it's more important for you to have a single place where all components are configured, you can resort to using the components.xml configuration file discussed at the end of this section, rather than the Seam code annotations.

These @Name annotations aren't completely automatic, however. In order for Seam to process these code annotations, you need to include a seam.properties file (an empty one, if necessary) in the root of your archive file. If you place a seam.properties in your archive, Seam will check every Java class packaged in that archive for component annotations, and bind them to names according to their @Name annotations. If there is no seam.properties file, no checking will be done, and your components won't be bound to JSF names.

Why does Seam force you to flag your archives this way? Well, if an archive contains a significant number of classes, parsing all of them for Seam annotations can be an expensive operation. Even if it's only a one-time scan performed when an application is deployed, you might like to avoid this when possible (e.g., to speed up repetitive deployments during development). In our Gadget Catalog example, all of our Seam components are EJB components as well, and so they are all packaged within our EJB jar file. So we placed an empty seam.properties file in our EJB jar, making the directory structure look as shown in Figure 3-3.

---

1. Seam component names are case-sensitive, so be sure to use the exact name when referencing components in EL expressions or directly in your code. There also seems to be a general trend to name components beginning with lowercase letters, to avoid confusion with class names, which are typically uppercase.

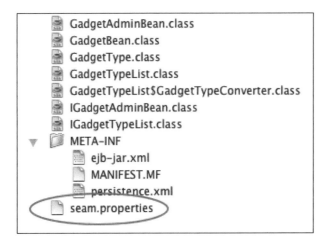

Figure 3-3. *Seam-enabled EJB jar structure*

■**Note** The more inquisitive readers might be asking at this point, "How exactly does Seam trigger the scan for component names?" Well, like most things in life, it's really pretty simple once you see how it's done.

In Chapter 2, you saw that configuring an application to use Seam included the addition of a listener to the web.xml deployment file:

```
<listener>
    <listener-class>org.jboss.seam.servlet.SeamListener</listener-class>
</listener>
```

This listener is the key to the component-naming magic (as well as several other Seam capabilities). When the web container starts up the web context for the application, it initializes any listeners configured in the web.xml file. The SeamListener, in its initialization routine, checks each archive that has been loaded with the application for a seam.properties file (it does this through some class loader games that I won't go into here). If an archive contains this file, it's a simple matter (through other class loader games) to iterate through all the classes loaded in that archive for @Name annotations. Each one that's found is inserted into a list of name bindings with the appropriate details needed to manage the component at runtime.

Configuring Seam Components with XML

As mentioned earlier, you can opt to configure Seam components using an XML file. Rather than use an @Name code annotation, you can use a component entry in the Seam components.xml file. You first saw this configuration file in Chapter 2 when I discussed general Seam installation and configuration. In that chapter, you saw how this configuration file is used to configure core Seam services, which are themselves implemented as Seam components. Now, you'll see how this same configuration file can be used for application components as well. A quick reminder: the components.xml file must sit in the WEB-INF directory of web archives and the META-INF directory of EJB archives.

In our Gadget Catalog application so far, we have two Seam components: gadget, a GadgetBean instance, and gadgetAdmin, a GadgetAdminBean. We configured both of these using @Name annotations, as discussed previously. The equivalent configuration using components.xml would look like the following:

```
<components>
    <!-- Install the Seam core internal components -->
    . . .
    <!-- Configure Gadget Catalog components -->
    <component name="gadget" class="GadgetBean"/>
    <component name="gadgetAdmin" class="GadgetAdminBean"/>
</components>
```

These two component entries have the same effect as the @Name annotations we had in the GadgetBean and GadgetAdminBean classes. The Seam runtime will bind instances of each of these classes to the component names "gadget" and "gadgetAdmin", respectively, and we can reference them in our JSF pages.

The components.xml file supports other configuration options as well, but you'll get a chance to explore those when I discuss the various other Seam services, in this chapter and later in the book.

Life Cycle and Callbacks

Similar to other component frameworks, like EJB and web components in Java EE, Seam provides life-cycle management services for its components. Once Seam knows about your component (either through an @Name annotation or an entry in the components.xml configuration file), it takes on the responsibility of managing your component's life cycle to some degree. In the case of EJB components that are also Seam components, this life-cycle management needs to be compatible with the life-cycle services provided by the EJB container. But the goal of Seam is to provide the services described here consistently across all of its components.

During the life of the component, specific life-cycle events will occur. Seam allows you to register callbacks that can be invoked when these events occur. These callbacks are registered using code annotations in your component code.

Component Creation

Seam is responsible for creating components when needed during the lifetime of an application. The creation of a component can be triggered by a number of things, such as a form being submitted (requiring the associated backing bean to be created) or the injection of a component value that hasn't been initialized yet (as you'll see in the section "Bijection" later in this chapter).

You can annotate a method in your component as a creation-time callback, using the @Create annotation. You can only have one create callback method per component. The create callback will be invoked by Seam just after it instantiates your component. That makes it useful for various initialization tasks, like priming data collections or connections to databases or other external resources.

Note that create callbacks can only be used on Seam components that are stateful session EJBs or JavaBeans/POJOs. Entity beans can be constructed directly by clients, so there is no way for Seam to guarantee that a create method would be called at the appropriate point in the bean life cycle. Stateless session beans, on the other hand, don't really support the concept of create callbacks because of their very simple life cycle.

Suppose we wanted to perform initialization like this on our GadgetAdminBean component from the Gadget Catalog application. We would simply add an appropriate method to our class and annotate it using the Seam annotation:

```
@Stateful
@Name("gadgetAdmin")
public class GadgetAdminBean implements IGadgetAdminBean {

    . . .
    @Create
    public void init() {
        // Do any initialization here . . .
    }
    . . .
}
```

Our GadgetAdminBean component is also a session EJB with a local interface (IGadgetAdminBean) defined for it, so we also need to declare our init() method there:

```
@Local
public interface IGadgetAdminBean {

    . . .
    public void init();
    . . .
}
```

Why? Because when the Seam runtime acquires an instance of our session bean from the EJB container, it will usually be given a proxy class generated by the EJB container. In order to ensure that the create callback is callable through the EJB proxy, we need to include it in the local interface (just like any other business method we want to be callable on our EJB component). You see, from the perspective of the EJB container, the Seam runtime is just like any other client, so it can only invoke operations that are declared in the interface for the EJB component.

In this example, since the Seam component is also a session EJB, our init() method will be invoked by Seam just after it's acquired an instance of our bean from the EJB container. If our component were a simple JavaBean, Seam would invoke the create callback just after it had instantiated an instance of the JavaBean.

Component Destruction

Seam also provides callbacks for component destruction. Seam only destroys components when the scope/context that contains them is destroyed.

A destroy callback method is annotated using the @Destroy annotation from Seam. In the case of our GadgetAdminBean session EJB, the destroy() method was our Seam destroy callback:

```
. . .
@Remove
@Destroy
public void destroy() {}
. . .
```

Destroy methods are only supported on Seam components that are stateful session beans or JavaBeans/POJOs. When the component is a stateful session EJB, the destroy method must also be an EJB remove method, annotated with an @Remove annotation, as shown in the preceding code snippet.

Destroy methods serve largely the same role as remove methods in EJB, but like Seam's create methods, they can be used with non-EJB Seam components as well.

Component-Driven Events

Seam also supports callbacks tied to a "life-cycle" service of sorts—component-driven events. A component can register one or more callback methods for any component-driven event, using either an @Observer annotation on the method or an entry in an events.xml configuration file. I'll discuss component-driven events in detail in Chapter 5, which covers structured pageflow services provided by Seam.

Using EJBs As JSF Managed Beans

In standard JSF, all managed beans (action listeners and backing beans) are treated as regular JavaBeans/POJOs. In terms of life-cycle management, for example, when the bean is first needed, an instance is constructed directly by the web container and placed into the JSF scope specified in the managed-bean entry in faces-config.xml.

The assumption that managed beans are POJOs means EJB components can't be used directly, because they have different container contracts. Session beans, for example, should always be created by the container, so that it can do all the required instance pooling and other runtime services for the EJB. In short, if you try to use EJB components directly as managed beans in standard JSF, bad things may happen.

Instead, without Seam to help you out, you need to resort to creating POJO façades around your EJB components when you need to integrate them into your JSF event handling. You saw this in Chapter 1 in the Java EE (non-Seam) version of our Gadget Catalog. Since we were using standard JSF in that case, we needed to wrap our GadgetAdminBean session EJB and GadgetBean entity EJB with a GadgetAdminAction POJO. In addition, we needed to create a JavaBean value object (Gadget) analogous to the GadgetBean EJB to use as the backing bean for our JSF forms. The GadgetAdminAction translated Gadget objects into GadgetBeans (and vice versa) and acted as a proxy action listener for the GadgetAdminBean EJB. The result was the (overly complex) class relationships shown in Figure 3-4.

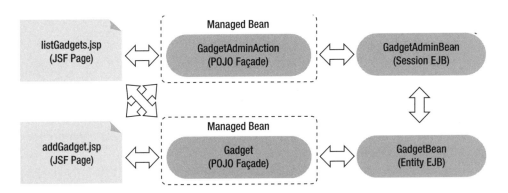

Figure 3-4. *Typical integration of EJBs into JSF without Seam*

Seam bridges the JSF component model with the EJB component model, allowing you to use EJB components directly as JSF managed beans. Seam ensures that the EJB container contracts are honored when EJB-based managed beans are required, allowing the EJB container to manage the services it provides, while still allowing the JSF environment to safely pass along UI data and events to these components.

You've already seen this in action in the Seam version of our Gadget Catalog. In Listing 3-2, you can see that we've annotated the same GadgetBean class as an entity EJB and named it as a JSF component using a Seam @Name annotation. This is equivalent to specifying the EJB class in a managed-bean entry in the faces-config.xml configuration file, which isn't possible without Seam.

With Seam in the mix, the class design of our Gadget Catalog application becomes a lot simpler, as shown in Figure 3-5.

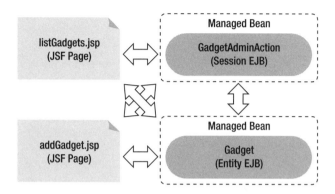

Figure 3-5. *Simplified class design under Seam*

■**Note** Again, astute readers might be wondering at this point exactly how Seam manages to bridge EJB components and JSF managed beans. And again, I have to say that it's all pretty simple once you are exposed to the details. Part of the puzzle is provided by the same SeamListener that handles the @Name annotations discussed in the previous section. The other part of the puzzle is the Seam JSF phase listener, configured in the faces-config.xml. As I mentioned earlier, the SeamListener runs when the web application is loaded, locating all the named components in your application and registering them as Seam components. The JSF phase listener ensures that, when a reference to a managed bean is made, through an EL variable or some other means, and if that bean is actually a Seam component, then the proper runtime handling of the component is made, depending on its component type. If the component is a session EJB, for example, the necessary EJB container interactions are made to ensure that the component's EJB services are managed properly at runtime.

Extending the Gadget Catalog

Now, we're supposed to be extending the Gadget Catalog to support user-defined gadget types, as described earlier. Making this change is quite a bit simpler in Seam than without it. We want to store gadget types in the database to make them both persistent and extendible, and the obvious approach to doing that would be to change the GadgetType enumeration into an entity EJB. The result is shown in the GadgetType entity EJB in Listing 3-3.[2]

---

2. You'll notice that all of our entity beans implement the java.io.Serializable interface. While not strictly necessary in all cases, it's a good practice to follow, since many EJB containers will attempt to serialize your entity beans for caching and other reasons.

Listing 3-3. *Entity Bean for Gadget Types*

```java
@Entity
@Table(name="GADGET_TYPE")
public class GadgetType implements Serializable {
    private long mId;
    private String mLabel;
    private String mDescr;

    public GadgetType() {}

    @Id @GeneratedValue
    @Column(name="TYPE_ID")
    public long getId() {
        return mId;
    }

    public void setId(long id) {
        mId = id;
    }

    @Column(name="DESCR")
    public String getDescription() {
        return mDescr;
    }

    public void setDescription(String descr) {
        mDescr = descr;
    }

    @Column(name="LABEL")
    public String getLabel() {
        return mLabel;
    }

    public void setLabel(String label) {
        mLabel = label;
    }

    public boolean equals(Object comp) { . . . }
    public int hashCode() { . . . }
};
```

This is a simple entity bean, with a generated id field acting as the primary key for the types, and both a label and description for the type. The label will be used in situations where a short type description is needed (e.g., menus in a web form), and the description will serve as a more detailed description of the meaning and scope of the gadget type.

The next step in our refactoring exercise would be to adjust the GadgetBean entity EJB to use a GadgetType for its type property, rather than the string used in the earlier version. This change matches up with the updated database model we saw back in Figure 3-1 for the revised Gadget Catalog, and it also makes sense from a design perspective. The changes to our GadgetBean entity bean are fairly straightforward, as shown in Listing 3-4.

Listing 3-4. *Updated GadgetBean Entity EJB*

```
@Entity
@Table(name="GADGET")
@Name("gadget")
public class GadgetBean implements Serializable {
    . . .
    private GadgetType mType;
    . . .
    @ManyToOne(optional=false)
    @JoinColumn(name="TYPE_ID")
    public GadgetType getType() {
        return mType;
    }
    public void setType(GadgetType t) {
        mType = t;
    }
    . . .
}
```

The type property has been changed to be a GadgetType, and the persistence annotations on the getType() accessor have been updated to specify that this is a many-to-one relationship to the GadgetType entity, keyed by the TYPE_ID column in the updated GADGET table. The remainder of our GadgetBean has remained unchanged from the earlier version, and those parts of the code have been omitted here for brevity.

Up until this point, all of the changes we've made would have been necessary whether we were using Seam or not. But now we need to plug our GadgetType entity EJB into the JSF UI, and that's where Seam helps us out in a few ways.

First, we need to create a JSF form to add gadget types to the Gadget Catalog. With Seam in the mix, this is a simple matter. First we create a form much like the one we used to add gadgets to the catalog. The addGadgetType.jsp page is shown in Listing 3-5.

Listing 3-5. *JSF Page for Adding New Gadget Types*

```
<%@ taglib uri="http://java.sun.com/jsf/html" prefix="h"%>
<%@ taglib uri="http://java.sun.com/jsf/core" prefix="f"%>
<%@ taglib uri="http://jboss.com/products/seam/taglib" prefix="s" %>

<html>
<head>
    <title>Add a Gadget Type</title>
</head>

<body>
    <f:view>
        <h:form>
            <table border="0">
                <tr>
                    <td>Label:</td>
                    <td>
                        <h:inputText value="#{gadgetType.label}"
                                     required="true" />
                    </td>
                </tr>
                <tr>
                    <td>Description:</td>
                    <td>
                        <h:inputText value="#{gadgetType.description}"
                                     required="true" />
                    </td>
                </tr>
            </table>
            <h:commandButton type="submit" value="Create"
                             action="#{gadgetAdmin.newGadgetType}" />
        </h:form>
    </f:view>
</body>
</html>
```

In this new JSF form, we're referencing a new backing bean, "gadgetType", to hold the values of the label and description fields being entered by the user. Seam allows us to use our GadgetType entity EJB directly as this backing bean by simply putting an @Name annotation on our class:

```
@Entity
@Table(name="GADGET_TYPE")
@Name("gadgetType")
public class GadgetType implements Serializable { . . . }
```

If we were using straight JSF, we would have had to create another proxy POJO for our GadgetType EJB, and added converters for it somewhere so that the managed bean could be converted into a GadgetType to be persisted, and vice versa. With Seam, none of that is necessary, and our new form to create gadget types is ready to go.

We also need to adjust our "add gadget" JSF page, addGadget.jsp, so that the drop-down list of gadget types is pulled from the new GADGET_TYPE table. This is where Seam helps us in a more subtle way. Our addGadget.jsp page uses a JSF selectOneMenu component to render the drop-down list of types, with a selectItems child element that pulls in the list of choices for the menu. In the Gadget Catalog version in Chapter 1, we used the selectOneMenu like so:

```
  . . .
<tr>
    <td>Type:</td>
    <td>
        <h:selectOneMenu value="#{gadget.type}"
                              required="true">
            <f:selectItems value="#{gadget.gadgetTypes}" />
        </h:selectOneMenu>
    </td>
</tr>
  . . .
```

The value attribute on a selectItems component needs to be either a single SelectItem object, an array or Collection of SelectItem objects, or a Map containing keys and values that can be used as labels and values (respectively) on select items. When the gadget types were represented by an enumeration, we were able to map the type values into the UI component by simply generating a Map<String,String> collection that used the enumeration labels as the keys, and the enumeration names as the values in the map. The value chosen in the selectOneMenu component was the unique name of the enumeration, which was just fine for our purposes in that version, since that's all we needed to populate the type property on our GadgetBean class (the value stored in the TYPE column of the GADGET table). The Map of labels and names was accessed through a getGadgetTypes() utility method on the GadgetBean class:

```
. . .
@Transient
public Map<String,String> getGadgetTypes() {
    Map<String,String> types = new HashMap<String,String>();
    for (GadgetType value : GadgetType.values()) {
        types.put(value.label(), value.name());
    }
    return types;
}
. . .
```

In our new model, however, our GadgetBean.type property isn't a simple string name anymore. It's a reference to an instance of our new GadgetType entity bean. Ideally, we'd like to have JSF map the user's type selection in the "add gadget" form to an appropriate GadgetType value, and assign that to the GadgetBean.type property directly. In order to make this work, we can't just use a simple Map<String, String> anymore. We want to use a Map<String, GadgetType>, mapping menu selections to actual GadgetType instances. JSF supports this, but we'll need to define a JSF javax.faces.convert.Converter that will map GadgetType objects into unique string values for the select list, and then back again from selected strings into GadgetType instances. This is straightforward enough to do—we simply need to define a JSF Converter subclass and implement its getAsString() and getAsObject() methods to do the appropriate conversions. The converter will need to maintain a list of valid GadgetType instances in order to implement the getAsObject() conversion from type IDs to GadgetType instance. The GadgetTypeConverter shown in Listing 3-6 accepts a list of valid GadgetType values in its constructor and uses this reference list in getAsObject().

Listing 3-6. *Converter to Allow* GadgetType *Objects to Be Used in JSF Select Lists*

```
public class GadgetTypeConverter implements javax.faces.convert.Converter {
    private List<GadgetType> mTypes;

    public GadgetTypeConverter(List<GadgetType> types) {
        this.mTypes = types;
    }

    public String getAsString(FacesContext ctx, UIComponent comp,
                              Object obj)  {
        if (obj == null) return null;

        GadgetType type = (GadgetType) obj;
        String val = String.valueOf(type.getId());
```

```
        return val;
    }

    public Object getAsObject(FacesContext ctx, UIComponent comp,
                              String strVal)
        throws ConverterException {
        if (strVal == null || strVal.length()==0) {
            return null;
        }

        long id = Long.valueOf(strVal).longValue();
        for (GadgetType type : mTypes) {
            if (type.getId() == id) {
                return type;
            }
        }

        return null;
    }
}
```

Next, we need to load the set of GadgetType values from the database to populate the select list, and also to initialize the GadgetTypeConverter. The list of GadgetType values is going to be changing on the fly, however, because of the introduction of the addGadgetType.jsp page. We need to be sure that the latest set of GadgetType values is used to populate the select list whenever it is displayed.

The obvious next step is to assign these responsibilities to a class that can be used as a component by the JSF page. This class will be responsible to get the current values for the select list from the database, and to manage the Converter to ensure that it has the latest set of GadgetType values to use for the conversions.

This is where Seam's EJB-to-JSF bridge helps us out (again). Some of the EJB container capabilities are useful here. For one thing, we need to cache the GadgetType list in such a way that any updates to the list will be loaded automatically. Using the EJB life-cycle services along with entity EJB persistence seems like a good idea. We also need this component to be fairly scalable, since every user hit on the "add gadget" page will depend on it. Session beans with instance pooling seem like a great fit for this. But without a way to directly use an EJB as a JSF component, we'd need to create a POJO/JavaBean façade around our EJB layer, much like the GadgetAdminAction POJO we were forced to create in the non-Seam example in Chapter 1.

With Seam, we can create a single session EJB that handles all the responsibilities we just described, and also serves as our JSF component backing up the GadgetType select list. Our solution to this, the GadgetTypeList bean, is shown in Listing 3-7.

Listing 3-7. *Session EJB That Manages GadgetType Lists for the UI*

```
@Stateful
@Name("gadgetTypeList")
@Scope(ScopeType.EVENT)
public class GadgetTypeList implements IGadgetTypeList, Serializable {
    // All gadget types pulled from the database
    private List<GadgetType> mGadgetTypes;
    // Map to be used for select lists in the UI
    private Map<String,GadgetType> mGadgetTypeMap;
    @PersistenceContext
    EntityManager em;
    /** When this bean is created, load up the types and
     *   populate the internal map */
    @Create
    public void loadTypes() {
        // Load up the types from the database, ordering them by label
        mGadgetTypes =
            em.createQuery("select gt from GadgetType gt order by gt.label")
                .getResultList();
        // Convert the list into a map.  We use a TreeMap in order
        // to preserve the ordering we asked for in the query
        // above.
        Map<String,GadgetType> results = new TreeMap<String,GadgetType>();
        for (GadgetType type: mGadgetTypes) {
            results.put(type.getLabel(), type);
        }
        mGadgetTypeMap = results;
    }
    public Map<String,GadgetType> getAllTypes() {
        return mGadgetTypeMap;
    }
    /*
     * Get a converter initialized with the current list of types
     */
    public Converter getConverter() {
        return new GadgetTypeConverter(mGadgetTypes);
    }
```

```
    @Remove @Destroy
    public void destroy() {}
}
```

We've made this a stateful session EJB with an @Create method, loadTypes(), that loads up all the current GadgetType values from the database when the bean is created by the EJB container. This method creates a list of these types to be used with the GadgetTypeConverter, as well as Map from the type labels to their corresponding GadgetType instances. This Map will be used by the JSF UI in its select menu, through the getAllTypes() accessor method.

The getConverter() accessor method provides access to the GadgetTypeConverter. Here, the GadgetTypeList component initializes a converter with the current list of GadgetType instances and returns it. We tie this all into the JSF UI by referencing this component in the selectOneMenu JSF element in addGadgets.jsp. The relevant portion of this JSF page is shown here:

```
        . . .
        <tr>
            <td>Type:</td>
            <td>
                <h:selectOneMenu value="#{gadget.type}"
                                 converter="#{gadgetTypeList.converter}"
                                 required="true">
                    <f:selectItems value="#{gadgetTypeList.allTypes}" />
                </h:selectOneMenu>
                <!-- Link to add a new gadget type -->
                <s:link action="addGadgetType">
                    <h:outputText value="[Add a new gadget type]"/>
                </s:link>
            </td>
        </tr>
        . . .
```

We're linking the selectOneMenu input field to the type property on the gadget component, which is now a GadgetType value. We set the converter property on the select menu to be the converter property on our GadgetTypeList component, using the JSF expression #{gadgetTypeList.converter}. In Listing 3-7 you can see that we've bound an instance of our GadgetTypeList to the component named "gadgetTypeList", which is how this component reference works. Finally, we're using a selectItems child element that references the allTypes property on our GadgetTypeList, which returns the Map that was generated in the loadTypes() method.

This takes care of the GadgetType conversion, and the initial loading of the GadgetTypes from the database, but how, you may ask, are we dealing with the caching issue? What happens when someone uses the addGadgetType.jsp page to add a new type to the database, invalidating the list of GadgetType instances loaded up by this component? Well, we're using a little EJB and a little Seam to solve that problem. First, as you can see in the class annotations in Listing 3-7 we've declared the GadgetTypeList as a stateful session bean. That may seem a bit odd, since this component doesn't really keep any client-specific state. But this allows us to put the component into the Seam event context, using the @Scope annotation. You'll learn more about Seam scopes in the next chapter when I discuss Seam contexts and the concept of conversations, so for now you'll have to take my word on this part of the solution. In effect, the combination of a stateful session bean and event scope creates a simplistic but effective cache flushing scheme. The type data is loaded in to support the user event, flushed when the event is over, and then reloaded again the next time around. This isn't the most scalable solution in the world, since the cache only lasts for the duration of a request, but it demonstrates how Seam allows us to make direct use of EJB services without additional design overhead.

Bijection

Several Java EE APIs (EJB, JSF, etc.), as well as popular open source frameworks like Spring, make use of the concept of *dependency injection*. Injection involves the automatic, runtime insertion of a property value into a bean. This simple concept can greatly simplify development, especially in a Java EE environment. Tedious things like JNDI resource lookups, for example, can be eliminated and replaced with a simple annotated member variable on a bean class, or an entry in an XML configuration file. In fact, we made use of Java EE injection capabilities in the Java EE version of our original Gadget Catalog in Chapter 1. Our action listener POJO, GadgetAdminAction, used the @EJB annotation defined in EJB 3.0 to inject a reference to a stateless session EJB, GadgetAdminBean:

```
public class GadgetAdminAction implements IGadgetAdminAction {
    @EJB
    private IGadgetAdminBean mGadgetAdmin;
    . . .
}
```

At runtime, the web container picked up this annotation and injected a GadgetAdminBean instance, assigning it as the value of the annotated mGadgetAdmin instance variable. This saved us the trouble of doing a JNDI lookup to get a GadgetAdminBean instance in our code.

Seam's bijection model expands on this basic injection concept in a few significant ways, to create what they call their *bijection* model:

- It supports injection as well as what Seam calls *outjection*, meaning that a component can also "export" a value out as the value of a named component.

- Seam performs ongoing, dynamic injection of a given value during the life of a component. Many injection models simply inject a value once, for example, when the target component is initialized or when some specific life-cycle event occurs. Seam updates an injected value on an ongoing basis.

- It supports Seam's context/scope model. You'll learn more about this aspect in the next chapter, where I cover contexts and conversations.

Let's start with Seam's version of simple injection, and then move on to the extended services that make up their bijection model.

Simple Injection

As you might expect, you can also use injection with Seam components. After all, the goal of Seam is to add value, not take it away. In Seam, the @In annotation is used to inject Seam components into other Seam components. The simplest use of this annotation is demonstrated here:

```
@Name("handler")
public class MyHandler {
    @In
    private SomeBean formBean;

    public SomeBean getFormBean() { return formBean; }

    public void setFormBean(SomeBean b) {
        formBean = b;
    }

    public String myAction() {
        Object data = formBean.getSomeProperty();
    }
}
```

Here, we're annotating the formBean property on the Seam component MyHandler, telling Seam to inject the value of this property whenever MyHandler is invoked. In this case, we haven't specified any details about where the value of this property should be injected from—we're using @In with no arguments. By default, Seam will search all of its contexts for a component with the same name as the annotated property, "formBean". The first one it finds (in an ordered search of contexts, starting from the event context

and ending with application context) is used as the value of the annotated property. If no
component of the given name is found anywhere, the injection will not happen, and the
property will remain uninitialized.

The `@In` annotation can be applied on class data members or accessor methods.
In the preceding example, we could have also chosen to annotate the `getFormBean()`
accessor:

```
@In
public SomeBean getFormBean() { return formBean; }
```

As you might expect, you can also explicitly specify the Seam component name to be
used for the injection. If we had a component named "productDetails" that we wanted
injected into our `MyHandler`, we'd use the `value` attribute on the annotation to specify that:

```
@Name("handler")
public class MyHandler {
    @In(value="productDetails")
    private SomeBean formBean;
    . . .
}
```

You can also use JSF expressions to specify the value to be injected into the field or
property. In the preceding example, suppose there was a component named "product"
that had a property named "details" that we wanted injected instead. We could then use
an expression for the `value` attribute:

```
    . . .
    @In(value="#{product.details}")
    private SomeBean formBean;
    . . .
```

The `@In` annotation supports three other attributes. The `scope` attribute specifies
which Seam context to search for the component. I'll discuss Seam contexts in more
detail in the next chapter. The other two attributes allow you to control when and how
Seam deals with uninitialized components during injection.

The `required` attribute specifies whether the injected component must be nonnull
or not. By default, this attribute is `true`, which means that if the component to be injected
is not initialized when the injection occurs, an exception is raised by Seam. If you set the
`required` attribute to `false`, Seam will allow the injected value to be null.

The `create` attribute specifies whether Seam should create an instance of the specified component when it's found to be uninitialized during injection. By default, this
attribute is `false`, meaning that Seam will not attempt to do any initialization of its own
during injection.

We have made good use of simple Seam injection in our Gadget Catalog application. On our `GadgetAdminBean` session EJB, we're injecting the value of the named "gadget" component:

```
@Stateless
@Name("gadgetAdmin")
public class GadgetAdminBean implements IGadgetAdminBean {
    . . .
    @In(value="gadget", create=true)
    private GadgetBean mActiveGadget;
    . . .
}
```

Remember that the component named "gadget" is the `GadgetBean` instance we're using as the backing bean for the `addGadget.jsp` page. We're using the `value` attribute on `@In` here because the name of the component we want injected ("gadget") does not match the name of the property we want set ("mActiveGadget"). We're also setting the `required` attribute to false, because depending on the page flow the user takes, we may invoke action listener methods on our `GadgetAdminBean` before the `gadget` component has been initialized in the UI.

Outjection

As mentioned at the start of this section, Seam extends simple injection by introducing the concept of outjection, or the export of a component value from one component back into the scope where the component lives.

In our earlier example, we injected the `formBean` component into the `MyHandler` component, and then used the injected bean value in the `myAction()` action listener method. Suppose that method was extended to update the value of the `formBean` component:

```
    . . .
    public String myAction() {
        Object data = getSomeData();
        formBean.setSomeProperty(data);
    }
    . . .
```

If we wanted the other parts of the application to see this change, we could outject our `formBean` property back out into the Seam context, using the `@Out` annotation:

```
    . . .
    @In
    @Out
    private SomeBean formBean;
    . . .
```

The `@Out` annotation can also be applied to either fields or property accessors on Seam components. If you want to annotate the accessor method, however, you need to place the `@Out` annotation on the getter rather than the setter, since we're exporting the value from the component. And similar to injection, outjection occurs each time the Seam component is invoked, but at the end of the invocation rather than at the beginning.

The `@Out` annotation has `value`, `required`, and `scope` attributes that behave analogously to the `@In` attributes of the same names. The differences are related to the export versus import of data values.

The `value` attribute specifies the name of the component that should have its value set to the annotated field or property. If no `value` attribute is specified (as in the preceding example), the name of the annotated field or property is used as the name of the target component. In our case, the component named "formBean" will be set to the value of the `MyHandler.formBean` field, since we haven't used the `value` attribute, and the annotation is on the `formBean` field.

The `required` attribute also behaves similar to the `required` attribute on `@In`. If this attribute is `true` (the default), the outjected bean value must be nonnull, or an exception will be raised by Seam. If `required` is `false`, the bean can be null, and the target bean will have its value set to null as well.

The `@Out` annotation also has a `scope` attribute that allows you to specify the target context of the outjection. Again, you'll get a detailed look at Seam contexts in the next chapter, but here's a quick summary of how outjection works in terms of the target component's scope:

- If you specify the target scope, Seam will look for a component of the correct name in the specified scope and assign the exported value to it if found.

- If you don't specify a scope, Seam searches bottom-up (starting from the event context and moving up through the page, conversation, session, business process, and application contexts) for a component with the appropriate name. That component will have its value set to the exported value.

- If no scope is specified and no matching named component can be found in any scope, the exported value is assigned to a new component in the event scope.

In the updated Gadget Catalog, we made use of Seam's outjection to improve usability when new gadget types are added to the catalog. We've made the assumption that, when users add a new type to the catalog, they probably intend to use that type when they add their next gadget in the "add gadget" page. Making this happen is just a matter of exporting the value of the `activeType` property on our `GadgetAdminBean` component:

```
@Stateless
@Name("gadgetAdmin")
```

```
public class GadgetAdminBean implements IGadgetAdminBean {

    . . .

    @In(value="gadgetType", required=false)
    @Out(value="#{gadget.type}", required=false)
    private GadgetType mActiveType;

    . . .

}
```

Remember that the GadgetAdminBean.newGadget() method is used as the action listener for the addGadgetType.jsp form. The preceding @In annotation injects the value of the gadgetType backing bean from that form into the activeType property before the newGadgetType() method is invoked. After the newGadgetType() method completes, the @Out annotation tells Seam to export the value of the new GadgetType to the type field on the gadget component. When the addGadget.jsp form is rendered, this property on the gadget component is used as the value for the type menu, as you saw earlier:

```
    . . .
    <h:selectOneMenu value="#{gadget.type}"
                     converter="#{gadgetTypeList.converter}"
                     required="true">
        <f:selectItems value="#{gadgetTypeList.allTypes}" />
    </h:selectOneMenu>
    . . .
```

The result is that the newly created gadget type will be preselected in the "add gadget" form.

Dynamic Bijection

As opposed to some injection models, Seam's model is dynamic in nature, not a one-time injection event. The injection and outjection specified in the @In and @Out annotations on a given component will be carried out every time a Seam component is invoked.

If this weren't the case, the bijection wouldn't have been much use to us for setting the default gadget type in the previous section. We need to have the GadgetAdminBean. activeType property exported to the type property of the gadget component every time the GadgetAdminBean is invoked, because the user is going to add new types over time as they are needed. The same component, gadgetAdmin, is being used as the action listener for all these transactions, so we need to export the value every time.

If bijection was a one-time event, we would be forced to play games with the scope of the gadgetAdmin component so that it goes out of scope and is reinitialized, triggering the injection/outjection again. But this isn't the case, luckily for us.

Summary

In this chapter, we've explored the fundamentals of Seam's component model, which serves as the core of all of the Seam framework features that we'll examine in the rest of this book. The Seam component model serves as a bridge between the JSF and EJB component models, allowing EJBs to be used directly as JSF managed beans. The Seam component model also serves as a unified model for the other Seam framework capabilities, such as pageflow, security, and business process management.

Seam components can be bound to names using `@Name` annotations. You also have the option to use the `components.xml` configuration file, if you'd prefer to use external XML configuration. The `@Name` annotations also publish components as JSF managed beans, allowing you to avoid `faces-config.xml` configuration entries.

Seam components also support bidirectional dependency injection, or what Seam calls "bijection." With bijection, in addition to injecting components into properties on other components, you can also outject components into the various Seam contexts after action methods and other life-cycle methods are completed.

CHAPTER 4

■ ■ ■

Contexts and Conversations

In this chapter, we explore Seam's context support, which is an extension of the contexts supported by Java EE web containers. Most of the focus will be on Seam conversations, which is a key new capability provided by the Seam framework. But first, as background, I introduce you to all of the new contexts supported by the Seam component model.

Seam Component Contexts

One of the keys to the Seam component model is its extended set of *scopes*, also referred to as *runtime contexts*. These contexts are familiar to anyone who has developed web applications based on servlets, JSPs, and/or JSF. Runtime data can be assigned to various contexts, and the scope of the data is defined by the duration of the context and the access that is allowed to the context. *Session* contexts, for example, last for the duration of a single user's session with an application, and the data contained in a session is only accessible to a single user. *Application* contexts, on the other hand, last for the duration of the entire application, and the data contained in them is potentially accessible to all users using that application.

Session data is probably the most commonly used context in servlet/JSP/JSF applications. Each user is given a session context when he or she enters an application, and your server-side code can put data associated with the user into his or her session context. The scope of the session is the user's active period with the application, and the access to the session is limited to just the user who owns the session.

Figure 4-1 depicts the contexts that are defined within the standard JSP/JSF environment. A global application context covers all runtime data managed by a particular application. Application data is available during the processing of any user request. Every user is given a session context, as I already mentioned. The session starts when the user first interacts with the application from his or her browser, and lives until it is either automatically or explicitly ended. A session can be ended by several events—the application can explicitly kill off a session because the user hits a "logout" link, or the requests from the user might stop for an extended period of time, causing the session to be expired by the server.

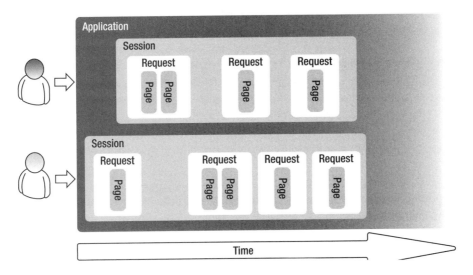

Figure 4-1. *Standard JSP/JSF contexts*

Within each user session are subcontexts that arise as the user interacts with the web application. Every user request has its own context and can hold data that lives only for the duration of that request. Any given request might involve multiple pages (a JSP may include other JSPs in its view, and/or a user request might be forwarded on the server to other pages). Each page can have its own runtime context, with data that only lives within that page invocation.

Seam's component model extends the runtime context structure, as shown in Figure 4-2. The application, session, request, and page scopes are essentially the same as what is supported by standard JSP/JSF containers.[1] Seam adds the concept of a *user conversation*, which segments a user's session into independent data contexts, as well as a context that covers the scope of an entire business process, which is in effect broader in scope than even the application scope, because it can persist across the lifetime of the application.

---

1. Note that JSF and JSP use the term "request" scope, while Seam uses the terms "request" and "event" intermittently in its documentation to refer to this same context. In this chapter and for the rest of the book, I will try to use the term "request" consistently.

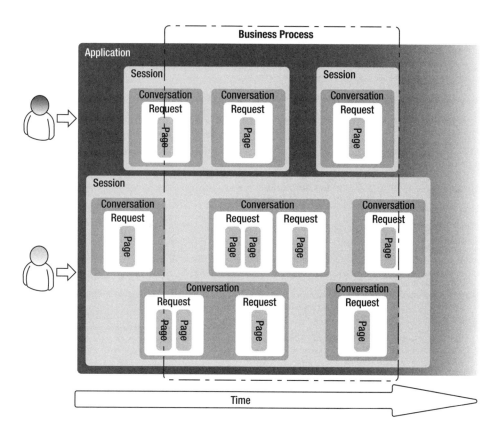

Figure 4-2. *Seam's extended context model*

I'm going to defer discussion of the business process context until Chapter 7, which dives into business process modeling (BPM) with Seam. For the remainder of this chapter, we're going to take a look at Seam's conversation model and what practical benefits it brings to the table.

Seam Contexts and the JSF Life Cycle

Before we dive deep into the practical aspects of Seam conversations, it's important to take a brief foray into some background material. Seam manages the various contexts in its component model within the larger structure of the JSF life cycle. When you first start to experiment with Seam contexts, the interaction of Seam with the JSF process is probably going to be the first place that you scratch your head and wonder, "Why isn't this working the way I expect?" So take a few minutes now and get to know a little about how Seam integrates with JSF.

Figure 4-3 shows the standard phases of the JSF request processing life cycle, and how Seam plugs itself into these phases with its JSF phase listener. You've already seen how Seam's phase listener is installed in the `faces-config.xml` file of your web application. This figure depicts what the listener is actually doing at runtime to manage the Seam contexts (among other things).

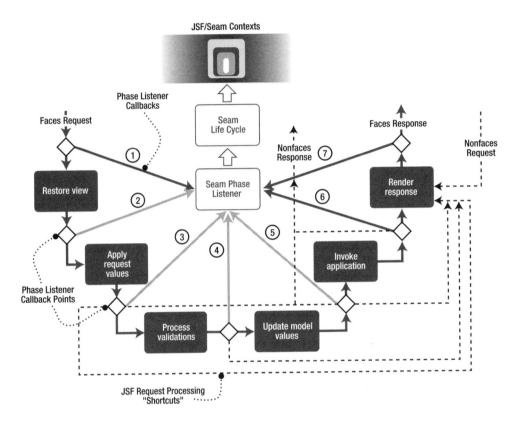

Figure 4-3. *JSF request processing phases and Seam's phase listener*

As shown in the figure, JSF-registered phase listeners are invoked before and after each phase in the JSF request life cycle, through an event notification pattern. This allows frameworks like Seam (or your own application code, if you want) to perform their own life-cycle processing. In the case of Seam, these phase events are used to implement Seam's own context life cycle, including the management of Seam's extended set of contexts.

I won't go into a lot of detail here about the JSF request life cycle itself (that's better covered in material specifically on JSF). But the following are short descriptions of what generally happens in each of the JSF phases:

- *Restore view*: Determine the intended target view for the request, and either create it (if it doesn't exist yet) or restore it (if it does exist already).

- *Apply request values*: Update all the UI components involved in this request with the data passed in with the request (form fields, cookie values, etc.).

- *Process validations*: Run all registered validators against the data values set by the request.

- *Update model values*: If the previous phases were successful (i.e., all UI component fields have been set and validated), the registered managed beans in your application model will be updated in this phase, using the values processed in the previous phases.

- *Invoke application*: Any registered application callbacks are invoked in this phase. This includes any action listeners you may have configured.

- *Render response*: Once all the application processing is complete, the view and all of its UI components are asked to render the intended response for the client.

As the figure shows, Seam's phase listener receives phase events before and after each JSF life-cycle phase, and it uses these event notifications to implement key elements of its component model. Although Seam receives notifications at all phase boundaries in the JSF life cycle, the key activities are performed in the three stages highlighted in Figure 4-3, namely:

- *Before "restore view"*: At this point, Seam simply initializes its internal references to the various contexts. For contexts that are shared with JSF (such as the session context), the context reference is extracted from the `FacesContext`. Seam-specific contexts, such as the conversation context, are initialized if needed, or pulled from storage if they already exist (e.g., long-lived, explicit conversations).

- *After "restore view," before "apply request values"*: Seam initializes the current conversation context. Seam ensures that the conversation state is in sync with the session and the request parameters. If, for example, a request was made to switch to another conversation, the conversation ID is pulled from the request parameters, and the referenced conversation is restored.

- *After "render response"*: Seam removes any expired contexts, stores any long-lived contexts (like explicit conversations), and cleans up the internal structures used to manage the various contexts.

The practical implications of the actions performed by the Seam phase listener will become clear in the rest of the chapter, as we explore Seam's contexts, especially the support for conversations.

Gadget Catalog: Conversational Gadgets

In keeping with this book's practical treatment of Seam, let's define some extensions to our Gadget Catalog application that demonstrate the conversation features of Seam.

While the Gadget Catalog has served this book's purpose so far in terms of demonstrating Seam's basic component model, it's ridiculously simple. The model for gadgets isn't very realistic—a single string type, name, and description associated with a gadget. Even with this simplistic model, the UI is very limited. All we can do is create new gadgets and view them in a list. No update or delete operations, and no searching. In order for our Gadget Catalog to become truly useful, both the model and the operations supported in the UI need to be extended.

We'll start with the object model. We haven't used object models in our design so far, but now that we're pushing for a realistic application, it's a good time to start keeping a UML class diagram for our object model. The revised object model we'll target for this revision of the Gadget Catalog is shown in Figure 4-4. Our Gadget now supports multiple types (e.g., a printer can be a copier and a fax machine at the same time, a mobile phone can be a media player, etc.). In addition, each Gadget can have a set of features, represented as a GadgetFeature. Features will represent the various nuances of gadgets within the same type (e.g., a mobile phone can have Bluetooth capabilities, a laptop can have a built-in web camera, etc.). Each feature can also have one or more parameters associated with it. These parameters serve as a basic way to record details of the various features, where applicable (e.g., Bluetooth version 1.2 versus 2.0).

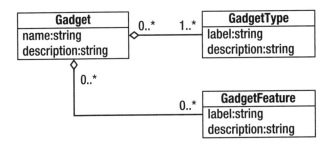

Figure 4-4. *Object model for conversational Gadget Catalog*

Naturally, we'll need to extend our database model to support our new object model, since all of these details about gadgets will need to be persisted in the catalog database. Figure 4-5 shows the new schema for our Gadget Catalog database. Gadgets, types, and features are maintained in the GADGET, GADGET_TYPE, and GADGET_FEATURE tables, respectively. Types and features are linked to gadgets through association tables (GADGET_TYPE_ASSN and GADGET_FEATURE_ASSN), allowing them to be associated with multiple gadgets if needed (as specified in our object model).

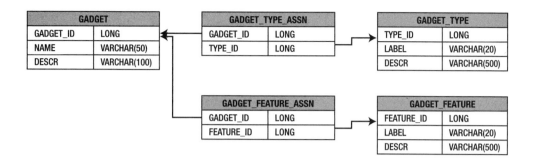

Figure 4-5. *Database model for conversational Gadget Catalog*

Finally, we come to the user interface. Our web application will need to be extended as well, to allow administrators to create, edit, and delete all of these model entities. Our extended pageflow is depicted in Figure 4-6.

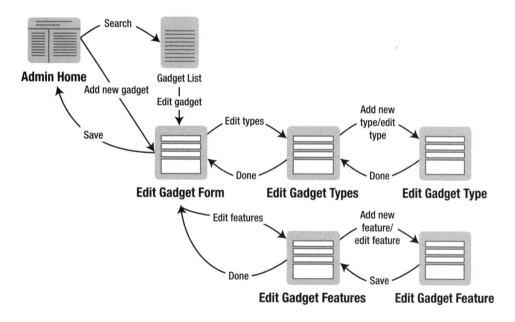

Figure 4-6. *Pageflow for the conversational Gadget Catalog*

We've reorganized the UI around a new administrative home page that acts as a launching point for the various administrative functions. From the home page, administrators can choose to create a new gadget or search for existing gadgets to be edited. Both paths lead to an "Edit Gadget" page that is used to both create new gadgets and edit existing ones. From this page, the administrator can edit the core attributes of a gadget (name and description, currently), and also invoke other screens for editing gadget types and features. From these subscreens, the user can create new types and features, and assign/remove these from the gadget being edited.

Conversation Basics

A conversation is a new context scope introduced by Seam. Before we look at the technical details behind Seam conversations, let's examine the practical motivations for introducing a new context in web applications.

The Motivation for Conversations

If you've developed web applications before, looking at the extended Gadget Catalog pageflow in the previous section should remind you of some common issues with basic create/update/delete systems like this. One obvious issue that comes with more complicated pageflow is state management. When the user chooses to edit a gadget (using the "Edit Gadget Form"), and then moves into editing types and/or features for that gadget on other pages, we need to remember the gadget that he or she is editing. By itself, that would be a relatively simple thing to handle using session data, but what about more problematic or complicated actions the user might perform? As the user moves into the various branches of the flow, there's the chance that he or she may want to back up and start working on something else. The user may start up another tab/window in the browser and start a new path through the pageflow. How do we deal with these gracefully and maintain consistent state data for the user?

With just a single session context for each user, we have to juggle the state data within the session when these events happen. If the user starts a new path through the flow, we have to either reset the state data (e.g., flush the edits the user has made so far and start a fresh gadget edit session), or we need to maintain multiple sets of state data for the user. Neither of these options is very appealing. Flushing the state and starting over is fairly simple from a development standpoint, but the user may lose valuable work that he or she actually meant to go back and finish. Maintaining multiple sets of state data is appealing to the user, but it will get complicated quickly in terms of the application code. We'll need to create a way to identify these various sets of state data and somehow determine which set the user wants to work on at any given point. We may also have to create additional navigation functions to allow the user to jump between the different sets of state data.

Many readers have probably had to deal with this issue themselves in the past using standard MVC frameworks like Struts or vanilla JSP/JSF, and may have been successful to various degrees. But these same issues led the Seam framework developers to devise a better way to deal with more complex user interactions, and their solution became the conversations that are in Seam today.

Conversations and Other Contexts

As you saw in the earlier section "Seam Component Contexts," the conversation context is, in one sense, just a subdivision of the standard session context. In regular Java EE environments, all web interactions happen within a short-lived event context that falls within a long-lived session context. And each page that is involved in a given event has its own even shorter-lived page context. Seam conversations provide another context that wraps one or more user events within a given session. The key phrase here is "one or more." If a conversation could only include a single event, it wouldn't be very useful. But conversations can span multiple user events. Just as a verbal conversation between two people consists of one or more exchanges of words, a Seam web conversation consists of one or more request/response exchanges between a user and a web application. And since a conversation is like any other context, it can hold state data, and that state data spans all the events that fall into the conversation.

While a conversation is more than just an event, it's also less than an entire user session, and that makes it useful for other reasons. A user can start and end multiple conversations during a given session, which provides the capability to group multiple requests into something like "subsessions." Seam also supports multiple active conversations, allowing a user to have simultaneous workspaces. Each conversation can be kept independent of the others, and since each one has its own set of state data, a Seam application can actually remember (and forget) each conversation separately.

Conversation Life Cycle

As you saw in the earlier section "Seam Component Contexts," Seam manages conversations (and other contexts) within the overall JSF request processing life cycle. The Seam phase listener drives the conversation management at each stage in the JSF request life cycle.

Before the "restore view" phase, Seam performs some basic housekeeping for its overall context management scheme. After the "restore view" phase completes, Seam determines whether a conversation context needs to be created or restored, and then initializes the active conversation. The result of this initialization will be one of two things:

- If the request contains a reference to an existing conversation, and that conversation hasn't expired, then that conversation will be restored.

- If there's no conversation to be restored, a new conversation will be created.

There are two concepts that I just mentioned that need to be explained a bit more: conversation *references*, or IDs, and conversation *expiration*.

Conversation IDs

First, I mentioned that a request could contain a *reference* to a conversation. Conversations can span across multiple web requests, so there needs to be a way to track the conversation in the stateless world of HTTP requests. This is the same issue faced with the session context—Java EE web containers need to track the user's session across requests. And the solution that Seam uses for sessions is largely the same. Each conversation is given a conversation ID, and this conversation ID needs to be passed along with each request so that Seam knows which conversation to initialize after the "restore view" phase.

Normally, you don't need to worry about conversation IDs, because Seam handles them for you when it's involved in generating links or directing the user to views after an action completes. But in cases where you are generating nonfaces links in your UI, and you need to propagate the conversation ID to the target page, you do need to ensure that the conversation ID is attached to the link. I'll discuss these details in the section "Starting or Ending Conversations on Page Links."

While conversation IDs are typically generated for you automatically by Seam, you can specify your own conversation IDs explicitly, if needed. You'll see how this is done when we look at the various ways of starting conversations. Specifying your own conversation IDs is especially useful when you want the "identity" of a conversation to be tied to specific state data. If a user is editing his or her profile in one conversation, for example, and then asks to edit his or her profile in another conversation, it doesn't make much sense to have both conversations happening at the same time. It would be much better to automatically jump the user to the existing profile editing conversation. This can be accomplished by giving the conversation an ID that's based on the action being performed (e.g., "editing") and a unique identifier for the target entity (e.g., the user ID that owns the profile).

You should also note here that conversation IDs (explicit or otherwise) are only necessary because Seam supports multiple active conversations for each user. If Seam only supported one conversation at a time, the active conversation reference could simply be kept in the user's session, and Seam would just have to check to see whether an active conversation existed each time a request occurs. But since Seam supports nested conversations, as well as concurrent conversations, for the same user, it needs to know which conversation each request is running under.

Conversation Expiration

The other important life-cycle concept that I mentioned is that conversations can *expire*. Again, just like with sessions, Seam needs to detect when a conversation isn't needed any longer. Sometimes a conversation is ended explicitly, but sometimes a conversation needs to be expired, because we just stop getting requests from the user who owns the conversation. If this wasn't done, old conversations would start to pile up within the Java runtime, eating up precious resources until eventually the application server would choke.

The expiration time for conversations (i.e., the duration of inactivity that has to occur before a conversation is expired) is a Seam configuration parameter. It can be set in the `components.xml` or in the `seam.properties` file, both of which I discussed in Chapter 2 when I described Seam configuration. Seam's built-in manager component has a property called "conversationTimeout" that specifies the conversation expiration in milliseconds (the default value is 10 minutes, or 600,000 ms). To set conversations to expire in 3 minutes, for example, you would add the following entry to `components.xml`:

```
<components>
    . . .
    <!-- Set the conversation timeout to 3 minutes -->
    <component name="org.jboss.seam.core.manager">
        <property name="conversationTimeout">180000</property>
    </component>
    . . .
</components>
```

Implicit vs. Explicit Conversations

As I just discussed, Seam ensures that every user event happens inside a conversation context. If you don't tell Seam anything about when to begin and end conversations, each individual request will be wrapped with its own conversation, and the conversation will be destroyed when the request ends. These conversations are *implicit* ones—you didn't ask for them to be created, but Seam creates them automatically when the request occurs, and ends them when the request ends. More specifically, in terms of the JSF life cycle depicted in Figure 4-3, Seam creates implicit conversations just after the "restore view" phase, and then removes them after the "render response" phase.

Looking back at our Gadget Catalog pageflow in Figure 4-6, let's suppose that the user is on the gadget list page, selects a gadget to edit, and then adds a feature to that gadget. If we haven't given Seam any clues about when to begin and end conversations, Seam will create implicit conversation contexts around each request, as shown in Figure 4-7. Anything we put into the conversation context during our page processing will be lost once the page rendering has completed.

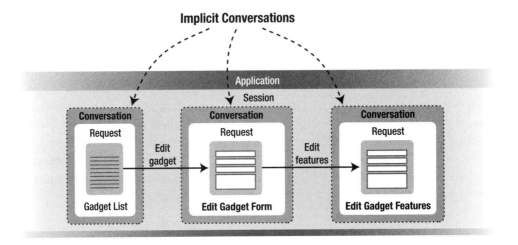

Figure 4-7. *Implicit conversations*

In some cases, this might be sufficient, but you're not really using the power of Seam conversations unless you explicitly define the boundaries of the conversations. Explicit conversations can span multiple page requests, allowing conversation state to be carried across requests. Explicit conversations also allow you to keep multiple conversations active at the same time, supporting the workspace features in Seam.

Explicit conversations are defined by specific begin and end events. In the next section, we'll examine the various ways that you can specify these begin and end events.

Starting and Ending Conversations

You can start and end explicit conversations in two ways: when you execute an action listener method, and when you follow a link to a page. It's much easier, and therefore more common, to annotate action listener methods to control conversations, so we'll start there.

@Begin and @End on Action Listener Methods

Any action listener method can be marked with the Seam @Begin or @End annotations to indicate that they should begin or end the current conversation. If an action listener method is marked with @Begin, Seam will attempt to start an explicit conversation when the method completes successfully (i.e., if it does not generate an exception, and if it returns a nonnull result). New explicit conversations can only be started outside of any other explicit conversation. Since an @Begin annotation is handled when the action listener method is invoked by Seam, and since action listener methods are invoked during the JSF request life cycle (during the "invoke application" phase, to be precise), there will be either an implicit or explicit conversation active. If the conversation is implicit, Seam promotes it to an explicit, long-lived conversation, and all is well. If there is an explicit conversation already active, Seam raises an exception, unless the @Begin annotation includes either the join or nest options discussed in the later sections.

You can also specify explicit conversation IDs in the @Begin annotation, using the id attribute. The id can be a literal value, like "editGadget", or it can use component references to base the conversation ID on state data, like "edit-#{gadget.name}".

To demonstrate the use of the @Begin annotation, let's look again at our extended Gadget Catalog. The pageflow in Figure 4-6 has a branch that's used for editing a chosen gadget, starting with the "Edit Gadget Form" page. There are several pages that the user could visit while editing a gadget—one or more types or features could be assigned to the gadget, and new types or features could be created on the fly. As the user bounces between these pages, we need to keep track of the gadget being edited. We could do this by inserting the gadget into the user's session, and then plucking it out again once the user is done. But then we'll face all the limitations discussed earlier—the user can only edit one gadget at a time, or we have the difficult task of juggling multiple gadgets at the same time for the user. Seam's conversations are the perfect solution. What we want to do is start a conversation when the user chooses to create or edit a gadget, and then end the conversation when that user is finished.

The path to create a new gadget, leading from the "Admin Home" page to the "Edit Gadget Form" page, is handled by the editGadget() action listener method on the gadgetAdmin component, as you see in the code in the page that generates the "Add a new gadget" link:

```
. . .
<s:link action="#{gadgetAdmin.editGadget}">
    <h:outputText value="[Add a new gadget]"/>
</s:link>
. . .
```

The gadgetAdmin component is an instance of our GadgetAdminBean session bean. We want to start a new conversation when the user creates a new gadget, so we can simply annotate the editGadget() method with an @Begin marker:

```
. . .
// Start a (new) conversation when the user selects a gadget to edit
@Begin
public String editGadget() {
    return "success";
}
. . .
```

That's about all we need to do. When the user clicks the "Add a new gadget" link on the home page, the editGadget() method will be invoked. This method always returns a nonnull outcome, so when it completes, Seam will create a new explicit conversation context. We have our pageflow configured in our faces-config.xml so that the editGadget() action takes us to the editGadget.jsp page:

```
<faces-config>

    . . .

    <navigation-rule>
        <navigation-case>
            <from-action>#{gadgetAdmin.editGadget}</from-action>
            <from-outcome>success</from-outcome>
            <to-view-id>/editGadget.seam</to-view-id>
        </navigation-case>
    </navigation-rule>

    . . .

</faces-config>
```

The editGadget.jsp page has been extended to include support for multiple types and for gadget features, but it's otherwise similar to the previous version. It references the gadget component as the backing bean for the form, much as it did before:

```
    . . .
    <table border="0">
        <tr>
            <td>Name:</td>
            <td>
                <h:inputText value="#{gadget.name}"
                             required="true" />
            </td>
        </tr>
        <tr>
            <td>Description:</td>
            <td>
                <h:inputText value="#{gadget.description}"
                             required="true" />
            </td>
        </tr>
    </table>
    <h:commandButton type="submit" value="Save"
                     action="#{gadgetAdmin.saveGadget}" />
    . . .
```

The gadget component is bound to an instance of our Gadget entity EJB using the @Name annotation in the code, just as we did in earlier versions:

```
@Entity
@Table(name="GADGET")
@Name("gadget")
public class Gadget implements Serializable {
    . . .
}
```

By default, Seam binds entity bean components to the current conversation context, which is exactly what we want to happen here. Our editGadget() action listener method caused an explicit conversation to get started, and when the editGadget page references the gadget component, it is initialized (since until this point in the pageflow it hasn't been referenced yet) and placed in the conversation context. In earlier versions of our Gadget Catalog, the conversation context was implicit and was destroyed after the editGadget page request was processed. That was fine before, because all we were doing in earlier versions was setting the gadget's name, description, and single type value, all in one form submission. So as long as the gadget component was persisted before the request completed, it was fine to have the implicit conversation destroyed along with the Gadget backing bean. But now, we're going to be editing the Gadget across multiple page requests, so we need to have an explicit conversation scope that extends across these requests, in order to keep our Gadget active.

We've managed to start our conversation, now we have to worry about when and how to end it. You'll notice in the snippet from the editGadget page earlier that the form is backed by the saveGadget() action listener method on our gadgetAdmin bean. That's the obvious place to end the conversation, since that's the point when the user is saying, "I'm done working on this gadget." Ending a conversation with action listeners is similar to beginning them; we simply annotate the listener method in our GadgetAdminBean class with an @End annotation:

```
    . . .
    @End
    public String saveGadget() {
        saveGadget(getActiveGadget());
        return "success";
    }
    . . .
```

Just like the @Begin annotation, Seam will end the current conversation if the annotated method returns a nonnull value, without generating an exception. That means that the current conversation is still active while the method is running, allowing you to complete any necessary tasks before the conversation ends. In our case, the saveGadget()

method does just what you'd expect—it persists the current active `Gadget` sitting in the conversation context, by calling the `saveGadget(Gadget)` utility method on `GadgetAdminBean`:

```
.   .   .
public void saveGadget(Gadget g) {
    try {
        if (gadgetDatabase.find(Gadget.class, new Long(g.getId())) != null) {
            gadgetDatabase.merge(g);
        }
        else {
            gadgetDatabase.persist(g);
        }
    }
    catch (Exception e) {
        e.printStackTrace();
    }
}
.   .   .
```

Assuming that this is successful, the `saveGadget()` method returns a "success" value, and Seam will then destroy the active conversation context, along with the `gadget` component. Our pageflow is set up so that the `saveGadget()` action takes us back to the home page, where we can start the whole pageflow over again.

Starting or Ending Conversations on Page Links

Seam also allows you to start and end conversations on page links. By providing Seam-specific request parameters on your page links, you can instruct the Seam phase listener to begin and end conversations prior to rendering the requested page.

If you look back at the extended Gadget Catalog pageflow in Figure 4-6, you'll notice that there are two ways a user can transition into the gadget editing branch. I just covered one of them (the "Add a new gadget" link on the home page). The other path involves performing a search against the database, and then clicking an "Edit" link next to one of the gadgets in the list of results, to edit that gadget.

Before I discuss the conversation-related aspects of the search function, let's take a brief detour and run through how we've implemented the search function itself in our extended version of the Gadget Catalog. First, we added a search box to the home page, allowing users to search for gadgets by matching the input text against the name and description fields of the gadget. The entire home page is shown in Figure 4-8.

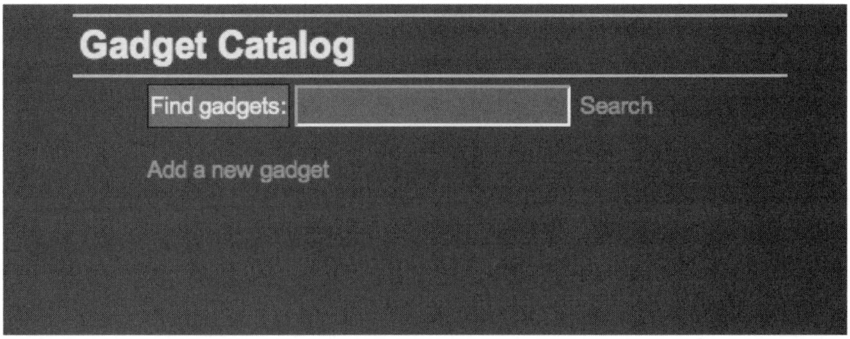

Figure 4-8. *Administrative home page for Gadget Catalog*

The code for the home page is pretty simple:

```
<html>
<body>
    <%@ include file="header.jsp" %>
    <f:view>
        <h:messages/>
        <!-- Link to add a new gadget -->
        <h:form>
            <table border="0">
                <tr>
                    <td class="formLabel">Find gadgets: </td>
                    <td class="formInput">
                        <h:inputText value="#{gadgetAdmin.searchField}"/>
                    </td>
                    <td><h:commandLink type="submit" value="Search"
                                       action="#{gadgetAdmin.search}"/></td>
                </tr>
            </table>
        </h:form>
        <s:link action="#{gadgetAdmin.editGadget}">
            <h:outputText value="[Add a new gadget]"/>
        </s:link>
    </f:view>
    <%@ include file="footer.jsp" %>
</body>
</html>
```

Note that I've removed all the CSS style references for the sake of clarity. If you'd like to see the full version with the CSS styles, check out the code examples for the book.

Handling the search itself is pretty simple. If you look at the preceding JSP code, you see that the text input field in the search form is tied to the searchField property of the gadgetAdmin component, and the form is handled by the search() action listener method on this same component. On our GadgetAdminBean class, we defined the searchField property to accept the value of the input field, and the search() method is implemented to perform the appropriate search, using the EntityManager injected into the bean:

```
. . .
private String mSearchField;

public String getSearchField() { return mSearchField; }
public void setSearchField(String sf) { mSearchField = sf; }

public String search() {
    String searchField = "%" + getSearchField() + "%";
    try {
        Query q =
            gadgetDatabase.createQuery("select g from Gadget as g " +
                                       "where g.name like :searchField " +
                                       "or g.description like :searchField " +
                                       "order by g.name")
                    .setParameter("searchField", searchField);
        mGadgetMatches = q.getResultList();
    }
    catch (Exception e) {
        e.printStackTrace();
    }

    mSelGadget = null;

    return "listGadgets";
}
. . .
```

Now, how do we actually display the list of matching gadgets? Well, in the preceding search() method, you'll notice that we're taking the list of Gadget beans returned from the query and assigning it to our mGadgetMatches member variable. We're also setting the mSelGadget member variable to null. Why? Well, these member variables have been annotated with a few other Seam annotations:

```
. . .
@DataModel(value="gadgetMatches")
List<Gadget> mGadgetMatches;
```

```
@DataModelSelection
private Gadget mSelGadget;
. . .
```

The @DataModel annotation publishes a collection (a Map, List, Set, or an array of Objects) as a JSF DataModel that can be used with a JSF dataTable UI component. The annotation causes Seam to wrap the tagged collection with a DataModel and put it into the scope of the component that owns it, under the name given by the value attribute (if no value is provided, the name of the member variable is used). You can then reference the DataModel in a dataTable component in your JSP. In our case, we've configured the pageflow to take the user to the listGadgets.jsp page when the search() action listener returns, so in that page we display the search results by referencing the "gadgetMatches" DataModel:

```
<body>
    <f:view>
        <h:messages/>
        <!-- Show the current gadget catalog -->
        <h:dataTable value="#{gadgetMatches}" var="selGadget"
                    columnClasses="dataCell">
            <h:column>
                <f:facet name="header">
                    <h:outputText value="Name" />
                </f:facet>
                <h:outputText value="#{selGadget.name}" />
            </h:column>

            <h:column>
                <f:facet name="header">
                    <h:outputText value="Description" />
                </f:facet>
                <h:outputText value="#{selGadget.description}" />
            </h:column>
            <h:column>
                <s:link linkStyle="button" value="Edit"
                        action="#{gadgetAdmin.pickGadget}" />
            </h:column>
        </h:dataTable>
        . . .
</body>
```

A sample view of the search results page is shown in Figure 4-9.

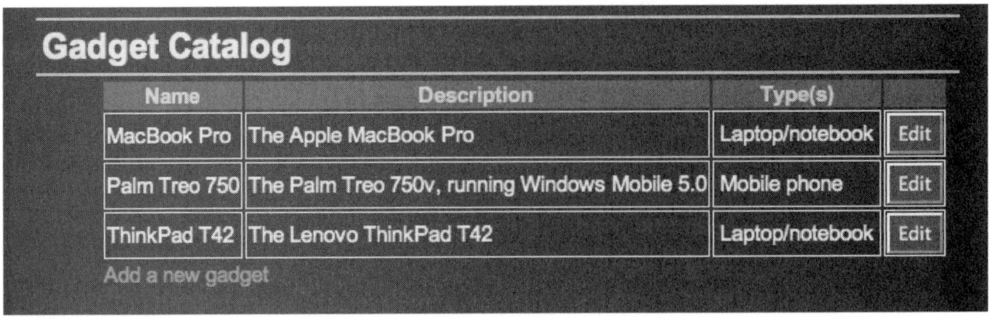

Figure 4-9. *Search results page*

The other annotation we showed previously was the @DataModelSelection on the mSelGadget member variable. This annotation will cause Seam to inject the selected object from the DataModel when a Seam link tag is used in the dataTable. In our case, we've put an Edit button at the end of each row of the search results, allowing the user to edit any Gadget found in the search. When the user clicks one of the "Edit" links, the corresponding Gadget for that row of the dataTable will be injected into our mSelGadget data member, and then the pickGadget() action listener method will be called, as specified in the s:link tag in our listGadgets.jsp page. The pickGadget() method is simple enough:

```
. . .
public String pickGadget() {
    setActiveGadget(mSelGadget);
    return "editGadget";
}
. . .
```

Here, we take the selected Gadget that was injected into the mSelGadget member and set it as the value of our activeGadget property. We've annotated the activeGadget property so that it will be outjected as the value of the gadget component that's used in our editGadget.jsp page:

```
. . .
@In(value="gadget", create=true)
@Out(value="gadget", required=false)
private Gadget mActiveGadget;
. . .
```

Our pageflow is set up in `faces-config.xml` to take the user to the `editGadget.jsp` page when the `pickGadget()` action listener returns "editGadget":

```
. . .
<navigation-rule>
    <navigation-case>
        <from-action>#{gadgetAdmin.pickGadget}</from-action>
        <from-outcome>editGadget</from-outcome>
        <to-view-id>/editGadget.seam</to-view-id>
    </navigation-case>
</navigation-rule>
. . .
```

When `pickGadget()` returns, the user will be brought to the edit page with the selected `Gadget` set as the active target of the edit page.

Finally, after all that preface, we can get back to the conversational aspects of our search function. For a number of reasons, we want the entire search/edit pageflow to be enclosed by a conversation context. If the search results (the "gadgetMatches" `DataModel` on our `GadgetAdminBean`) are held in an explicit conversation, we can allow the user to return to the results after editing a `Gadget` and pick another `Gadget` to edit. In addition, we want the editing segment of the pageflow to be contained in a conversation for the same reasons discussed earlier, namely, the user can then bounce between pages in the editing section of the pageflow while the active `Gadget` remains in place.

We want the explicit conversation to start when we initiate the search from the home page. There are a number of ways we could do that, but we wanted to see how to initiate a conversation over a page link, so that's what we'll do. Looking back at the code for the `adminHome.jsp` page, we see that the "Search" link is implemented using a JSF `commandButton`:

```
<h:commandLink type="submit" value="Search" action="#{gadgetAdmin.search}"/>
```

Seam allows us to control conversation propagation over links like this, using a special request parameter called "conversationPropagation". We begin a new conversation by setting this parameter to "begin". In this case, we'd add a JSF `param` tag to our `commandButton`:

```
. . .
<h:commandLink type="submit" value="Search" action="#{gadgetAdmin.search}">
    <f:param name="conversationPropagation" value="begin"/>
</h:commandLink>
. . .
```

This has the same general effect as annotating an action listener method with `@Begin`. When the user clicks the "Search" link, the Seam phase listener will pick up the `conversationPropagation` parameter and begin a new explicit conversation context. Then the `search()` action listener method will be invoked, which will populate the `DataModel` within the conversation.

It's important to note that there is an important difference between annotating an action listener method and using a page link to begin a conversation. When we annotate an action listener method, the conversation will be started after the method completes (assuming it returns a nonnull result). When we use the `conversationPropagation` parameter on a link, the conversation is started when the request is received, before any action listener is invoked. In our case, the conversation begins before the `search()` method is run. If we had annotated the `search()` method with `@Begin`, the conversation would have been started after the search was performed, and that would have left the `DataModel` and `DataModelSelection` outside of our new conversation. This definitely isn't what we want, so we have to use the link approach to begin the conversation.

There are several other ways to control conversation propagation over links in Seam. When you use the Seam `link` tag, you can use the `propagation` attribute on the tag:

```
<s:link value="Search" action="#{gadgetAdmin.search}" propagation="begin"/>
```

You can also specify conversation propagation for all requests to a given page, using attributes on a `page` element in the `pages.xml` configuration file:

```
<page view-id="/listGadgets.seam" action="#{conversation.begin}">
    List all gadgets
</page>
```

This approach will make more sense when I discuss Seam page actions and pageflow in Chapter 5, but essentially this entry in `pages.xml` tells Seam that every request for `listGadgets.jsp` should cause a new conversation to begin. The reference to `#{conversation.begin}` uses a special built-in component named "conversation" that provides access to conversation-specific actions.

Of course, in all these cases, we can also "end", "join", or "nest" conversations over the link. We can also specify that no conversation propagation should be done over the link, using the value "none" for the propagation parameter. This tells Seam to run the request inside of a new implicit conversation, and outside of any explicit conversation that was active when the link was chosen.

Joining Conversations

As mentioned earlier, a new explicit conversation can only be started outside of any other explicit conversation. If you try to start a new top-level conversation inside of another one, an exception will be thrown by Seam. You can, however, choose to join an existing conversation when an action listener or page is invoked.

The @Begin annotation provides a join parameter that can be used for joining an existing conversation. If you specify

```
@Begin(join=true)
```

on an action listener method, a new explicit conversation will be started if one doesn't already exist, and if one does already exist, this request will be subsumed into it and will have access to all the data stored in the existing conversation context.

It's important to remember the distinction between implicit and explicit conversations. If a request is operating within an implicit conversation, a join=true option will have the same effect as a regular @Begin annotation—the implicit conversation will be promoted to an explicit one. If a request is operating within an explicit conversation already, the join will cause the request to be run inside the existing conversation.

To see this in action, let's look back at the search path in the Gadget Catalog pageflow in Figure 4-6. In the previous section, you saw how the link from the home page to the search results page was configured to start a new conversation. You also saw how we had to set up a new action listener to handle the "Edit" links on each gadget in the results list. The editGadget() action listener method on GadgetAdminBean has an @Begin annotation already, so if the "Edit" links were handled by that action listener, we'd be trying to start a new explicit conversation inside the one that was started by the search link, and an error would be thrown. So we created the new pickGadget() action listener method on our GadgetAdminBean bean, with no @Begin annotation, and we set up our pageflow in faces-config.xml so that this action would also bring the user to the editGadgets.seam page.

The option of joining an existing conversation, however, allows us to remove this additional action listener method and have both the "Add a new gadget" links and the "Edit" links use the same editGadget() method as their action listener. All we have to do is change the @Begin annotation on editGadget() to use the join option, and move the handling of the selected Gadget into this action listener:

```
. . .
@Begin(join=true)
public String editGadget() {
    if (mSelGadget != null) {
        setActiveGadget(mSelGadget);
    }
    return "success";
}
. . .
```

With these changes, we can use `editGadget()` as the action listener for the "Edit" links on the search results screen:

```
. . .
<h:dataTable value="#{gadgetMatches}" var="selGadget">
    . . .
    <h:column>
        <s:link linkStyle="button" value="Edit"
                action="#{gadgetAdmin.editGadget}" />
    </h:column>
</h:dataTable>
. . .
```

Now both the "add new gadget" and "edit gadget" paths in our pageflow are being handled by the same `editGadget()` action listener method. When the user clicks an "Add a new gadget" link on the home page, `editGadget()` is invoked as before. There is no selected gadget set, so the logic to set the active gadget is bypassed, and the method returns successfully. The `@Begin` annotation causes a new explicit conversation to be started, because there is only an implicit conversation active at this point.

When the user performs a search from the home page, the `conversationPropagation` parameter on the search link causes a new explicit conversation to be created, as before. When the user clicks an "Edit" link, the selected gadget is injected into the `mSelGadget` member, as before, and the `editGadget()` method is called. In this case, the `activeGadget` property is set to the selected gadget, causing the gadget component to be outjected at the end of the method call. The `@Begin` annotation is checked as well, but since an explicit conversation is already active, and the `join=true` option has been used, the conversation context is left in place, and the gadget edit session is subsumed into the current conversation.

Nesting Conversations

Until now, we've only dealt with a flat conversation model. In all our examples, a conversation is a singular context, with no child conversation contexts, and no concurrent conversations. This is more than sufficient for most situations. But Seam also supports both *nested* conversations, where a conversation contains one or more child conversations, and *concurrent* conversations, where multiple conversations are active in a user's session. This section will cover nested conversations, and the next section will cover the broader topic of concurrent conversations, also called *workspaces*, in the Seam framework.

Nested conversations are begun using the same techniques discussed previously (namely code annotations or link parameters), but with additional parameter options that indicate to Seam that the conversation to be started should be nested within any existing conversation context. A nested conversation behaves just like any other conversation, except that it leaves the parent conversation active, and it also has read access to the context data stored in its parent conversation.

What is the practical use for nested conversations? Well, just like a conversation is a well-defined subset of work within an overall user session, a nested conversation is a well-defined subset of work inside another conversation. You can allocate data specifically for this piece of work, have it cleaned up when it completes, and (using the persistence support provided by Seam) define transaction boundaries to coincide with conversation boundaries, making a conversation (nested or otherwise) into a true transaction. I'll discuss the transactional aspect of conversations in more detail in Chapter 5 when I cover structured pageflows in Seam, and then again in Chapter 7 when I discuss business process management. But even ignoring that (advanced) feature of conversations, nested conversations provide an even more powerful way to organize the interactions with users in Seam-enabled web applications.

Getting back to the practical case of our Gadget Catalog application, we can make good use of nested conversations in the path from the search results screen into the gadget editing branch. In the last section, we changed the conversation structure so that an explicit conversation was created when a search is executed, and if the user picks a gadget to edit from the results list, we ensure that the editing session is performed within the overall conversation. But, by using the `@Begin(join=true)` annotation on the `editGadget()` action listener method, we also ensured that the creation of a new gadget will establish a new explicit conversation.

Well, if a user searches for a set of gadgets and starts editing one of them by clicking the Edit button on its row of the table, what's keeping him or her from using the back button on the browser to go back to the list and start editing another gadget? If the user does this, the `editGadget()` action listener will be called again, and the `@Begin(join=true)` annotation will cause the edit session to occur within the same overall conversation. The selected gadget will be set to the new gadget, and the user will drop back into the `editGadget.jsp` page with the new gadget active. In the current version of the Gadget Catalog, this isn't a problem, but in the future, we expect the complexity of gadget editing to increase as we increase the complexity of the model. We may need to have interim state data held within the conversation while the user manipulates the various aspects of the gadget. If we just set the active gadget and ignore all this other state data, there's a good chance we'll mix data for two gadgets and end up in an inconsistent state. This is similar to the kinds of issues commonly seen in non-Seam applications when state data is stored in a single session context. In this case, the inconsistencies are limited to the conversation context, but the same issue exists.

To resolve this, we simply need to make two small changes to the Gadget Catalog code. First, we change the @Begin annotation on the editGadgets() action listener method to specify that the editing conversation should be nested, if necessary:

```
. . .
@Begin(nested=true)
public String editGadget() {
    if (mSelGadget != null) {
        setActiveGadget(mSelGadget);
    }
    return "success";
}
. . .
```

The nested=true option on @Begin tells Seam to create a nested conversation if an explicit conversation has already been started (e.g., when the user edits a gadget from the search results screen). Otherwise, a new explicit conversation will be started (e.g., when the user chooses the "Add a new gadget" link from the home page).

As mentioned earlier, we can also specify the conversation ID for the nested conversation, by setting the id attribute on the @Begin annotation. In our case, we might want to have the conversation ID based on the ID of the gadget:

```
. . .
@Begin(nested=true,  )
public String editGadget() {
    if (mSelGadget != null) {
        setActiveGadget(mSelGadget);
    }
    return "success";
}
. . .
```

This way, if the user tries to edit the same gadget twice, he or she will be brought back into the first conversation that was created, rather than creating a new, redundant, and potentially confusing one.

We also need to make sure the nested conversation is ended at the right point in the pageflow. In our case, the user can return to the search results list from the gadget edit page by choosing the Back to list button at the bottom of the page, as shown in Figure 4-10.

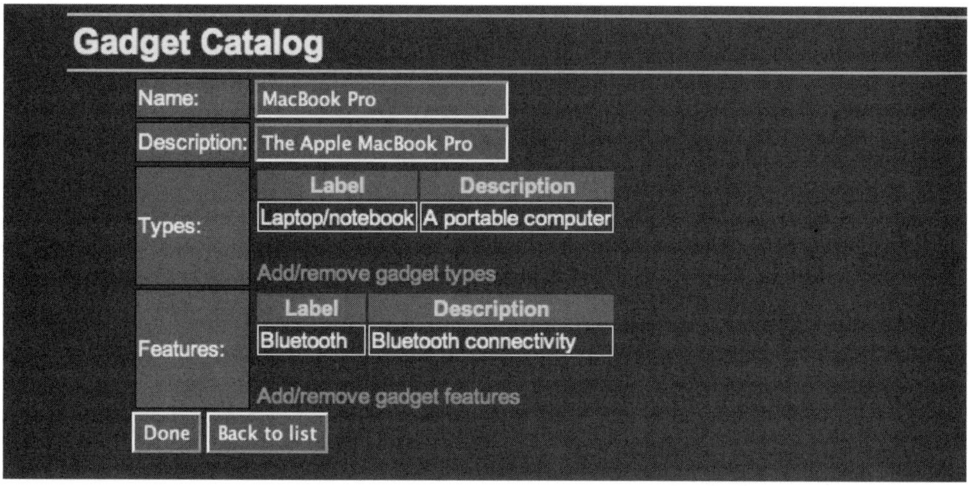

Figure 4-10. *Gadget editing page*

This button is handled by the listGadgets() action listener method on the GadgetAdminBean. We need to annotate this listener with @End to ensure that the nested conversation is ended:

```
. . .
@End
public String listGadgets() {
    setActiveGadget(null);
    return "success";
}
. . .
```

This is fine in terms of keeping the various workstreams separate, but we still haven't provided the user with any way to go back and forth between these conversations. If the user backs up in the browser, picks a new gadget, and starts editing it, the earlier nested editing conversation will be irrecoverable. It will just get cleaned up when the topmost explicit conversation is ended.

Seam's support for workspaces helps to fill this gap, as discussed in the next section.

Workspaces: Managing Concurrent Conversations

Saying that Seam "supports multiple conversations" isn't really accurate. It's more appropriate to say that Seam recognizes that a user can create multiple conversations whether you (the application developer) like it or not, and the framework gives you a reasonable way to deal with it. In addition to the "controlled" creation of nested conversations, described in the previous section, users can also do funny things like open multiple tabs in their browser and navigate through the application in multiple pageflows at the same time. Or, simpler still, they can use that perfectly innocent-looking back button on their browser to backtrack a few steps, and then take a completely different path through the application.

Seam helps you manage this situation by providing the following features that, in combination, provide the support for *workspaces* built into Seam:

- Every view (i.e., page) in your application can be given a stateful description, using an entry in pages.xml.

- When a view is encountered within an explicit conversation context, it is noted by the Seam phase listener, by setting the description of the conversation to be the description of the view pulled from pages.xml.

- Seam provides a built-in component named "switcher" that contains a list of the active conversations that have descriptions assigned to them.

- At any point during an active session in a Seam application, a user can ask to switch to another conversation by providing its ID.

Put this all together, and you have the means to provide some interesting concurrent workspace functions for the user.

The first piece of the puzzle is providing what I referred to as *stateful descriptions* for key views in your pageflow. That term refers to a description that is composed from key state data in the conversation. In other words, you can (and should) use information that uniquely identifies the conversation, from a workspace point of view, to construct the description of the key views in your pageflow. But, since the user will also be shown these descriptions, they need to be human-readable and understandable. These descriptions are specified in the pages.xml configuration file that you first encountered in Chapter 2 when we looked at configuring Seam applications. At that stage, I brushed off pages.xml as an optional configuration file that I'd describe in more detail later in the book. Well, we've reached that point now. I provide some cursory details about pages.xml here, and I'll dive into even more detail in Chapter 5, which covers structured pageflow.

Let's make this concrete by looking at the Gadget Catalog. There are a few key page views in our pageflow, and we've already flagged them in a sense by defining our conversation boundaries around them. There's the search results page (listGadgets.jsp) and the gadget editing page (editGadgets.jsp). Given what I just said about providing stateful descriptions for page views, Listing 4-1 shows what we've put into pages.xml for this version of the Gadget Catalog.

Listing 4-1. *The* `pages.xml` *Configuration File, with View Descriptions*

```
<pages>
    <page view-id="/editGadget.seam">Editing gadget: #{gadget.name}</page>
    <page view-id="/listGadgets.seam">
        All gadgets matching "#{gadgetAdmin.searchField}"
    </page>
</pages>
```

We defined a description for the `editGadget.jsp` page using the `name` property of the current gadget being edited, and the description for the `listGadgets.jsp` page is based on the text entered into the search box. Seam supports the use of JSP/JSF EL expressions in the descriptions of pages in `pages.xml`, which allows us to include state information in the descriptions.

As mentioned earlier, when a view is hit by a user during an explicit conversation, and that view has a description specified in `pages.xml`, Seam takes the page description, applies the current conversation state to it, and sets the result as the description of the current conversation. With this `pages.xml` file in place, if we do a search for "Apple", edit one of the gadgets, and then back up in the browser and do another search for "Palm", we'll end up with three conversations with descriptions set on them, as shown in Figure 4-11. An explicit conversation will be started when we hit the "Search" link on the home page and request `listGadgets.jsp`. The description for this view will be pulled from `pages.xml`, and the conversation description will be set to "All gadgets matching 'Apple'", and the Seam workspace switcher component will record the named conversation. When we choose to edit the gadget named "MacBook Pro", we start a nested conversation, and the description for `editGadget.jsp` is pulled from `pages.xml`. The nested conversation description is set to "Editing gadget: MacBook Pro", and the workspace switcher stores it in its workspace list. Finally, if we go back in the browser to the home page and search for "Palm", another conversation is started, its description is set to "All gadgets matching 'Palm'", and the switcher records this conversation in its list as well. Note that the implicit conversation that was started when we went back to the home page was not recorded by the workspace switcher. This conversation is not an explicit one, and even if it was, there is no description provided for it in `pages.xml`.

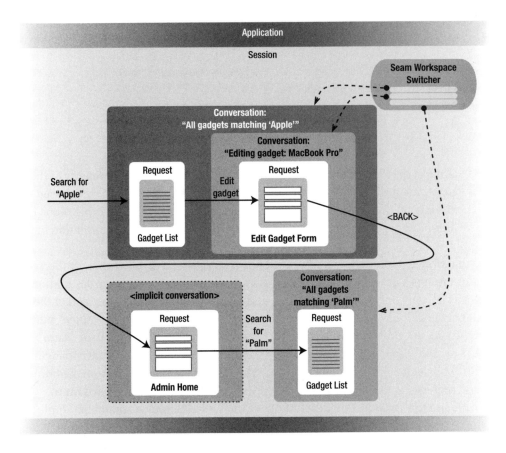

Figure 4-11. *Recording workspaces in the Gadget Catalog*

Now, if we want to make these workspaces useful to the user, we'll need to give the user some way to see them and jump between them. The Seam workspace switcher is published in each request context under the name "switcher", so we can access it and use the stored conversations to generate workspace links for the user.

■**Note** You may have noticed that I depicted the workspace switcher in Figure 4-11 as sitting in the session context, when in fact it's a component in the request context. The conversation list that backs the workspace switcher is in session scope, however, and all the switcher does is convert the list of workspaces into a select list that can be used in UI components. But it's still important to know that the component itself is in the request scope.

The switcher component has a property named "selectItems" that contains a list of JSF SelectItem objects, each of which maps a conversation ID to its description. The switcher also has an action listener method named select() that implements all the logic to switch the user's view to the workspace whose ID matches the value of the switcher's conversationIdOrOutcome property. So it's a simple matter for us to put a select menu into our home page that allows the user to pick an active workspace to jump to:

```
. . .
<!-- Switch workspaces, if any exist -->
<h:form rendered="#{!empty switcher.selectItems}">
    <h:commandButton action="#{switcher.select}" value="Jump to:"/>
    <h:selectOneMenu value="#{switcher.conversationIdOrOutcome}">
        <f:selectItems value="#{switcher.selectItems}"/>
    </h:selectOneMenu>
</h:form>
. . .
```

First, we insert a JSF commandButton that invokes the switcher.select action listener. Then we insert a JSF selectOneMenu that uses the switcher's selectItems list as its set of choices. The value of the chosen item will be the conversation ID of the workspace, which will be set to the switcher's converstionIdOrOutcome property.

If we put the preceding menu into our home page, and then follow the page sequence depicted in Figure 4-6 the result will be the workspace choices shown in Figure 4-12.

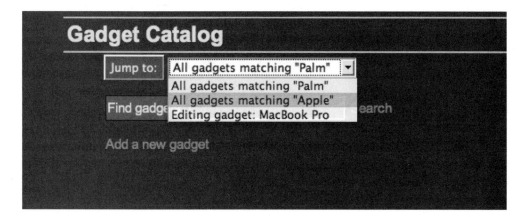

Figure 4-12. *The workspace switcher in action*

When a workspace is chosen, the switcher will switch the current conversation context to the chosen one, and then take the user to the view that generated the description of the workspace. So in our case, if we pick the "All gadgets matching 'Apple'" workspace, that conversation context, including the GadgetAdminBean instance containing the results of the search in its gadgetMatches property, will be restored. Then we'll be taken to the listGadgets.jsp page, which will display the results for us again, as you see in Figure 4-13.

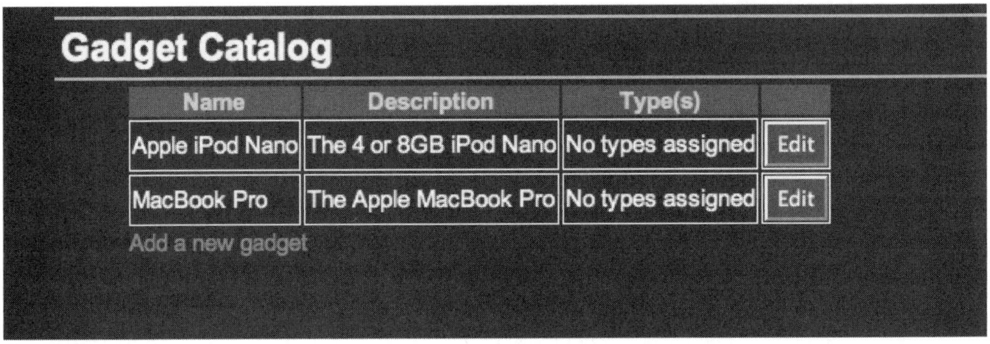

Figure 4-13. *Returning to an in-process conversation*

Summary

This chapter has introduced you to the concept of conversations, a powerful feature provided by the Seam component model. More than just another web context, more than just a subset of the session context, conversations provide an effective way to parcel user activity into discrete interaction scenarios.

All web requests in a Seam application are handled within a conversation context, but conversations are only made explicit and long-lived when you tell Seam where to begin and end them. You saw two general ways to set conversation boundaries: using @Begin and @End annotations on action listener methods, and using request parameters on page links. You also saw how options on the conversation boundaries can cause requests to be optionally merged into existing conversations (called "joining" the active conversation), or you can define nested conversations that live within the duration of their parent conversations, and can read (but not write) the context data in their parents.

Finally, you saw how Seam leverages the conversation model to provide user workspaces, allowing a user to switch dynamically between independent, concurrent activities.

I'll expand on the concepts I introduced in this chapter in Chapter 5, when I discuss Seam's support for structured pageflow and jPDL, and also in Chapter 7, where I'll discuss business process modeling and transactional conversations.

CHAPTER 5

■ ■ ■

Structured Pageflow

In earlier chapters, we explored the core features of the Seam framework, namely its component model (bridging JSF and EJB, among other things) and its extended set of runtime contexts/scopes (providing the concept of conversations, among other things). In this chapter, we begin to look at the ancillary features of the framework. I label these as "ancillary" not to downplay their importance or practical value. Quite the contrary, they are eminently useful. I call them "ancillary" because it is not likely that you will choose to adopt Seam simply to use these features. Under normal circumstances, you'll adopt the core Seam features (Seam components and conversations), and then pick and choose from among the ancillary features (pageflow, business process modeling, AJAX support) to suit your needs.

This chapter is focused on Seam's support for managing application pageflow using the jBPM Process Definition Language (jPDL). As the name implies, jPDL is part of jBPM (Java Business Process Management), which is the JBoss tool for defining workflows and orchestrating tasks within a business process. Roughly speaking, jPDL plays the same role as the Business Process Execution Language (BPEL)[1] standard. Both are XML languages for defining process/task flows within a larger BPM environment.

The jBPM support found within Seam can be used in two general ways. Within the scope of a single user session (actually, within the scope of specific conversations) in a web application, jPDL can be used to specify the valid pageflows that a user can take in the user interface. This limited application of jBPM provides a form of pageflow configuration that is richer and more expressive than the standard JSF navigation rules found in faces-config.xml.

This in itself can be very useful for managing the view layer of your web application, but jBPM is capable of doing much more. If you generalize the concept of flow between pages to flow between general-purpose tasks, and consider that these tasks could be implemented as web services, web pages, rules in a rules engine, business objects, or whatever, you've made the progression from pageflow to workflow. If you further expand

---

1. At the time of this writing, JBoss has released a beta version of jBPM that includes support for BPEL as an alternative to its custom jPDL syntax. You can expect to find this support make its way into a future release of Seam.

the concept to allow for long-lived workflows, involving multiple users acting across multiple user sessions, you've entered the realm of business process management. This is the broader realm of jBPM.

This chapter focuses on the more limited (but still very useful) application of jBPM to manage pageflow (i.e., the use of jPDL to define the navigation of a single user between pages within a single conversation). To do this, I first discuss the basics of jPDL itself, and how it is integrated and extended by the Seam framework. Then we'll return to our Gadget Catalog so you can see how pageflow can be used to define more structured user scenarios in the application.

In Chapter 7, I'll discuss the broader applications of jBPM for full-blown business process management within Seam.

The Basics of Pageflow with jPDL

Before diving into the details of Seam's pageflow support and its practical use in the Gadget Catalog application, you need to understand the concepts behind jBPM's pageflow definition language, jPDL.

The Language of jPDL

Description languages, typically based on XML, are at the heart of most current workflow environments, whether they are simple pageflow schemes or full BPM frameworks. You've already become very familiar with a simple pageflow description language—the navigation rules found in the JSF `faces-config.xml` file. And in these navigation rules, you also saw the basic components of these flow description languages, just geared specifically for pageflow rather than more general process flow. Here's a sample set of JSF page navigation rules for a hypothetical user interface used for editing users in an application:

```
    . . .
  <navigation-rule>
      <from-view-id>/users/addUser.jsp</from-view-id>
      <navigation-case>
          <from-action>#{userAdmin.saveUser}</from-action>
          <from-outcome>success</from-outcome>
          <to-view-id>/users/userHome.jsp</to-view-id>
          <redirect/>
      </navigation-case>
      <navigation-case>
          <from-action>#{userAdmin.editRoles}</from-action>
          <to-view-id>/users/editUserRoles.jsp</to-view-id>
      </navigation-case>
```

```
</navigation-rule>
<navigation-rule>
    <from-view-id>/users/editUserRoles.jsp</from-view-id>
    <navigation-case>
        <from-action>#{userAdmin.addRole}</from-action>
        <from-outcome>success</from-outcome>
        <to-view-id>/users/addUser.jsp</to-view-id>
        <redirect/>
    </navigation-case>
</navigation-rule>
. . .
```

This pageflow is represented graphically in Figure 5-1.

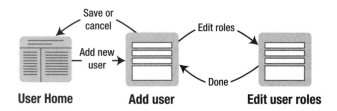

Figure 5-1. *New user pageflow*

This section of the faces-config.xml defines the pageflow used to add a new user, add roles for that user, save the user's information, and return to a home page. The flow starts when the user lands on the /users/addUser.jsp page. From this view, the user can either save the user information (by invoking the userAdmin.saveUser() action listener method) or jump to the /users/editUserRoles.jsp page. From the editUserRoles.jsp page, if the user invokes the userAdmin.addRole() action listener with a "success" outcome, he or she is brought back to the addUser.jsp page.

You can see here the same basic concepts that are used in other flow description languages, namely:

- *States*: The flow progresses from one state to another. States are represented here as JSF views, implemented by specific pages.

- *Events and outcomes*: Various activities can occur during the course of the flow. These activities can have different outcomes: success or failure is a common choice, but others can be defined to suit the context. In the case of JSF, events are JSF action methods, and outcomes are the return values from those action methods.

- *Transitions*: Events and their outcomes, combined with starting states, can be used to define transitions to other states. If the flow is in state A and event E occurs with outcome X, take the flow to state B. Or, in the case of JSF, if the user is on view A and action listener E is invoked with return value X, take the user to view B.

These same concepts are present in jPDL, but under different terms, using a different syntax, and with more options. And since jPDL is meant to be a full business processing modeling language, it supports these concepts in a much more general way than what's needed for simple pageflow.

I won't go through a full primer on jPDL syntax here, but let's look at a simple pageflow example to demonstrate. The jPDL configuration in Listing 5-1 is roughly equivalent to the JSF navigation rules you saw previously, and this pageflow is also represented in Figure 5-1.

Listing 5-1. *Example jPDL Pageflow Definition*

```
<pageflow-definition name="new-user">
    <start-page name="add-user" view-id="/users/addUser.jsp">
        <transition name="save" to="home">
            <action expression="#{userAdmin.saveUser}"/>
        </transition>
        <transition name="editRoles" to="edit-roles"/>
        <redirect/>
    </start-page>
    <page name="edit-roles" view-id="/users/editUserRoles.jsp">
        <transition name="success" to="add-user"/>
        <redirect/>
    </page>
    <page name="home" view-id="/users/userHome.jsp">
        <end-conversation/>
        <redirect/>
    </page>
</pageflow-definition>
```

This configuration describes a pageflow that begins on an "add-user" page, with two possible transitions—to a "home" page or to an "edit-roles" page. From the "edit-roles" page, there is only one possible transition, back to the "add-user" page. When the user transitions to the "home" page, the flow ends (as indicated by the end-conversation element). Notice that each state in the flow is bound to a physical page/view in the web application, using view-id attributes. But state transitions always reference logical state names, not physical pages, because the same physical page can be used to implement multiple logical flow states.

Again, you see all the elements of general pageflow here. Flow states are represented using page and start-page elements (there's also the option to use a start-state element, as you'll see in the section "Initiating Pageflows." Events are specified as optional action elements of the definition of state transitions, and they are bound to JSF action listeners using their expression attributes. Transitions themselves are defined using transition elements, whose name attributes reference the outcomes of action listeners.

■**Practical Tip** When they integrated jBPM into their framework, the Seam developers took some liberties with the jPDL XML schema, ostensibly to make it seem more "page-like" and less "process-driven" (the "P" in jPDL stands for "process," not "page"), but also to provide a way to explicitly specify JSF views within process nodes (something standard jPDL does not support). By inserting their own parsers and node classes into the jBPM configuration, they added the root pageflow-definition element (in addition to the standard jPDL process-definition root element), and also added the page and start-page elements (to extend the standard elements such as start-state, state, node, etc. in jPDL). This can cause some confusion if you attempt to reference the jPDL XML schema provided with jBPM, and then use these page-related elements as specified in the Seam documentation. Your jPDL documents will not validate correctly against the standard jPDL schema, because in effect, Seam is not using the standard jPDL schema. Instead, if you want to use these pageflow-specific elements introduced by Seam, you must remove the jPDL schema reference from your jPDL XML file, which eliminates the validation features of XML editors. Hopefully in the future JBoss Seam and JBoss jBPM will converge on a common jPDL schema, or simply jump entirely to the industry standard BPEL schema for process definitions. In either case, they would need to map general BPM concepts into the pageflow context through some other means.

Besides the more expressive nature of jPDL pageflow definitions (which you'll see in more detail as this chapter unfolds), jBPM supports a state-oriented pageflow model, as opposed to the event-oriented nature of JSF navigation rules. I discuss that aspect in more detail in the section "Seam's Pageflow Model" later in this chapter.

When to Use jBPM Pageflow

JSF comes with perfectly good page navigation support, as you've seen many times. So why would you want to use jBPM pageflow rather than JSF navigation rules? The answer to this lies in the pageflow models each option provides.

First, this choice isn't a complete "either/or" situation. You can mix JSF navigation and jBPM pageflow in the same Seam application. You'll see more about how the transition between the two is handled in the section "Making Sense of 'Pages' in Seam, jBPM, and JSF." But understanding the pageflow models of JSF and jBPM will help you decide whether it makes sense to introduce this additional pageflow scheme to your application.

JSF navigation rules use a model centered on the logical outcomes of events. With a JSF `navigation-rule` entry, you can say things like, "When action X generates outcome Y, take the user to this view." The state within the overall pageflow is implicit. I might, for example, take several paths through the pageflow to get to a specific physical page. JSF sees all of these as ending up in effectively the same state, because the user's location within the pageflow can only be represented using `view-id` attributes. But in reality, the state of the user in the flow depends on the specific transitions that landed the user there.

When defining pageflow in jPDL, states are defined as logical entities, using named `start-page` or `page` elements in the jPDL configuration. These states are bound to physical views, to indicate what view should be presented to the user at this stage in the pageflow, but the state is a separate entity. Different transitions can lead to different states, and these states can have their own transitions, and can be bound to the same or different physical views, as needed.

There are pros and cons with both types of pageflow. As you'll see in the rest of this chapter, jPDL is more expressive, allowing you to define everything about the pageflow within the XML configuration. This can simplify both the JSP pages and the backing beans in your application, and provides a cleaner separation of pageflow rules and application/view logic. But jPDL pageflows are more restrictive in terms of controlling the user's "motion" in the application. Once the user enters a state in the flow, he or she can only transition from that state using one of the transitions specified in the jPDL configuration. If the user tries to go back in his or her browser, the jBPM handler in Seam detects this and (by default) brings the user back to his or her current state in the pageflow.

Although it's possible to bypass this restriction on using the back button (see the section "Managing the Back Button" later in this chapter), jBPM's pageflow model is generally more restrictive and lends itself best to modal navigation, such as wizards and other controlled workflow situations.

You can implement a form of stateful pageflow when using JSF page navigation by carefully defining rules that cover every possible transition path the user might make into and out of a particular view, and specializing the navigation-case entries to define implicit states within the pageflow. But if you find the need for a truly modal interaction with the user in your application, why not make use of a tool that directly supports that?

The upshot of all this is that there are generally two situations when you'll find jBPM pageflow to be useful:

- You need to implement a controlled, modal interaction with the user, as either a subset of the overall user interface or across the entire interface.

- You prefer the clean separation of pageflow rules out of your component and page code, and your interface can still work effectively with the more restrictive pageflow provided by jBPM.

If neither one of these applies in your situation, you probably don't need jBPM pageflow, and can live with regular JSF navigation rules.

Gadget Catalog: The "New Gadget" Wizard

We've now spent far too much time in this chapter on purely technical details, without looking at a practical example (we must always remember the title of this book, no?).

First, let's review where our Gadget Catalog application stands at this point. In Chapters 1 and 3, we created the basics of the tool, allowing users to create new gadgets and store them in the database. Chapter 4 introduced the concept of Seam conversations and used them to implement a number of extensions to both the data model and the pageflow. In that version, gadgets were assigned one or more types and features, along with their core properties (a name and description). The user can search for gadgets with a simple keyword search and can edit the properties of gadgets. Users can also add new gadget types and features, as needed.

Our Gadget Catalog still has a long way to go before it could be considered "practical" in a real-world sense, however. There are a number of improvements we could imagine, but let's start with the glaring problems first. If you deploy the Gadget Catalog application from Chapter 4 and actually try to use it, you'll notice pretty quickly that creating new gadgets is a bit clumsy. If you hit the "Add new gadget" link on the home page, you're presented with the gadget-editing screen, with everything blank to start. This is probably what you'd expect. If you're anything like me, you'll probably type something into the Name and Description fields on the form to start. Then you'll notice the sections for Types and Features. You'll click one of them to see what the options are and pick a few to add to your new gadget. Then you'll hit the Set button and return to the main gadget edit screen. To your dismay, you'll see that your name and description values have been lost. Why? Because we don't persist the state of the gadget when we make the page transitions from editing the gadget to editing the gadget's types or features. We expect the user to enter the name and description for a new gadget, save it, then find it again and edit it to add the types and features. Of course, that's just silly. A user should be able to initialize a new gadget with whatever details he or she has on hand at the time, within a single conversation. Jumping in and out of the edit conversation multiple times to set up a new gadget just won't do.

There are a number of ways we could solve this interface problem. If we wanted to maintain a modeless interface for creating gadgets (as well as editing them), we'd want to ensure that all the page transitions within the gadget editing conversation committed any data entry to the current Gadget object. But suppose that, to start, we wanted to take the easy route and create a "new gadget" wizard. This wizard will step the user through the stages of creating a new gadget, asking for specific pieces of information along the way, and incrementally store the results in the active Gadget object. Then, at the end of the wizard, we will save the Gadget to the database.

We'll use the implementation of this wizard as the backdrop for our discussion of using jPDL pageflows in Seam in this chapter.

Seam's Pageflow Model

Seam uses jBPM to implement its pageflow capabilities, but these capabilities have been tightly integrated into Seam's overall framework. To accomplish this, the Seam developers extended jBPM to provide direct support for web page views as the target of flow transitions (e.g., they created a flavor of jBPM where flow events are triggered by web events, and "state transition" is equated to "web page transition"). I mentioned earlier that Seam extended the XML syntax of jPDL files to allow you to directly bind JSF views to flow states. They also extended the concept of actions in pageflows, allowing you to link actions directly to action methods on any Seam component using JSF's expression language syntax. We saw an example of this in Listing 5-1. The start page includes a transition named "save", and the action defined for this transaction is linked directly to the addUser() method on the userAdmin component.

The Seam developers also integrated jBPM flow control into the Seam conversation model. The boundaries of a pageflow are always defined by the boundaries of a conversation—you optionally start a pageflow when you start a conversation, and that pageflow will end when the conversation ends. The reverse is also true: when you end a pageflow, you also end the surrounding conversation.

Linking pageflow with Seam's conversation model like this provides a few advantages. Aligning pageflows with conversations also aligns them nicely with workspaces, allowing a user to have multiple pageflows active at a given time, each within a conversation that can be swapped in and out using the workspace features discussed in Chapter 4. The link between a pageflow and a conversation also makes a lot of sense, conceptually. After all, a pageflow is meant to be a well-defined interaction with the user as a subset of his or her overall session, which is exactly what a conversation is meant to represent. So aligning pageflow with a conversation simplifies the handling of context data and avoids unnecessary complexity in the overall framework.

In a sense, you should really think of Seam's jBPM pageflow features as an extension of the conversation model of the framework. In other words, you can choose to use jBPM pageflow within a conversation if you want, by providing a jPDL configuration for the pageflow, and then referencing that pageflow when you start the conversation.

Configuring jPDL Pageflows

You've already seen what jPDL configuration files look like, but how do we configure our Seam application to use it? First, you need to enable jBPM support in Seam, by adding an entry to the Seam components.xml file. An example is shown in Listing 5-2.

Listing 5-2. *Configuring jBPM in* `components.xml`

```
<?xml version="1.0" encoding="UTF-8"?>
<components>
    . . .
    <!-- Install jBPM support -->
    <component class="org.jboss.seam.core.Jbpm">
        <property name="pageflowDefinitions">
            <value>newGadget.jpdl.xml</value>
            <value>anotherPageFlow.jpdl.xml</value>
        </property>
    </component>
    . . .
</components>
```

This entry ensures that Seam initiates the jBPM component when your application starts up, and the `pageflowDefinitions` property entry specifies one or more jPDL configuration files for the jBPM component to load.

The Seam jBPM component looks for the jPDL files specified here in two general locations. First, it tries to find the files as resources loaded through the JSF `ExternalContext`, which resolves to the current `ServletContext` if the application is running in a servlet/JSP environment, or to the `PortletContext` if the application is actually running as a portlet. So in our case, we could place our jPDL files into the root of our web archive along with the other web files (HTML, JSP, etc.). But this raises security concerns, since users could inadvertently gain access to the pageflow XML files, and you probably don't want that.

Alternatively, the Seam jBPM component also searches the application's class path by attempting to load the jPDL file as a resource using the application's class loader. If you want to use this approach, your jPDL files need to sit either in the root directory of an EAR or EJB jar file, or in the `WEB-INF/classes` directory of a web archive. This is the approach we've taken with the updated version of the Gadget Catalog code, where we place our jPDL file in the root of the application archive file.

Making Sense of "Pages" in Seam, jBPM, and JSF

By now you have probably noticed that there are several configuration files in Seam that deal with pages in various ways. Before we go any further, you should be clear about the relationship among these various page configurations.

First, we have the JSF page navigation rules that Seam inherits from JSF, typically specified in the `faces-config.xml` file. We've been using these throughout the book for our Gadget Catalog application. We also have page definitions that are specified in the Seam pages.xml file. I discussed these in the latter half of Chapter 4 when I covered Seam conversations and workspaces. Finally, we have jPDL XML files that define the flow states in jBPM that can be backed by web pages, which is the topic of this chapter.

The fact that there are exactly three of these configurations available makes perfect sense, since we're looking at the integration of three pageflow-related technologies: JSF, Seam, and jBPM. And the configurations link together the way you'd expect given the services each of these technologies provides.

JSF navigation entries provide basic rules about where to go when specific actions are fired from pages. Some of these JSF transitions can lead you into pageflows defined by a jBPM jPDL file. While this jPDL pageflow is in effect at runtime, Seam takes its flow cues from jBPM, based on the rules defined in your jPDL. If there is any overlap (e.g., if a given page/action/outcome combination is referenced in both the jPDL file and in the JSF faces-config.xml file), the jPDL rules take precedence if the user is operating within a conversation where the pageflow is still active. If the user arrives at this same page outside of the pageflow defined in the jPDL file, the JSF navigation rules will be used to control the navigation.

On top of all this flow management, Seam's pages.xml file allows you to make use of Seam's page-related services, such as conversation-based workspaces (discussed in Chapter 4), and page actions, which are action listeners that can be fired whenever a given page is accessed. As discussed in Chapter 4, you'll define various points in your application where conversations will begin and end. If you decide to use jBPM pageflow in your Seam application, some of these conversations will have their pageflow controlled by jPDL-defined rules. If you decide to make use of Seam's extended page-related services, you can also define some of these conversations to be named workspaces and/or add actions to pages, whether they fall within jBPM pageflows or not.

Initiating Pageflows

In general terms, starting a pageflow in Seam involves telling Seam, during the processing of a user request, that a particular named pageflow should be started. Seam will then look for the named pageflow by checking the name attributes on the pageflow-definition elements in all jPDL files that it loaded up at startup. If it finds the named pageflow, it checks the starting point defined in the pageflow, and based on that and how the pageflow was started, it decides where to put the user as the first view in the pageflow.

The starting point of the pageflow is specified in the jPDL file using either a start-state or start-page element. You saw an example of a start-page element in Listing 5-1. A start-state element is similar, except that it isn't tied to a specific view ID using a view-id attribute:

```
<pageflow-definition name="checkout">
    <!--
    <start-state name="start">
        <transition name="one-click" to="step1a"/>
        <transition name="classic" to="step1b"/>
    </start-state>
    . . .
</pageflow-definition>
```

What's the difference? Put simply, you define the entry point for your pageflow using a `start-page` element if the flow will always start from a predetermined page. If the starting point for the pageflow needs to be determined using the outcome of an action method, you use a `start-state` element. So in the preceding example, we're saying that the "checkout" pageflow should start on the node named "step1a", if the action method that kicked off the pageflow returns a result of "one-click". But if the action method returns "classic", the pageflow should start on node "step1b".

This tells us what happens when users come into a pageflow, but how do we move a user into the pageflow in the first place? How do we arrange for an action method to kick off the `start-state` of the pageflow, or for a page link to fire the `start-page`? I mentioned earlier that jBPM pageflows are aligned with Seam conversations. So it makes sense that a pageflow can be (optionally) started whenever a conversation is started. In Chapter 4, you saw how conversations are begun in two fundamental ways. You either use an `@Begin`[2] annotation on an action method or arrange for a page link itself to start a conversation (using either attributes on the page link in the JSF view or attributes in a `page` element in Seam's `pages.xml` configuration file). These same approaches can be used to trigger a named pageflow.

Starting Pageflows with Annotations

When using `@Begin` (or related) annotations to enter a pageflow, you specify a `pageflow` attribute on the annotation. The value of the attribute must reference the name of a pageflow defined in a jPDL file deployed with your application. In the Gadget Catalog, as mentioned earlier, we want to change the "Add a new gadget" link on the home page to take the user into the "new gadget" wizard. In the previous version of the application, that link invoked the `editGadget()` action on our `GadgetAdminBean`, the same action we use for editing existing gadgets. But now we want this link to take the user to a pageflow, and we want to use the `@Begin` annotation to specify this. To make this happen, we'll need to define a new action method so that we can annotate it independently of the `editGadget()`

---

2. You can also start pageflows using the `@BeginTask` and `@StartTask` method annotations. These are used to resume/start a task when using jBPM for more general jBPM process management. You'll see these in action in Chapter 7.

method. We want regular gadget editing to continue using the free-form navigation style implemented earlier, and only new gadgets will be created through the "new gadget" wizard.

To make this all happen, we first need to adjust the "Add a new gadget" link in the home page to use the new action method:

```
. . .
<s:link action="#{gadgetAdmin.newGadget}" value="Add new gadget"/>
. . .
```

Then we define a `newGadget()` action method on our `GadgetAdminBean` and use the `pageflow` attribute on an `@Begin` annotation to take the user into our named pageflow:

```
@Begin(pageflow="new-gadget")
public String newGadget() {
    setActiveGadget(null);
    return "start";
}
```

When this action method is triggered during a JSF request, Seam picks up the `@Begin` annotation and looks for the pageflow named "new-gadget". So our jPDL configuration has to have a matching `name` attribute on the root `pageflow-definition` element:

```
<pageflow-definition name="new-gadget">
    . . .
</pageflow-definition>
```

And of course, we have to ensure that our jPDL file is deployed properly in our Seam application, as described in the section "Configuring jPDL Pageflows" earlier.

We're using an action method to start our pageflow, so the jPDL has to use a `start-state` element as the entry point for the pageflow, as just discussed at the start of this section. If the action method completes successfully, Seam will start an explicit conversation (as specified by the `@Begin` annotation itself). Then Seam takes the return value of the action method and checks the `start-state` node in the jPDL file to determine where to take the user next. In our case, we've defined the `start-state` for our "new gadget" wizard as follows:

```
<pageflow-definition name="new-gadget">
    <!--
    <start-state name="entry">
        <transition name="start" to="core-data"/>
    </start-state>
    . . .
</pageflow-definition>
```

The `start-state` element has a single transition defined. It says that a result of "start", coming from the action method that landed the user here, should cause that user to transition to the node named "core-data" in the pageflow. From there, further transitions will determine how the user makes his or her way through the rest of the pageflow. I'll talk more about page transitions in the next section.

Now, `@Begin` annotations can be used with other types of methods on Seam components as well, like `@Create` and `@Factory` methods. In these cases, the next page has already been determined, because these methods are run during the RENDER_RESPONSE phase of the JSF request cycle. So if you use an `@Begin(pageflow="...")` annotation (or `@BeginTask` or `@StartTask`) on one of these methods, the target pageflow has to start with a `start-page` element that specifies the same page. In our case, suppose the first page in our "new gadget" wizard is `/wizard/start.jsp` (it is, actually, but you haven't actually seen it yet at this point, so you'll just have to assume I'm telling the truth). If we wanted to start our conversation and pageflow on an `@Create` or `@Factory` method for some reason, our jPDL pageflow has to use a `start-page` entry point, referencing the first) page in the wizard:

```
<pageflow-definition name="new-gadget">

    . . .

    <start-page name="entry" view-id="/wizard/start.jsp">

        . . .

    </start-state>

    . . .

</pageflow-definition>
```

The disadvantage here is that, as mentioned previously, `@Create` and `@Factory` methods aren't called until the target page has been determined already. In fact, the target page is what causes the `@Create` or `@Factory` method to be invoked in the first place. So somehow we have to navigate the user to the target page (using JSF navigation rules, or using an explicit view ID as the return value of an action method) to trigger the method that will start the pageflow. This usually isn't as clean as using an action method, because you're mixing two navigation models (JSF rules and jPDL) pageflow) in the same request. But this option is still there if you need it.

Starting Pageflows with Page Links

In Chapter 4, you saw that conversations could be started using page links, and that there were a few ways to make this happen: using attributes directly on JSF controls in the page, or using parameters on a `page` element in the Seam `pages.xml` file.

If you are using one of the Seam JSF controls, like `<s:link>` or `<s:button>`, you can use the `pageflow` attribute on these to name the pageflow to be started when the link is traversed. In our case, we could adjust our `<s:link>` control in the home page to specify the pageflow to start:

```
<s:link action="#{gadgetAdmin.newGadget}"
        propagation="begin" pageflow="new-gadget"
        value="Add a new gadget"/>
```

Note that we need to also specify the start of a conversation, using the `propagation` attribute. A pageflow has to line up with the boundaries of a conversation, so we can't enter a pageflow without starting a new conversation. Now that we're beginning the conversation and pageflow using `link` attributes, we have to remove the `@Begin` annotation from the `newGadget()` action method. If we don't, we're telling Seam to start two explicit conversations on the same request, and an error will occur.

We can also start a pageflow using a standard JSF `<h:commandLink>` control. As you saw in Chapter 4, Seam supports a special link parameter called "conversationPropagation" for controlling conversation boundaries using standard page links. As you saw in that chapter, we'd use a value of "begin" on this parameter to start a conversation. You can also use this parameter to specify a pageflow to start with the conversation, using the syntax `begin.<pageflow-name>` for the value of the parameter. So, in our case, we could replace our Seam `<s:link>` with a JSF `<h:commandLink>` like so:

```
<h:commandLink action="#{gadgetAdmin.newGadget}">
    <f:param name="conversationPropagation" value="begin.new-gadget"/>
    <h:outputText value="Add a new gadget (commandLink)"/>
</h:commandLink>
```

The other way to kick off a pageflow across a page link is to use a `page` element in the Seam `pages.xml` configuration file. As discussed in Chapter 2, the `pages.xml` file is placed in the `WEB-INF` directory of the web archive for our application, and it's used to configure workspaces and page actions in Seam applications. In Chapter 4, you saw how we could also begin and end conversations whenever a referenced page is reached by the user by using a page action that references the built-in `conversation` component in Seam:

```
<page view-id="/somePage.jsp" action="#{conversation.begin}"/>
```

An alternative way to accomplish the same thing is to use a `<begin-conversation>` child element on the page:

```
<page view-id="/somePage.jsp">
    <begin-conversation/>
</page>
```

If you use this approach, you can also instruct Seam to start a named pageflow on this page:

```
<page view-id="/somePage.jsp">
    <begin-conversation pageflow="some-pageflow"/>
```

```
</page>
```

For our Gadget Catalog, we would add the following entry to our `pages.xml`:

```
<page view-id="/wizard/start.jsp">
    <begin-conversation pageflow="new-gadget"/>
</page>
```

Why would we use this approach rather than using the links to the page? An entry in the `pages.xml` file is more efficient and easier to manage, in the situation where you know that you want to start a pageflow every time a specific page is hit by the user. Otherwise, you'd have to make sure every link in the user interface that leads to that page is marked up with the necessary attributes.

What about using `start-page` vs. `start-state` when initiating pageflows over links? The rules that I discussed earlier with method annotations also apply here. Namely, if the target page is already determined when the pageflow is started, you should use a `start-page` in your jPDL file; otherwise, you should use a `start-state`. In our first link example, we used an action method on our link:

```
<s:link action="#{gadgetAdmin.newGadget}"
        propagation="begin" pageflow="new-gadget"
        value="Add a new gadget"/>
```

No target view is specified here: the action method will be invoked and then the next page in the navigation will be determined based on the outcome. So we need to use a `start-state` element in our jPDL definition of the "new-gadget" pageflow, and the transitions there will determine the starting view for the pageflow.

With page entries in the `pages.xml` file, on the other hand, the target page has already been determined and used to look up the corresponding page entry. The target page may have been specified using a `view-id` attribute on a link control, for example. In this case, the jPDL for the pageflow needs to use a `start-page` to start the flow.

Defining Page Nodes and Transitions

Typically, the trickiest part of jPDL pageflow in Seam is setting up the start of the pageflow. Once the user is in the pageflow, the contents of the jPDL file are used to specify the states and transitions of the flow the user will take. Pageflow states are specified using `page` elements, and transitions between states are specified using `transition` child elements on these `page` elements.

To demonstrate, let's implement the "new gadget" wizard discussed earlier. The proposed pageflow for our wizard is shown in Figure 5-2. The user starts the wizard from the administrative home page when he or she clicks the "Add a new gadget" link. In the first step of the wizard, we'll ask the user to enter the core data fields for the gadget, which at this point in the evolution of the Gadget Catalog just includes the name and description fields. The next step asks the user to pick the relevant types for this gadget, and the step after that asks the user to choose the relevant features. In both cases, we'll give the user the option to define a new type or feature, if needed. Finally, the user will be asked to confirm the entire gadget entry with a confirmation page. Any time along the way, the user can back up using "previous" links in the wizard.

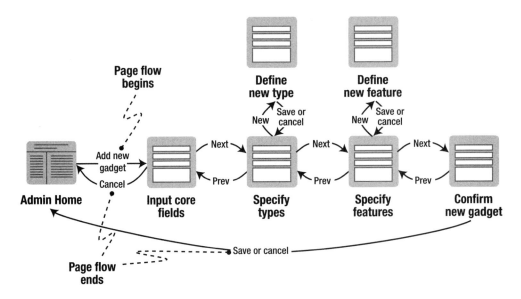

Figure 5-2. *"New gadget" wizard pageflow*

The complete jPDL definition of our "new gadget" wizard pageflow is shown in Listing 5-3.

Listing 5-3. *Complete jPDL for the "New Gadget" Wizard*

```
<pageflow-definition name="new-gadget">
    <start-state name="entry">
        <transition name="start" to="core-data"/>
    </start-state>
    <page name="core-data" view-id="/wizard/start.jsp">
        <redirect/>
        <transition name="next" to="types">
            <action name="interim-save"
                    expression="#{gadgetAdmin.interimSaveGadget}"/>
        </transition>
        <transition name="cancel" to="end">
```

```xml
            <action name="cancel" expression="#{gadgetAdmin.cancelGadget}"/>
        </transition>
    </page>
    <page name="types" view-id="/wizard/types.jsp">
        <redirect/>
        <transition name="next" to="features">
            <action name="interim-save"
                    expression="#{gadgetAdmin.interimSaveGadget}"/>
        </transition>
        <transition name="prev" to="core-data"/>
        <transition name="new" to="new-type"/>
    </page>
    <page name="new-type" view-id="/wizard/newType.jsp">
        <redirect/>
        <transition name="save" to="types">
            <action name="save-type"
                    expression="#{gadgetAdmin.saveGadgetType}"/>
        </transition>
        <transition name="cancel" to="types"/>
    </page>
    <page name="features" view-id="/wizard/features.jsp">
        <redirect/>
        <transition name="next" to="confirm">
            <action expression="#{gadgetAdmin.interimSaveGadget}"/>
        </transition>
        <transition name="prev" to="types"/>
        <transition name="new" to="new-feature"/>
    </page>
    <page name="new-feature" view-id="/wizard/newFeature.jsp">
        <redirect/>
        <transition name="save" to="features">
            <action name="save-feature"
                    expression="#{gadgetAdmin.saveGadgetFeature}"/>
        </transition>
        <transition name="cancel" to="features"/>
    </page>
    <page name="confirm" view-id="/wizard/confirm.jsp">
        <redirect/>
        <transition name="save" to="end">
            <action name="save" expression="#{gadgetAdmin.saveGadget}"/>
        </transition>
        <transition name="cancel" to="end">
            <action name="cancel" expression="#{gadgetAdmin.cancelGadget}"/>
        </transition>
    </page>
```

```
    <page name="end" view-id="/adminHome.jsp">
        <redirect/>
        <end-conversation/>
    </page>
</pageflow-definition>
```

Among all the options discussed in the previous section about initiating the page-flow, we decided in the end to use an @Begin annotation on our newGadget() action method, and reference this action from an <s:link> control in the home page. So in our jPDL in Listing 5-3, we start the flow with a start-state element. The start-state has a single transition defined; specifying a "start" outcome from the action method should bring the user to the state named "core-data".

The "core-data" state is defined in the next page element. It's tied to the /wizard/start.jsp page using the view-id attribute. This is what brings the user to the first page of our wizard when the link on the home page is clicked. The "start" outcome from the newGadget() action method triggers the transition on the start-state node, bringing the pageflow to the "core-data" node. The user will be taken to the view for this node at the end of the request, because this is the state of the pageflow at the end of the request.

If you refer back to Figure 5-2, where I graphically show the pageflow we want for the wizard, the "core-data" node corresponds to the "Input core fields" page shown there. In the figure, I've shown two possible transitions from this state. A "next" trans-ition should take the user to a page for defining the types for the gadget. A "cancel" transition should take the user back to the home page and end the pageflow. These two transitions are defined in our jPDL in the "core-data" node, using transition child ele-ments. We've named each transition with the name attribute and indicated the destination node when the transition is followed using the to attribute. The destination node refer-ences the name attribute for a page element in the pageflow. For the "next" transition, we specify that the destination node is "types", and for "cancel", we specify "end" as the destination node.

We've also specified action child elements on each of these transitions. These specify action methods that should be invoked when the transition is followed. In the case of a "next" transition, we want the interimSaveGadget() action method on our GadgetAdminBean to be invoked, so we can do any interim persistence that is necessary for the data col-lected by the wizard. For a "cancel" transition, we want the cancelGadget() method to be invoked to clean up before the wizard is ended.

Obviously, we need to give the user a way to actually trigger these transitions. When operating within a jPDL pageflow, the transition names in the configuration can be refer-enced as the action attributes on page links. So, in the start.jsp page of our wizard, we've put two JSF commandButton controls at the bottom of the page:

```
    <h:commandButton value="Cancel" action="cancel"/>
    <h:commandButton value="Next" action="next"/>
```

Clicking the Next button will trigger the "next" transition on the "core-data" node, because that is the state we are in within the pageflow. The `interimSaveGadget()` method will be invoked, and then the user will be transitioned to the "types" state and the page that is associated with it. Similarly, clicking the Cancel button will invoke the `cancelGadget()` action and then take the user to the "end" state and its view. The "end" state actually ends the pageflow, but I'll discuss that in the next section.

Most of the remainder of the pageflow just uses these same concepts to implement the remainder of the flow depicted in Figure 5-2. Each page in the flow is represented in the jPDL with a `page` element whose `view-id` references the JSP file that implements the appropriate view for that state. Each transition between the states/pages is specified in the jPDL using `transition` elements, and then we add links in the views that reference these transition names in their `action` attributes. Any processing we need to do can be handled by action methods referenced using `action` elements on the transitions. If no processing is needed across a transition, we just leave out the action. The "prev" transitions present on most of the pages are a good example. Any interim persistence of gadget parameters has been done in our `interimSaveGadget()` action method, so there's really nothing we need to do when the user asks to go to the previous stage in the wizard.

Conditional Flow

So far we've only used unconditional transitions in our pageflow. If a user chooses a form button in the wizard, the transition named in the `action` attribute of the control is triggered, and the transition is followed, period. But there are situations where we want to conditionally follow different transitions from a given state, depending on various factors (input from the user, the state of context and/or persistent data, etc.).

Suppose, for example, that we introduced a new business rule into our Gadget Catalog: a gadget can only have features if it has at least one type assigned. This business rule might be introduced because we want all features to be validated against the gadget's types, to make sure that nonsense combinations aren't created (like a mobile phone with a built-in DVD player). The implications of this on the "new gadget" wizard are that we should not take the user to the "features" state unless the user has added at least one type to the gadget while in the "types" state.

jPDL supports conditional flow rules with the decision element. A decision plays roughly the same role as a state node in the pageflow, but it's a temporary state, not associated with any specific view. If a transition leads to a decision node, the JSF expression specified on the decision is evaluated, and the result is used to determine which transition to make.

To implement our new "features require types" business rule in the Gadget Catalog, we introduce a new decision node, and change the "types" node so that the "next" transition leads to the decision node rather than directly to the "features" state:

```
<page name="types" view-id="/wizard/types.jsp">
    <redirect/>
    <transition name="next" to="check-types">
        <action name="interim-save"
            expression="#{gadgetAdmin.interimSaveGadget}"/>
    </transition>
    <transition name="prev" to="core-data"/>
    <transition name="new" to="new-type"/>
</page>
<decision name="check-types" expression="#{empty gadget.types}">
    <transition name="true" to="confirm"/>
    <transition name="false" to="features"/>
</decision>
```

With this adjustment to the jPDL, the pageflow of the "new gadget" wizard will now follow the path shown in Figure 5-3.

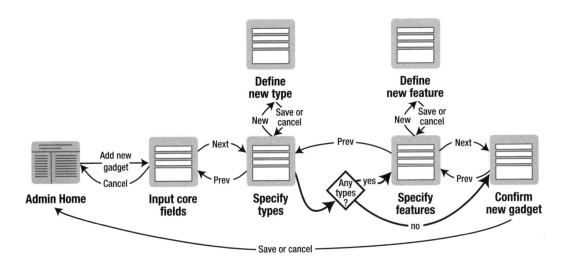

Figure 5-3. *Updated "new gadget" pageflow, with decision node*

Now, when the user clicks the Next button on the "Specify types" page, he or she is taken to the "check-types" state, which is a decision node. The expression "#{empty gadget.types}" is checked, and if it's true (i.e., there are no types on the gadget), the user is taken to the final "confirm" state. If the user did pick some types for the gadget (i.e., the expression is false), he or she is taken to the "features" state to pick some features for the gadget. Again, no application or page code changes were needed to make this happen, just some tweaks to the jPDL. However, if we wanted to implement the validation of features against types, we would want to adjust the action that's taken when the user moves on from the "features" state.

Note that you aren't limited to `Boolean` true/false expressions for the decision. You can also make transitions conditional on action method outcomes. As an alternative implementation of the condition in our pageflow, we could add a new `checkTypes()` action method to our `GadgetAdminBean`:

```java
public String checkTypes() {
    if (getActiveGadget() != null &&
        !getActiveGadget().getTypes().isEmpty()) {
        return "typed";
    }
    else {
        return "no-type";
    }
}
```

Then we could use this action method, and its outcomes, to configure the decision node:

```xml
<decision name="check-types" expression="#{gadgetAdmin.checkTypes}">
    <transition name="no-type" to="confirm"/>
    <transition name="typed" to="features"/>
</decision>
```

Managing the Back Button

By default, jBPM pageflow management effectively blocks the use of the browser's back button while a pageflow is active. If the user tries to back up, the jBPM component picks up the request, looks up the pageflow associated with the conversation of the request, and checks the user's current state in that pageflow. Then it brings the user to that state and its associated view. To the user, the effect is a disabling of the back button. The user can hit the back button as much as he or she likes, but Seam will keep putting the user on the same page.

This policy is a sensible default policy for jBPM-based pageflows, because they are modal by nature. The jPDL rules are meant to determine all states and transitions between states. The back button gives the user a way to bypass these rules and jump into another state without following the necessary transitions, which could leave the context data in an unpredictable state.

However, there are times when you do want to allow the user to back up during a jBPM pageflow. In our "new gadget" wizard, for example, we don't really depend on the sequence of the steps in the wizard. Each transition forward simply calls the same interimSaveGadget() action method to save the interim state of the Gadget being created. So it might be useful for us to enable the user to back up in the wizard, in addition to using the "prev" transition buttons we've put into the interface.

To accomplish this, we use the back attribute on the page elements in our jPDL configuration. If we set back="enabled" for a state in the flow, the user will be allowed to jump into that state whenever he or she likes by using the back button. We can enable the backing up to the first page of the wizard, for example, by enabling the back attribute like so:

```
<pageflow-definition name="new-gadget">
    . . .
    <page name="core-data"
          view-id="/wizard/start.jsp"
          back="enabled">
        <redirect/>
        <transition name="next" to="features">
            <action name="interim-save"
                    expression="#{gadgetAdmin.interimSaveGadget}"/>
        </transition>
        <transition name="cancel" to="end">
            <action name="cancel" expression="#{gadgetAdmin.cancelGadget}"/>
        </transition>
    </page>
    . . .
```

Obviously, if you allow the user to make asynchronous transitions in the pageflow like this, you'll need to handle this in your application logic, so that the state data held in the various contexts (session, conversation, etc.) is kept consistent. But this situation is no worse than standard JSF navigation. And Seam's context support (especially the concept of conversations within sessions) helps make this a bit easier to manage. By dividing up the user's session into well-defined conversation "segments," you reduce the problem to keeping the conversation data consistent. And assuming that your conversations are really well defined and represent a sensible grouping of interactions with the user, then keeping conversation data consistent should be relatively straightforward.

One situation that is important to expect with back-buttoning enabled is a user backing up into a state in a pageflow when that conversation has already ended. The conversation may have ended because the user ended it by following a transition that explicitly ended the conversation. Or, the conversation may have timed out. Either way, if you start to enable backing into states of your pageflow, it's a good idea to deal with this case for those states.

To help with this, Seam has extended jPDL to provide you a way to specify a view that should be used when the user hits a state in a pageflow with a conversation that has ended. There is another attribute that Seam has added to the page element, called no-conversation-view-id. A user will be taken to this view when he or she backs up to this pageflow state with an expired conversation. In our example, if a user backs up into the "new gadget" wizard with an expired conversation, the most logical place to put that user would be the administrative home page. So we would specify this on our page nodes like so:

```
<pageflow-definition name="new-gadget">
    . . .
    <page name="core-data"
          view-id="/wizard/start.jsp"
          back="enabled"
          no-conversation-view-id="/adminHome.jsp">
        <redirect/>
        <transition name="next" to="features">
            <action name="interim-save"
                    expression="#{gadgetAdmin.interimSaveGadget}"/>
        </transition>
        <transition name="cancel" to="end">
            <action name="cancel" expression="#{gadgetAdmin.cancelGadget}"/>
        </transition>
    </page>
    . . .
```

Ending Pageflows

Pageflows are aligned with conversations, so ending a pageflow involves ending its surrounding conversation. All the methods for ending conversations, as discussed in Chapter 4, will also end any pageflow associated with that conversation. These methods include executing an action method with an @End annotation, or traversing a link with attributes that end the conversation, or hitting a page with an entry in pages.xml that ends the conversation when that page is encountered.

Using jPDL, there is an additional way to end the conversation for a pageflow. Adding an end-conversation element to a state definition in the jPDL will cause the conversation (and pageflow) to end when that state is reached. We used this in our "new gadget" wizard to end the pageflow when the user landed on the "end" state:

```
. . .
<page name="end" view-id="/adminHome.jsp">
    <redirect/>
    <end-conversation/>
</page>
. . .
```

We used this state as the destination for the "cancel" transitions on the first page of the wizard and for the final confirmation page. If the user hits the Cancel button on either of these pages, he or she will transition to this state, which ends the conversation and lands the user back on the home page.

Advantages of jPDL

Now that we have our "new gadget" wizard fully implemented using jBPM, let's revisit some of the advantages of jPDL-based navigation versus JSF navigation rules.

Flexible Pageflow Through Encapsulation

One point in favor of jPDL is the way that it allows you to cleanly separate your application code (action listeners included) from the view navigation rules. It even allows you to separate the view display (i.e., the code in your pages) from the navigation rules. JSF navigation rules provide some degree of encapsulation, but since JSF navigation is defined in terms of concrete pages, it is tied more directly to the implementation details.

If you examine the action methods on GadgetAdminBean that are used as actions in our "new gadget" pageflow (namely, interimSaveGadget(), saveGadget(), cancelGadget(), saveGadgetType(), and saveGadgetFeature()), we've kept these free of any navigation information. These action methods don't know when or how they are being triggered, nor do they care. Some of them (saveGadgetType() and saveGadgetFeature()) are reused from elsewhere in the Gadget Catalog application, outside of the pageflow.

The view code in the wizard pages is also very clean. There are commandButton controls that reference logical transition names (like "prev" and "next"), but there's no hardcoded page transitions. Even the actions that are performed on the transitions are specified outside of the view code, in the jPDL.

One practical advantage of all this is the ability to alter the pageflow without making significant (or, in some cases, any) changes to the application code or the view code. Suppose that we decided it made more sense to add the features to a new gadget before we add the types. All we need to do is adjust the transitions in the jPDL to make this happen. We change the "next" transition on the first page to take the user to the "features" state:

```
<page name="core-data" view-id="/wizard/start.jsp">
    <redirect/>
    <transition name="next" to="features">
        <action name="interim-save"
                expression="#{gadgetAdmin.interimSaveGadget}"/>
    </transition>
    <transition name="cancel" to="end">
        <action name="cancel" expression="#{gadgetAdmin.cancelGadget}"/>
    </transition>
</page>
```

Then we change the "next" and "prev" transitions on the "features" state so that "next" leads to the "types" state and "prev" returns the user to the "core-data" page:

```
<page name="features" view-id="/wizard/features.jsp">
    <redirect/>
    <transition name="next" to="types">
        <action expression="#{gadgetAdmin.interimSaveGadget}"/>
    </transition>
    <transition name="prev" to="core-data"/>
    <transition name="new" to="new-feature"/>
</page>
```

Finally, we adjust the "types" state so that "next" takes us to the final "confirm" state and "prev" takes us back to the "features" state:

```
<page name="types" view-id="/wizard/types.jsp">
    <redirect/>
    <transition name="next" to="confirm">
        <action name="interim-save"
            expression="#{gadgetAdmin.interimSaveGadget}"/>
    </transition>
    <transition name="prev" to="features"/>
    <transition name="new" to="new-type"/>
</page>
```

That's it. Now the wizard will follow the new pageflow, with no changes to our application or view code.

Now, I should admit that we're getting off a bit easier than normal here, because in our wizard we're using the same action for all of our "next" transitions regardless of the destination state. That means we didn't have to tweak any of the transition actions when we changed the pageflow. But even if we did, those changes would have been fairly trivial as well. And being able to restructure the pageflow with minimal impact on the rest of the application can be a big advantage, especially with significant pageflows and ongoing adjustments being introduced because of user feedback, business requirements, and so on.

Expressiveness of jPDL

Compared to JSF navigation rules, jPDL provides a more direct representation of the logical pageflow of the application. We could easily take the jPDL configuration in Listing 5-3 and generate (manually or automatically) the graphical pageflow for our wizard in Figure 5-2. JBoss took this to the next level, providing a plug-in for the Eclipse IDE that allows you to graphically view and edit jPDL pageflows. Of course, the same could be done for JSF navigation rules (and, in fact, it has been done, since several tools exist to graphically edit JSF rules as well). The difference with jPDL is that, since jPDL distinguishes between logical states and physical pages, we have the option of creating either logical or physical pictures of our pageflow. In the case of our "new gadget" wizard, this isn't much of an advantage, because all of our logical states have a one-to-one relationship with our physical pages ("core-data" is mapped to `start.jsp`, "types" to `types.jsp`, etc.). But in more complicated modal interfaces, it's often necessary to use the same view at multiple states in the logical pageflow. jPDL allows you to express this directly, while it's only implicitly expressed in JSF rules since the logical states being implemented have to be inferred from the various navigation cases where the same view is used.

Summary

In this chapter, you've seen how Seam's integrated jBPM support has been used to implement a powerful alternative for defining pageflow in your application. Using jPDL XML files, you can define structured pageflow to be followed within specific Seam conversations. There are advantages (richer configuration syntax, better separation of navigation and application code) and disadvantages (more restrictive navigation) to jPDL over JSF navigation rules, but luckily you can mix-and-match the two within your Seam application fairly easily.

We explored how jBPM pageflows are configured using a jPDL XML file that's deployed with your Seam application, and how jPDL allows you to specify the states, transitions, actions, and conditional flows in your pageflow. And, as usual, you saw all of this in action in our Gadget Catalog application by implementing a "new gadget" wizard using jBPM pageflow.

CHAPTER 6

■■■

Security

Security is a natural part of nearly every online application. Any application that requires some kind of personal service needs to know the identity of the user. Preferences and data can't be associated with you unless the application knows who "you" are. This is the goal of authentication: securely identifying the users of a system.

Applications are typically put online so that many people can use them, not just one. It is very rare, however, that you want everyone using your application to have the same access rights. Some people have more or less access than others, depending on the roles and permissions that they have been given. Authorization provides the tools for assigning and verifying the access rights of users.

In this chapter, we are going to explore Seam's support for authenticating and authorizing users. First, I'll give you a high-level overview of the capabilities provided by Seam. Then I'll describe some security-related extensions required in the next version of the Gadget Catalog, and we'll implement them in the rest of the chapter using Seam's security services.

Seam Security Support

Seam directly supports the integration of security measures into your applications. Specifically, it facilitates adding authentication and authorization features to your Seam applications. As any security expert will tell you, there are many other aspects to be considered when it comes to security (identity management, encryption, intrusion detection, etc.). But Seam focuses on the most common application needs, and the rest can be integrated through other means.

Authentication

Seam helps you inject login functionality into your application, in areas where you need to identify users and/or check to see whether they have rights to access particular pages, functions, or data. Seam gives you the ability to require authentication at various levels (page, JSF control, component, action method) using configuration file entries and/or code annotations. The login process can be implemented using standard Seam components and JSF forms, in conjunction with built-in components provided by Seam. Seam also provides built-in components that support the handling of the user's identity for easy access from within the Seam contextual component model.

Authorization

You often need to authenticate users because you need to check their access rights. Again, Seam helps you to authorize users at various levels in the application—you can specify access limits for groups of pages, single pages, specific JSF controls, entire Seam components, or specific action methods on components. These access rights are specified using roles and/or permissions. Roles in Seam are simple named role assignments, like "admin" or "sales-rep", while permissions are named actions that can be performed in general or on specific entities. Like the authentication services within Seam, you can specify access rules for entities using configuration file entries and/or code annotations. It's also possible to do more advanced authorization management using JBoss Rules rulesets.

Seam Security vs. Java EE Security

Readers who are familiar with Java EE security features for web and EJB components might be wondering how Seam's security features relate to them. The short answer is that they don't. Seam's security services are an independent system that is not integrated with Java EE's declarative or programmatic security features. User identities and roles in Seam are sourced from Seam components and services, while Java EE uses the concept of realms configured in the application server. Seam's authentication is configured through `components.xml` and the identity is stored in a Seam component, while Java EE uses `login-config` elements in `web.xml` and stores the identity in the user's runtime web/EJB context. Seam's programmatic role checking is done through EL expressions and/or Seam component methods, while Java EE provides the `isUserInRole()` methods in web and EJB components. And so on.

Seam does offer some crude integration with the Java Authentication and Authorization Services (JAAS), which are the backing services behind the Java EE security services. In the current released version of Seam (version 1.2.1), however, this integration is definitely not seamless (pardon the pun) and involves some fairly complicated configuration gymnastics. These configuration details aren't provided here, because they seem to be very preliminary in nature, and not broadly useful in their current form. The integration is also limited, since it only provides a common source for identities and roles, but no shared authorization or authentication configuration.

In order to avoid complex configuration details, runtime conflicts, and potential confusion, my recommendation would be to stick to one security model or the other until there is better integration between the two. If you have a specific requirement to use

Java EE security, it's best to use that exclusively and avoid using Seam's security services. Otherwise, you should definitely look to Seam's security services for your Seam application, since it provides a simplified model that blends right into Seam's contextual component model.

Gadget Catalog: Expansion Through Security

Our Gadget Catalog has gone about as far as it can go (farther, actually) without integrating security services into the application. Without any authentication or authorization capabilities, all of our users are anonymous, and all users have equal access to all of the functions of the interface. This isn't practical, obviously. We may want to allow all users to browse the Gadget Catalog without identifying themselves, but we will definitely want to restrict access to the administrative functions of the system, such as adding new gadgets to the catalog and editing their features. At a minimum, we need to know who is performing these operations so that we have an audit trail for key transactions (to answer questions like, "Who deleted all of the mobile phones from the system?" or "Who has provided the most gadget entries in the system?"). It's also very likely that we will need to restrict access to some of the functions in the system. Some users will be allowed to perform some tasks, others will not.

The Gadget Catalog product development team has decided to implement the following security model for the application:

- Anonymous, unauthenticated users will be allowed to search the catalog and browse the contents.

- In order to add a gadget to the catalog (using either the "new gadget" wizard described in Chapter 5 or the basic gadget editing tools implemented earlier), users must be authenticated. The user must have an account in the system and will be required to log in before using these functions.

- The catalog will now record the identifier of the user who initially submitted the gadget to the catalog. This will be used in the future to support various administrative and community features, such as rewards for submitting large numbers of new gadgets (thus increasing the value of the catalog).

- There will be two roles defined in the Gadget Catalog: "USER" and "ADMIN". A "USER" is a general user who self-registers to use the system and can enter new gadgets into the catalog using the "new gadget" wizard. An "ADMIN" is a more knowledgeable user (typically, a person who works for the Gadget Catalog site as an employee) who performs administrative duties for the catalog. An "ADMIN" has access to all of the interface functions, including the more advanced gadget editing tools.

User Interface Access Control

The security model described previously implies some access-control restrictions on the pages of the user interface. Figure 6-1 shows the pageflow of the new version of the Gadget Catalog and depicts the new access restrictions being imposed on the application at this level. There are more fine-grained access control measures that will be necessary as well, but I'll describe those in detail in the sections that follow.

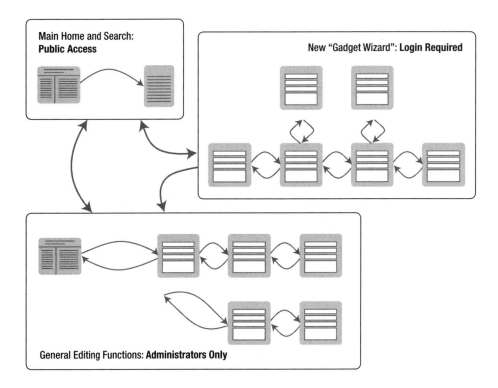

Figure 6-1. *Page-level access to the Gadget Catalog*

The only new page being introduced is a general-purpose home page, part of the "main home and search" section in the pageflow, which will be used for public and non-administrative users as their default entry point for the application. This page and the search results page will be publicly accessible, allowing any anonymous user to perform searches against the Gadget Catalog. The "new gadget" wizard, however, will require the user to be logged in, so that his or her ID can be recorded with the new gadget. The "Admin Home" and the general gadget editing pages will only be accessible to users who belong to the "ADMIN" role.

Data Model Changes

We will maintain the user and role information within the Gadget Catalog database, requiring the updates shown in Figure 6-2. A few new tables have been added to the schema: the USER table holds the essential attributes for users of the application, the ROLE table describes the various roles defined within the system, and the USER_ROLE_ASSN table associates users with the roles that they have been assigned. We've also introduced a new column in the GADGET table, SUBMITTER, that holds the identifier for the user who initially submitted the gadget.

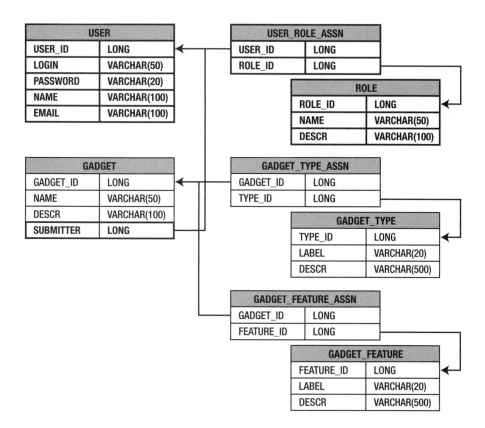

Figure 6-2. *Security-related extensions to the Gadget Catalog database*

Configuring Seam Security

Before you can use any of the Seam security measures described in the following sections, you need to enable the Seam security services in your application. There are some basic configuration steps you have to take no matter what features you're using from Seam's security services. Other details are only needed if you use specific parts of the Seam security services.

Minimal Configuration

In order to do any sort of authorization, you have to be able to identify the users of your application. In order to identify users, you have to authenticate them in some way. At a minimum, therefore, you'll need to enable some form of authentication support in Seam if you want to use Seam for any security operations. Authentication support is enabled by adding the `security:identity` element to your `components.xml` file. There are attributes on this element that allow you to specify the type of authentication you require. The following example shows the simplest use, where you plan to use Seam's internal login services with authentication handled by one of your Seam components:

```
<?xml version="1.0" encoding="UTF-8"?>
<components xmlns:security="http://jboss.com/products/seam/security"
            xmlns:xsi="http://www.w3.org/2001/XMLSchema-instance"
            xsi:schemaLocation=
                "http://jboss.com/products/seam/security
                 http://jboss.com/products/seam/security-1.2.xsd">
    . . .
    <security:identity authenticate-method="#{authenticator.login}"/>
    . . .
</components>
```

Notice that we've included the XML schema for Seam's security-related configuration elements in our `components.xml`. As mentioned in Chapter 2, Seam organizes the configuration details for individual services into separate schemas that can be referenced when needed in `components.xml`.

The `security:identity` element will cause Seam to initialize its basic security services, including the built-in `identity` component, and configure login services as specified in the configuration entry. In this case, we're using Seam's internal login module, and the `login` method on the `authenticator` component will be used to verify user identities. I'll discuss the authentication services in Seam in a later section.

Security EL Expressions

Seam provides some security-related EL expressions that can be used in your `pages.xml` configuration and in your JSF pages. If you want to make use of these EL expressions, you'll need to ensure that the EL libraries are available in the runtime environment of your application. This can be done by including the `el-ri.jar` and `el-api.jar` libraries bundled with Seam in your deployed archive. As discussed in Chapter 2, you can either put these in the root of your EAR file and reference them in the `application.xml` file as jar modules (making them available to all modules included in the application) or put them into the `WEB-INF/lib` directory of your web archive.

The JSF features of the security services also require that you include the `jboss-seam-ui.jar` library in your application classpath. This library can also be included in the web archive or the EAR file.

In order to use the extended Seam EL expressions in your JSF pages, you'll need to make use of the Seam Facelet view handler to process your JSF pages. This is done by adding the view handler to the application section of your `faces-config.xml` file, like so:

```
<faces-config>
    . . .
    <application>
        <view-handler>
            org.jboss.seam.ui.facelet.SeamFaceletViewHandler
        </view-handler>
    </application>
    . . .
</faces-config>
```

Doing this, however, sets off a chain reaction that might be a bit of a surprise. By installing the Seam Facelet view handler, you're also saying that all of your pages are implemented using Facelets instead of JSP, because that's what the Facelet view handler expects. This means that you'll need to convert your pages to Facelets if you want to use Seam's security-related EL expressions. This is an unfortunate dependency, especially if you have a lot of JSP pages in your application. But if you're already using JSF in your application, you should find that the conversion of pages to Facelets is fairly straightforward.

Facelets is a topic that's beyond the scope of this chapter, and the book for that matter. You can examine the pages in the sample code for this chapter, however, and compare them to the corresponding pages from earlier chapters, to see how pages can be converted from JSP to Facelets. For more information on Facelets and their use, refer to the Facelets project home page (`https://facelets.dev.java.net`).

JBoss Rules

As I'll discuss in the section "Authorization Services," you can optionally use JBoss Rules to define authorization rules for your application. If you decide to use this feature, there are a number of support libraries you'll need to include in the classpath of your application. These libraries are included in the Seam distribution, in the `drools/lib` directory. Add all of these as `jar` elements in the `application.xml` of your EAR file, or put them in the `WEB-INF/lib` directory of your WAR file.

Authentication Services

In the world of security, "authentication" refers to the identification of a user, based on credentials of some kind. Usually these credentials are a username and password, but more elaborate and more secure credentials can be used as well, like biometric scans (thumbprints, retinas, etc.) or hardware tokens. The discussion here will be limited to traditional username/password schemes.

This section is going to explore various details of Seam's authentication support. I'll first show you how to configure a simple login page with an authentication action method and how to access the authenticated user information from your Seam components. Then you'll see how to integrate authentication into a Seam application by adding login/logout links as well as requiring authentication for specific parts of the application.

Enabling the Authentication Services

If you've ever created your own login scheme in a web application, you know the usual approach that's taken to make this work: write a web form to collect the account and password information, and write a form handler to take that information and verify it against some back-end authoritative source (database, directory, etc.). If the user's credentials check out, you need to load up some basic identifying attributes (user ID, name, etc.) and make them available to the rest of the application. You might do this by tucking an object into session data, or putting an encrypted user ID into a cookie, or both.

Seam's security services simplify the creation of authentication features through some simple extensions of the Seam component and context models. In the section "Configuring Seam Security," you saw how to enable the basic Seam security services by putting an entry into the `components.xml` file like the following:

```
<security:identity authenticate-method="#{authenticator.login}"/>
```

In practical terms, this entry tells Seam that we want all authentication requests to be handled by the `login()` action method on the component named `authenticator`. So where do authentication requests come from? In Seam's security model, an authentication request comes from a JSF form that uses a specific, built-in Seam component named identity to handle the form attributes and the form submission. This component is initialized and made available in your Seam application when you add a security:identity entry to your components.xml.

Creating the Login Form

A typical Seam login form is shown in Listing 6-1. The username and password fields are collected through JSF input controls that are bound to the identity.username and identity.password properties, respectively. The form submission is handled by the identity.login action method.

Listing 6-1. *Basic Seam Login Form*

```
<!DOCTYPE html PUBLIC
    "-//W3C//DTD XHTML 1.0 Transitional//EN"
    "http://www.w3.org/TR/xhtml1/DTD/xhtml1-transitional.dtd">
<html xmlns="http://www.w3.org/1999/xhtml"
      xmlns:ui="http://java.sun.com/jsf/facelets"
      xmlns:s="http://jboss.com/products/seam/taglib"
      xmlns:h="http://java.sun.com/jsf/html"
      xmlns:f="http://java.sun.com/jsf/core">
<ui:composition template="template.xhtml">
    <ui:param name="title" value="Login"/>
    <ui:define name="main">
        <f:view>
            <h:form>
                <table border="0">
                    <tr>
                        <td class="formLabel">User name:</td>
                        <td>
                            <h:inputText value="#{identity.username}"
                                     id="name"
                                     style="formInput"/>
                        </td>
                    </tr>
                    <tr>
                        <td class="formLabel">Password:</td>
                        <td>
                            <h:inputSecret value="#{identity.password}"
                                     id="password"
                                     style="formInput"/>
```

```
                        </td>
                    </tr>
                </table>
                <h:commandButton value="Login"
                                  action="#{identity.login}"/>
            </h:form>
        </f:view>
    </ui:define>
</ui:composition>
</html>
```

■**Practical Tip** If you've got sharp eyes, you will have noticed that this page looks a bit different from our earlier examples. That's because we're using Facelets instead of JSP for the reasons described in the section "Configuring Seam Security."

A Facelets primer is beyond the scope of this book, as I said before, but you can easily follow these examples once you understand a few high-level differences between JSP and Facelets. Facelets uses XHTML in the page, and rather than importing JSP tag libraries, we import good old XML schemas. Facelets ties these XML elements back to view handlers through tag mappings provided by the providers of the JSF controls being used. In our pages, we're using standard JSF controls as well as Seam controls, so both the JSF implementation and the Seam framework have to provide these mappings, and in our case they do.

The other big difference here is that we're using the Facelets UI composition features to compose our page. We're importing a template file, `template.xhtml`, at the start of the page, in a Facelets `ui:composition` tag. This template defines the general structure of a page in our Gadget Catalog application, including any header and footer links and decorations. The template also defines a page section called "main", where we can plug in the specific content needed for this particular page. Here, we're plugging in the login form, within the element that starts with `<ui:define name="main">`, using standard JSF controls.

When this form is rendered, it will look like Figure 6-3.

Figure 6-3. *Gadget Catalog login form*

All of the decoration and header links (the CSS styles, the "Home" and "Log in" links, and the title) were defined in the page template, `template.xhtml`. The form elements defined in Listing 6-1 are rendered in the main part of the page.

Creating the Login Handler

When our login form is submitted, the Seam `identity` component referenced in the `commandButton` will invoke the action method that we configured in the `security:identity` entry in `components.xml`. In our example earlier, we specified this to be `authenticator.login`, so we'll need to provide a component named `authenticator` with a `login()` method.

The sample component listed here could serve as a handler for our login page:

```
@Stateful
@Name("authenticator")
public class SampleLogin implements Serializable {
    public boolean login() {
        boolean success  = false;
        Identity identity = Identity.instance();
        String username = identity.getUsername();
        String password = identity.getPassword();
        // AUTHENTICATE THE USER HERE
        return result;
    }

    @Destroy @Remove
    public void destroy() {}
}
```

The component is named "authenticator" using an @Name annotation to match the component reference we put into components.xml. The login() method returns a boolean value. This boolean value will be used by the Seam login service as the indication of whether authentication was successful or not. If the method returns true, the user is assumed to be authenticated and is taken to the appropriate page. If the method returns false, the default behavior is to generate a JSF message that simply says, "Login failed", and take the user back to the login page. Our page template displays any JSF messages just below the page title, so a failed login will result in what you see in Figure 6-4.

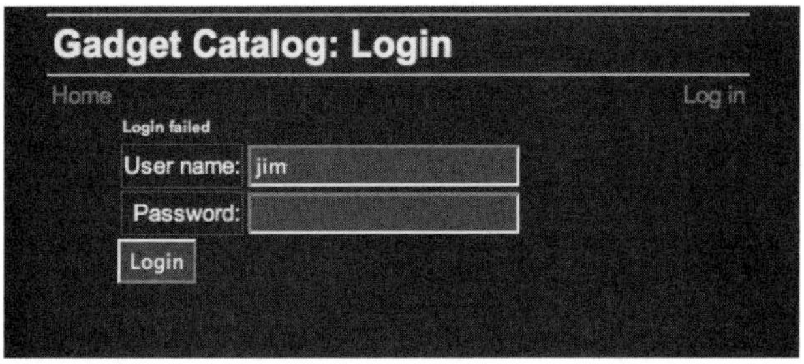

Figure 6-4. *Login error message*

The handling of successful and failed logins can be configured to some degree, and I'll get into those details in the next section.

You'll notice in our sample login() method that the username and password provided in the login form can be retrieved through Seam's Identity class. This class (in the org.jboss.seam.security package) has a singleton that is the implementation behind the identity component we referenced in the login form. You can get the Identity singleton using the static instance() method, as we're doing here, and then access the properties using standard accessors. With those fields, you can then do whatever authentication steps are necessary in your application.

In the Gadget Catalog, we're storing the user account information in the USER table in the database, shown in Figure 6-2. We need to compare the username and password fields from the login form to the LOGIN and PASSWORD columns in that table. The Seam-like way to do this is to create a new entity bean, User, that represents the data from the USER table, and then do an EJB-QL query in our login handler to verify the user's credentials.

Listing 6-2 shows our new User entity bean. It includes all of the appropriate JPA annotations to map its properties to the appropriate columns in the USER table. The bean is a straightforward mapping of the USER table, though for now we've left out the user roles stored in the ROLE table, linked through the USER_ROLE link table. I'll revisit that when I discuss authorization in the section "Authorization Services." Also, notice that we've used an @Scope annotation to make this a session-scoped component. We want the user's authenticated identity to last the duration of his or her session, not just for a single conversation. Otherwise, the user will be forced to log in whenever a conversation ends.

Listing 6-2. *The* User *Entity Bean*

```java
@Entity
@Name("user")
@Scope(ScopeType.SESSION)
@Table(name="USER")
public class User implements Serializable {
    private String mName = null;
    private String mEmail = null;
    private String mLogin = null;
    private String mPassword = null;
    private long mId;

    public User() {}

    @Id @GeneratedValue
    @Column(name="USER_ID")
    public long getId() {
        return mId;
    }

    @Transient
    public String getIdStr() {
        return Long.toString(getId());
    }

    public void setId(long id) {
        mId = id;
    }

    @Column(name="EMAIL")
    public String getEmail() {
        return mEmail;
    }

    public void setEmail(String email) {
        mEmail = email;
    }

    @Column(name="LOGIN")
    public String getLogin() {
        return mLogin;
    }
```

```
    public void setLogin(String login) {
        mLogin = login;
    }

    @Column(name="NAME")
    public String getName() {
        return mName;
    }

    public void setName(String name) {
        mName = name;
    }

    @Column(name="PASSWORD")
    public String getPassword() {
        return mPassword;
    }

    public void setPassword(String password) {
        mPassword = password;
    }
}
```

With the User bean in place, we can complete the implementation of the login handler for the Gadget Catalog. The full component class, Login, is shown in Listing 6-3. We've expanded on the sample component shown earlier to include an injected EntityManager that is used to make the necessary queries against the database. The query is straightforward enough—we select from the USER table, matching the username from the identity component with the LOGIN column and the password against the PASSWORD column. If there is a match, the user is authenticated, and we set the user property on our component to the resulting User object. The user property is annotated to be outjected into the session context, so that other components and pages can use it to render the user's name, e-mail address, and so on, as well as do any necessary queries against the database using the current user's details.

Listing 6-3. *Login Handler for the Gadget Catalog*

```
@Stateful
@Name("authenticator")
public class Login implements ILogin, Serializable {
```

```
@In(value="user", required=false)
@Out(value="user", required=false)
private User mUser;

@In(create=true)
private EntityManager gadgetDatabase;

public boolean login() {
    boolean result = false;
    if (getUser() == null) {
        try {
            Identity identity = Identity.instance();
            Query q =
                gadgetDatabase.createQuery("from User " +
                                            "where login = :userName " +
                                            "and password = :password")
                        .setParameter("userName", identity.getUsername())
                        .setParameter("password", identity.getPassword());
            setUser((User) q.getSingleResult());
        }
        catch (NoResultException nre) {
            FacesMessages.instance().add("Username/password do not match");
        }
    }
    result = (getUser() == null ? false : true);
    return result;
}

@Destroy @Remove
public void destroy() {}

public User getUser() {
    return mUser;
}

public void setUser(User user) {
    mUser = user;
}
}
```

In our `login()` method, a failed authentication is indicated when our query returns no results. This tells us that the information provided by the user in the login form doesn't match any records in the `USER` table. We catch the `NoResultException` thrown by the JPA query and put an appropriate error message into the JSF message list.

At the end of the `login()` method, we determine the success of the authentication by checking to see whether the user property has been set, and then return the appropriate value.

Adding Login and Logout Links

At this point, all we have is our login form, `login.xhtml`, and the component that handles the submissions from this form, `Login`. If we insert these pieces into our application, all we'll have is a login form that a user has to find manually. We need to make it easier for the user to log in, or else we're sure to hear complaints. One simple addition we can make is to add a login link to the application pages:

```
<h:outputLink value="login.seam"
              rendered="#{not identity.loggedIn}">Log in</h:outputLink>
```

This is a standard JSF `outputLink` that points to the `login.xhtml` page. There is one new detail here, however. We're making the display of this link conditional on the `identity.loggedIn` property. This property on the `identity` component is set to `true` if the authentication action method (in our case, the `Login.login()` method) returns `true` during a login. The `identity` component is scoped to the session context, so this property can be used to verify whether the current user is authenticated. In our case, we only want to display the login link if the user is not authenticated.

The user's authenticated session will eventually end, either through a session expiration because of inactivity or if the user closes the browser. It's good practice, however, to provide the user with a way to log out explicitly. That way he or she can be assured that his or her authenticated session is gone and not worry about leaving the browser open to do other work. Seam provides a `logout()` action method on the `identity` component that can be used for this purpose. We can add a logout link to our pages by including the following in our Facelets template file:

```
<s:link action="#{identity.logout}" value="Log out"
        rendered="#{identity.loggedIn}"/>
```

Notice that we're using the same `loggedIn` property on `identity` to determine whether to render this link or not. A logout link doesn't make any sense to a user who isn't logged in yet.

Restricting Pages

We still have some work to do if we want to implement the access control levels described in the section "User Interface Access Control," where I described the various sections of the pageflow and how they should be secured. The new requirements call for only authenticated users to be able to access the "new gadget" wizard pages, and only users with the administrator role are allowed to access the general editing pages. I haven't discussed how to do role-based authorization yet, so for now, we'll just require authenticated users for both sets of pages and add in the authorization rules later.

If you think about the various Seam configuration files, the obvious place to configure page-level security is in pages.xml. Luckily, the Seam developers saw it the same way, and they provide various security-related elements that you can use there.

In our case, we want all the "new gadget" wizard pages to require authentication. This can be accomplished by adding the following page element in our pages.xml configuration file:

```
<page view-id="/wizard/*">
    <restrict>#{identity.loggedIn}</restrict>
</page>
```

The view-id attribute specifies all of the pages that reside in the wizard subdirectory of the web application, which is where all the pages of the wizard live. In the page element, we use a restrict subelement to control access to the pages. A restrict element contains an EL expression. Technically, you can put any expression you like here, but for practical reasons, you'll typically want this expression to be a "security expression" (i.e., an expression that checks the user's authentication or authorization status using Seam's security components). I'll discuss the access control checks that you can use in the restrict element when I discuss authorization. Authentication checks, like the one we're doing here, are done using the same loggedIn attribute on the identity component that you saw earlier.

No matter what EL expression you place within the restrict element, Seam handles it the same way. If the expression evaluates to true, the user is taken to the page. If the expression evaluates to false, Seam checks the user's authenticated status. If the user is not authenticated, a NotLoggedInException is thrown. If the user is authenticated, Seam assumes the issue is access control and throws an AuthorizationException.

Another option for configuring authentication for a set of pages is to use the login-required attribute on the page element. If set to true, this attribute has the same effect as the restrict element shown previously:

```
<page view-id="/wizard/*" login-required="true"/>
```

The `restrict` element is more general-purpose, as you'll see when I discuss authorization, since it allows us to specify a range of restrictions that can be placed on access to the page(s). But if you simply need to ensure that users are authenticated before accessing a set of pages, the `login-required` attribute is a useful shortcut.

Our requirements call for the general gadget editing pages to be restricted to authenticated users as well. We can use page restrictions in `pages.xml` for this as well, but first we will move all of the pages we want restricted into their own `admin` directory. The pages had all been sitting in the root of our web archive, and to restrict them we would have had to use separate `page` elements for each page. With all the nonwizard editing pages moved into the `admin` directory, we can now restrict them all with a single `page` element:

```
<page view-id="/admin/*" login-required="\true"/>
```

Handling Authentication Exceptions

As just mentioned, if a page restriction check fails when a user visits a page, and the user isn't authenticated, a `NotLoggedInException` is thrown. We could let that exception go unchecked, generating a system error page, but that's not a very good user experience. It's much better to handle the exception in a user-friendly way. In this case, the most sensible thing from the user's perspective is to take him or her to the login form when this exception occurs. You can specify this kind of exception-handling behavior in Seam in `pages.xml`, using an `exception` element.

The `exception` element is a general-purpose way to handle runtime exceptions in Seam. You place an `exception` element in your `pages.xml`, specifying the type of exception you want to handle, and what to do when this exception is thrown. In the `exception` element, you can tell Seam to generate a specific HTTP error code, or you can redirect the user to a specific page.

In our case, when a user hits a restricted page and isn't authenticated, we want to send the user to the login page. That's much more helpful than generating a default error message and leaving it to the user to find the login page on his or her own. We can do this by adding the following element to our `pages.xml`:

```
<pages>
    . . .
    <exception class="org.jboss.seam.security.NotLoggedInException">
        <redirect view-id="/login.xhtml">
            <message>You must be logged in to access this page</message>
        </redirect>
    </exception>
    . . .
</pages>
```

With this exception handling[1] in place, a user who hits a restricted page will automatically be taken to the login page, and the message we specified within the redirect element will be put into the JSF messages list. Our login page displays these messages just above the login form, so the user will see the screen in Figure 6-5 after being redirected.

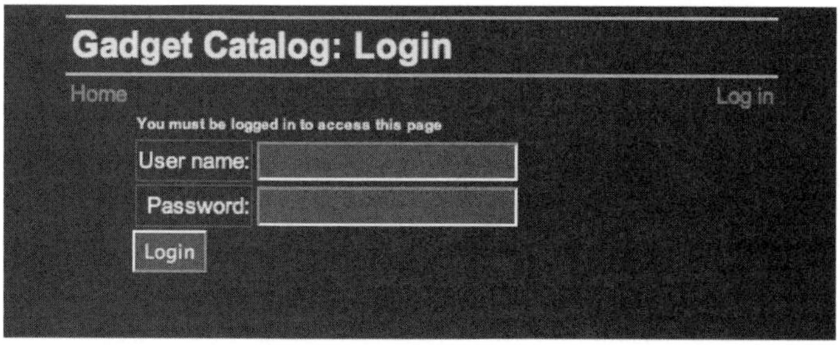

Figure 6-5. *Authentication exception message on login page*

Making a Smarter Login

The login scheme we've set up so far will ensure that only authenticated users will be allowed to access the gadget editing pages. Unauthenticated users will be taken automatically to the login page and asked to authenticate. But what happens after they log in?

As it stands, the user who logs in successfully will simply be left on the login page, with a message indicating that he or she has authenticated successfully. This user has to manually navigate back to the page he or she asked for in the first place. Ideally, we'd like the user to be taken back to the protected page that was requested automatically. Luckily, this is fairly easy to implement in Seam, using component-driven events.

Seam supports an event model where components can generate events, and other components can listen for them and react when they occur. Seam's internal components, including the security components, generate a set of built-in events that can be used to trigger application-specific behavior. In terms of authentication, Seam's security components fire two interesting events: a "notLoggedIn" event is fired when an unauthenticated user attempts to access a protected page, and a "postAuthenticate" event is fired when a user successfully authenticates through the Seam security services.

You can specify actions that should be taken when events are fired, in your components.xml file. The event element is used to specify an event, and an action child element is used to specify a component action method that should be fired when the event is fired. In our case, we want to catch the Seam notLoggedIn exception and have Seam remember the page that the user requested. Then we want to catch the

---

1. This exception-handling feature in pages.xml can be used for general exceptions as well, to send users to error-specific pages, or to cover all uncaught exceptions with a general-purpose error page.

postAuthenticate event and have Seam redirect the user to the page that it remembered for the user when he or she generated the notLoggedIn event. These can be achieved by adding the following two event elements to our components.xml:

```
<components>
    . . .
    <event type="org.jboss.seam.notLoggedIn">
        <action expression="#{redirect.captureCurrentView}"/>
    </event>
    <event type="org.jboss.seam.postAuthenticate">
        <action expression="#{redirect.returnToCapturedView}"/>
    </event>
    . . .
</components>
```

In these entries, we're using another built-in Seam component, redirect, to do the storage and retrieval of the user's target page. The redirect component has other utility methods available, but for our purposes, these two provide exactly the functionality we need.

With all this in place, the login behavior of our application is complete. When the user enters the application and requests a restricted page (e.g., by clicking the "Add a new gadget" link on the home page), he or she will not be authenticated yet, and two things will happen. A notLoggedIn event will be generated, causing the first event handler in components.xml to be triggered, saving the requested page through the redirect component. Then a NotLoggedInException will be thrown, causing our exception handler in pages.xml to be triggered, redirecting the user to the login.xhtml page. Assuming the user successfully authenticates with the login page, a postAuthenticate event will be generated, triggering our second event handler in components.xml. The stored page URL will be retrieved, and the user will be redirected to it.

Authorization Services

Now that the Gadget Catalog can authenticate users, we need to turn to the rest of our security requirements. If you refer back to the section "Gadget Catalog: Expansion Through Security," you'll see that we need to ensure that only administrators can access the general gadget editing pages. We know the identities of our users now (at least, we do once they try to access a protected area), so the next thing we need to do is assign them roles and make sure that Seam is aware of those roles. Once that's done, we can use these roles to specify access rights for users based on their roles.

Assigning Roles to Users

Seam knows whether the user is authenticated or not based on the `loggedIn` property on the `identity` component, which is set based on the return value of the authentication action method used to log in users (in our case, the `Login.login()` method). You also use the `identity` component to inform Seam about the roles belonging to a user.

Before we can tell Seam about the roles belonging to Gadget Catalog users, we need to map our `ROLE` and `USER_ROLE_ASSN` tables (refer back to Figure 6-2) to our object model. As you saw in Listing 6-2, our `User` entity bean only contains the data stored directly in the `USER` table. We'll create a new entity bean, `Role`, to hold the data stored in the `ROLE` table, and then define a new persistent property on the `User` bean to hold all the roles that the user has in the database.

The `Role` entity bean is shown in Listing 6-4. The JPA mappings being used are straightforward, so I won't discuss them in detail here.

Listing 6-4. Role *Entity Bean*

```
@Entity
@Table(name="ROLE")
public class Role implements Serializable {
    private long mId;
    private String mName = null;
    private String mDesc = null;

    public Role() {}

    @Id @GeneratedValue
    @Column(name="ROLE_ID")
    public long getId() {
        return mId;
    }

    public void setId(long id) {
        mId = id;
    }

    @Column(name="DESCR")
    public String getDescription() {
        return mDesc;
    }

    public void setDescription(String desc) {
```

```
        mDesc = desc;
    }


    @Column(name="NAME")
    public String getName() {
        return mName;
    }


    public void setName(String name) {
        mName = name;
    }
}
```

We then add a new `roles` property to the `User` bean, using a `@ManyToMany` relationship. The `USER_ROLE_ASSN` table is referenced in a `@JoinTable` annotation.

```
@Entity
@Name("user")
@Table(name="USER")
public class User implements Serializable {

    . . .
    @ManyToMany
    @JoinTable(name="USER_ROLE_ASSN",
                joinColumns=@JoinColumn(name="USER_ID"),
                inverseJoinColumns=@JoinColumn(name="ROLE_ID"))
    public List<Role> getRoles() {
        return mRoles;
    }


    public void setRoles(List<Role> roles) {
        mRoles = roles;
    }
    . . .
}
```

With these additions in place, the users that are created in the `Login.login()` authentication method will now have their roles loaded from the database. We can make Seam aware of the user's roles using the `addRole()` method on the `identity` component:

```
@Stateful
@Name("authenticator")
public class Login implements ILogin, Serializable {

    . . .
```

```
public boolean login() {
    boolean result = false;
    if (getUser() == null) {
        try {
            Identity identity = Identity.instance();
            Query q =
                gadgetDatabase.createQuery("from User " +
                                            "where login = :userName " +
                                            "and password = :password")
                    .setParameter("userName", identity.getUsername())
                    .setParameter("password", identity.getPassword());
            setUser((User) q.getSingleResult());

            if (getUser() != null) {
                // Register the user's roles with the Seam security system
                for (Role r : getUser().getRoles()) {
                    identity.addRole(r.getName());
                }
            }
        }
        catch (NoResultException nre) {
            FacesMessages.instance().add("Username/password do not match");
        }
    }
    result = (getUser() == null ? false : true);
    return result;
}
. . .
}
```

Remember that the identity component is a session-scoped component, so each user will have his or her own identity. The additional code that we added to the Login component tells Seam that the user who just logged in has all of the roles that are associated with his or her user record in the database.

Notice that Seam uses a simple string value for the roles. We're using the name property on the user's Role objects as the value for the roles on the user's identity, and this property on Role is mapped to the NAME column in the ROLE table. This is an important fact, because these role names are the same names that we will use to assign role-based access control in our application.

Specifying Page Access Rights

Now that Seam knows the roles assigned to the user in the Gadget Catalog database, we can use these roles to assign role-based access rights to pages and other parts of the Gadget Catalog.

Page-level authorization can be done using `restrict` subelements on `page` elements in `pages.xml`. This is the same element we used to require authentication for certain pages in our application.

Authorization restrictions are made using additional conditions on the security-related EL expression in the `restrict` element. Seam provides an EL function, `s:hasRole()`, that can be used to check whether the current user has a particular role. According to the security requirements listed in the section "Gadget Catalog: Expansion Through Security," we only want administrators to access the general gadget editing pages, which now sit in the `admin` directory of our web application. Assuming that we use the name "ADMIN" for the administrator role in its entry in our `ROLE` table, we would adjust the restriction on these pages in `pages.xml`:

```
<page view-id="/admin/*">
    <restrict>#{identity.loggedIn and s:hasRole('ADMIN')}</restrict>
</page>
```

Once this new restriction is in place, Seam will still check to see whether the user is authenticated (since we still have the `identity.loggedIn` clause in the expression). If the user is logged in, Seam checks the roles that have been associated with the user in the `identity` component. If any user without the "ADMIN" role attempts to access a page in the `admin` directory, an `AuthorizationException` will be thrown, and the user will see a default error page.

Ideally, we'd like to avoid having the user see raw error pages generated by the application server or the web server. The same way we customized the handling of the `NotLoggedInException` earlier, we can specify how we want an `AuthorizationException` handled using an `exception` element in `pages.xml`. In our case, an unauthorized user will be sent back to the main home page, with a message stating that he or she doesn't have access to the requested page:

```
<pages>
    . . .
    <exception class="org.jboss.seam.security.AuthorizationException">
        <end-conversation/>
        <redirect view-id="/index.xhtml">
            <message>We're terribly sorry, but you don't have the privileges
                    to access the page you requested.</message>
        </redirect>
    </exception>
    . . .
</pages>
```

We chose to send the unauthorized user to the main home page because it's guaranteed to be accessible to all users. With this exception handling in place, if an unauthorized user tries to go to any page in the admin area, he or she will see the message shown in Figure 6-6.

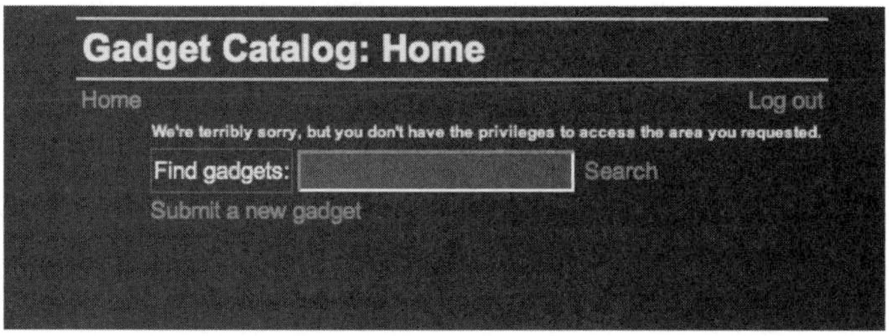

Figure 6-6. *Authorization exception message on home page*

Component-Level Restrictions

There are times when you will need to specify access-control restrictions on components and their methods, rather than at the page level. You may want to do this, for example, when a certain category of operations is performed by specific components in your application, and rather than enumerating all the places in the user interface where these operations are used, you simply want to restrict access to the components themselves. This allows the user interface and the page organization to change however it needs to, and your access restrictions will remain in force.

Back in the beginning of this chapter, we reorganized our pages so that all of the "new gadget" wizard pages are in the wizard directory of our application (where they always had been), and all of the general gadget editing pages are in admin. We did this to simplify our restrictions in the pages.xml file, allowing us to define one page element for each web directory and put the appropriate restriction on each.

Another approach we could take is to restrict access at the component level. Seam provides an @Restrict annotation that can be applied at the class or method level, and it allows you to restrict access to the entire component or specific methods on the component. The @Restrict annotation can include a security EL expression, similar to the EL expressions we used in the restrict elements in pages.xml. And, if you use an @Restrict annotation, it is handled the same way that the restrict elements are handled in pages.xml. When the user performs an action in the web interface that requires the component or method with the @Restrict annotation, the EL expression is evaluated. If it returns true, the access is allowed. If it returns false, Seam checks the user's status.

If the user is not authenticated, a `NotLoggedInException` is thrown. If the user is authenticated, an `AuthorizationException` is thrown.

In our Gadget Catalog application, all of the gadget editing functionality is provided by our `gadgetAdmin` component, which is implemented by the `GadgetAdminBean` class. Rather than putting restrictions on pages in `pages.xml`, we could also choose to restrict access to the `gadgetAdmin` component. We could add the following `@Restrict` annotation to our `GadgetAdminBean` class:

```
@Stateful
@Name("gadgetAdmin")
@Restrict("#{identity.loggedIn}")
public class GadgetAdminBean implements IGadgetAdminBean {

    . . .

}
```

This will restrict the `gadgetAdmin` operations to authenticated users only. If we look back at our original restrictions in `pages.xml`, we had two different restrictions for the two web directories: `wizard/*` was restricted with `#{identity.loggedIn}` (any authenticated user is allowed), while `admin/*` was restricted with `#{identity.loggedIn and s:hasRole('ADMIN')}` (only authenticated users with the "ADMIN" role are allowed). We could add the authorization clause to our `@Restrict` annotation, but this would apply the restriction to any use of the `gadgetAdmin` component, including the places in the "new gadget" wizard where `gadgetAdmin` is used. Instead, we could mix page-level restrictions with component-level restrictions, by leaving the `gadgetAdmin` restriction as it is earlier, and adding an additional authorization restriction to the `admin` directory in `pages.xml`:

```
<pages>
    . . .
    <page view-id="/admin/*">
        <restrict>#{s:hasRole('ADMIN')}</restrict>
    </page>
    . . .
</pages>
```

While this example demonstrates how component-level restrictions can be established with the `@Restrict` annotation, it won't actually meet our original security requirements at the beginning of this chapter. We wanted the main home page and the search results page to be unrestricted (no login required). But the main home page and search results page both reference the `gadgetAdmin` component in order to render the search form and display the results. Since the `gadgetAdmin` component has been restricted, users will be taken to the login screen when they access either of these pages as well. So in the end, we would have to revert back to the page-level restrictions in `pages.xml` after all.

Advanced Authorization

Sometimes user roles aren't sufficient for defining access control rules in an application. You may need to use more complex, dynamic logic to determine whether a user should be given access to specific pages, components, or methods.

Seam supports two approaches for implementing more complex authorization. The first, arguably the most straightforward, involves writing custom logic in your Seam components to check authorization. The second involves using JBoss Rules to implement your authorization rules, and is more involved.

Custom Authorization Expressions

You saw how EL expressions can be used in either the `restrict` element in `pages.xml` or a `@Restrict` annotation on a Seam component. As already discussed, this expression is evaluated, and if it is true, access is granted, and if not, the appropriate exception is thrown (`NotLoggedInException` if the user is not authenticated, `AuthorizationException` otherwise). So far, we've only used terms in these expressions from the Seam security services. Specifically, we've used `identity.loggedIn` to check the user's authentication status and `s:hasRole()` to check for roles. But there's nothing restricting us from using attributes and logic on our Seam components as terms in these restriction checks.

Suppose, for example, that we wanted users to have full access to edit gadgets that they submitted to the Gadget Catalog. In other words, users would need the "ADMIN" role to access the gadget editing pages, but any user can use the gadget editing pages to edit the gadgets that he or she submitted to the database. This logic can't be easily implemented using simple roles pulled from our `ROLE` and `USER_ROLE_ASSN` tables. A user's access to the editing pages has to be determined at runtime, using his or her `User` object and comparing it to the `submitter` property on the gadget being edited.

It's actually very easy to implement this dynamic access control logic. First, we add a new Boolean "property" to our `gadgetAdmin` component, called "gadgetSubmitter". This property should be true only if the `submitter` property of the current gadget (the `activeGadget` property on `gadgetAdmin`) is the same user as the current authenticated user. We implement this property with a single `isGadgetSubmitter()` method on `GadgetAdminBean`, where we dynamically determine the value of the property by checking the current user and the submitter of the active gadget:

```
public boolean isGadgetSubmitter() {
    boolean owner = false;
    if (getActiveGadget() != null &&
        getActiveGadget().getSubmitter() != null &&
        getUser() != null &&
        getActiveGadget().getSubmitter().equals(getUser())) {
        owner = true;
```

```
    }
    return owner;
}
```

We needed to add another property, user, to GadgetAdminBean, and we inject it from the session scope using an @In annotation:

```
@In(value="user", required=false)
private User mUser;
```

The user object is initialized and outjected into the session scope by the authenticator component, as you saw back in the section "Authentication Services."

With this new property in place, we can adjust the restriction expression for the admin directory in pages.xml to allow any user to use those pages to edit a gadget that he or she submitted:

```
<pages>
    . . .
    <page view-id="/admin/*">
        <restrict>#{identity.loggedIn and
                    (s:hasRole('ADMIN') or gadgetAdmin.gadgetSubmitter)}</restrict>
    </page>
    . . .
</pages>
```

Of course, we could use this same approach with an @Restrict annotation on a component or component method.

This use of custom component methods to implement authorization logic offers almost unlimited flexibility. You can use any available information to assess whether a user should have access to a specific portion of the application.

Authorization with JBoss Rules

Seam has also integrated its security services with JBoss Rules, allowing you to extend the authorization logic to include rules implemented in the JBoss Rules engine. A full tutorial on JBoss Rules is outside the scope of this chapter, but I can walk you through the basics of setting up JBoss Rules in your application and show you a simple example of using a rule to check permissions.

First we need to introduce the concept of Seam permissions. In addition to the s:hasRole() EL function that you've already seen, Seam also provides the s:hasPermission() EL function. This can be used to check whether a user has a specific permission. In Seam, a permission is defined as the combination of a name and an action. Usually, but not necessarily, the name refers to some entity in the application.

In our case, the name might be "gadget" or "user". The action refers to some action that the user might take, such as "edit" or "delete". You can check for a permission in a security expression (in either the `restrict` element in `pages.xml`, or in an `@Restrict` annotation) using the `s:hasPermission()` function. The `s:hasPermission()` function takes three arguments: an entity name string, an action string, and (optionally) a Seam component that is the target of the action to be taken. If you are simply checking a general permission, not specific to a particular component, you can specify the component argument as `null`.

In our case, we could change the access check on the admin directory from a role-based check to a permission-based check. Rather than checking for the "ADMIN" role using `s:hasRole()`, we can check for a permission with an entity name of "gadget" and the action "edit", using `s:hasPermission()`:

```
<pages>
    . . .
    <page view-id="/admin/*">
        <restrict>
            #{identity.loggedIn and s:hasPermission('gadget', 'edit', null)}
        </restrict>
    </page>
    . . .
</pages>
```

When you use the `s:hasPermission()` EL function, it triggers JBoss Seam to check for any rules that should be fired for the specific permission. Rules are defined in a JBoss Rules rule definition file, typically with the suffix `.drl`, and they are written in a rule language specific to JBoss Rules. Here's a sample `.drl` file that defines a rule for our permission check:

```
package org.jimfarley.gadgets;

import org.jboss.seam.security.PermissionCheck;
import org.jboss.seam.security.Role;

rule UserIsAdmin
    when
        p: PermissionCheck(name == "gadget", action == "edit")
        Role(name == "ADMIN")
    then
        p.grant();
end;
```

I can't provide a full primer on rule syntax, but this rule file shows you some of the basic details. The `.drl` file contains a single rule, "UserIsAdmin". The when clause of the rule specifies the conditions that must exist in "working memory" in order for the rule to fire. Working memory is essentially the set of runtime data that is made available to the rules engine for processing rules. The first condition in our when clause states that the working memory has to contain a permission with a name of "gadget" and an action of "edit". When you use the s:hasPermission() EL function in a security expression, it automatically injects a permission with the given arguments into the rule engine working memory. So in our case, a permission matching this first condition will be present when the security expression is encountered. The p: in front of the condition declares a variable named "p" and assigns it to the permission being checked for.

The second condition states that the working memory must contain a Role with a name of "ADMIN". Seam also inserts all of the current user's roles into the working memory, so this condition effectively says that the current user has to have the "ADMIN" role.

If all the conditions in the when clause are true, the then clause is executed. In our case, the then clause contains a single statement, p.grant();. This takes the permission variable declared in the when clause and grants the permission to the current user.

If we put this all together, here's what we have. When the s:hasPermission() function is used in a restriction EL expression, it injects the specified permission into working memory, along with the user's current roles, and then causes the JBoss Rules engine to check for any rules to fire. Our rule fires when a permission of "edit" on an entity named "gadget" is being checked, and when the user has the "ADMIN" role. When the rule fires, the permission ("edit" on "gadget") is granted to the current user. The s:hasPermission() function will return true, and the overall security expression will evaluate to true, thus allowing the user to access the admin directory of the web application. This rule, then, takes the place of our use of s:hasRole("ADMIN").

You can do much, much more with JBoss Rules than this. But this gives you a sense for the structure of rules, and for the interaction between Seam's security services and the JBoss Rules engine.

Summary

In this chapter, we explored the security services provided by JBoss Seam. We started by looking at how Seam supports the authentication of users using a simple component action method. We wrote a simple JSF page for the login form, tying the form to our authentication method. You also saw how to restrict pages in pages.xml, forcing Seam to authenticate the user before allowing him or her to access the pages. To make our Gadget Catalog login process more user friendly, we specified exception handlers in components.xml that will automatically redirect the user to our login form when he or she attempts to access protected areas. We also used Seam event handling to capture the target URL before sending the user to the login page, and then redirecting the user to the target URL once the login process completes successfully.

Once we had authenticated our users, we turned to authorizing them as specified in our application requirements. We adjusted our User component to load the user's roles from our database tables, and also adjusted our authentication method to register the user's roles with the Seam identity component. We then used the s:hasRole() EL function to check for these roles in our restriction expressions. We also saw how more complex authorization logic could be implemented using custom component methods and/or JBoss Rules.

More granular checks can also be applied at the component and method level, using the @Restrict annotation. The same security expressions that we used in pages.xml can be used in the @Restrict annotation.

■ ■ ■

CHAPTER 7

Business Process Management

In this chapter, we look at business processes and how business process management (BPM) is supported by Seam. I've already discussed JBoss Business Process Management (jBPM) in Chapter 5, when we explored Seam's pageflow features, which are built on jBPM. As mentioned in that chapter, while BPM can be applied effectively to manage pageflow, it's actually a much broader field, supporting tasks implemented in a variety of ways (web pages, business components, business rules, etc.), connected together with a structured workflow that can span multiple users across potentially long periods of time. In this chapter, we look at this broader application of BPM and how jBPM can be used within Seam to define and execute business processes.

Business Processes, jBPM, and Seam

In Chapter 5, I described pageflow as a specific subset of business process management. Pageflow is concerned with how a single user moves between web pages during a single session. And in the case of Seam, a jBPM pageflow is actually part of a single Seam conversation within a single session. This is just one very specific application of business process management.

In this section, I'll first introduce you to some of the basic concepts of business process management, then show you how jBPM models these concepts, and finally demonstrate how Seam integrates jBPM into its application framework.

Business Process Concepts

Business process management covers a broad realm using very general concepts that can be applied to many different practical situations. Any situation that involves structured workflow leading users through a series of tasks could be modeled using BPM. That's not to say that all these situations *should* be modeled using BPM. BPM frameworks bring their own overhead, and you need to be sure that the benefits are there before applying a process modeling tool. When such a situation arises, though, BPM can be a very powerful tool to help clarify and execute structured workflows that are defined by user experience goals, business rules, regulatory constraints, or all of the above.

In business process management, actions can be initiated by a variety of events beyond just users visiting web pages. Batch jobs can fire off messages to a queue, signaling the end of a task and a transition to a new state. Users can send e-mail messages to a target mailbox that triggers the start of an entire process. Any event that can be detected by the system can be used within a business process.

Business processes are also typically larger in scope, in terms of both timeframe and number of users involved. A pageflow involves a single user in a single web session, and web sessions typically last on the order of minutes. A business process can involve multiple users over a much longer period of time. Some processes take hours, days, weeks, even months to complete. Editing an article for a magazine or web site, for example, can be modeled as a business process, involving one or more authors, one or more editors, plus technical reviewers, production staff, and so on. The entire process can take several weeks or even months, involving interactions with several systems along the way.

Business Process Models

A business process consists of a set of *nodes*, or states, linked by various possible *transitions*. *Events* in the business process cause various *actions* to be executed. These events include arrival at a particular state in the process, a transition between states, or specific outcomes of other actions.

As a practical example, Figure 7-1 shows a graphical model of a simplified business process for editing articles. There are eight nodes in this workflow. Six of them are named states in the process: the starting state ("start-state"), a "write article" task, a "tech edit" task, a "copy edit" task, a "revise article" task, and the end state ("end"), signaling the completion of the article and the end of the process. The other two, unnamed nodes are a fork, between the article submission and the two parallel editing tasks, and a join, where the two parallel editing tasks transition to the article revision task. Various transitions exist between these nodes. Some of these are named, indicating specific actions that have to take place in order for the transition to take place. Others are not named, either because there is only one transition out of a given node, or the nature of the transition is obvious from the start and end nodes.

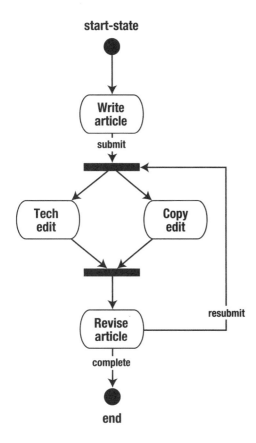

start-state

Write
article

submit

Tech
edit

Copy
edit

resubmit

Revise
article

complete

end

Figure 7-1. *Business process for editing articles*

Business Processes + Java = jBPM

A business process management framework, such as jBPM, supports the definition and orchestration of business processes in code. It maintains the process model in terms of the allowed states, the various transitions between states, and the actions and events that can trigger these transitions. BPM also includes the concept of actors, allowing you to specify what type of user can and should perform specific tasks in the process.

The jBPM framework is a Java-based BPM suite. It's aimed at configuring and managing business processes that are backed by Java-based processes, whether those are running in a Java EE application server or in a standalone Java workflow application of some sort. jBPM maps the BPM concepts discussed in the previous section into Java APIs and components, allowing your Java code to interact with workflows, and to implement tasks within the workflow.

The jBPM Process Model

In jBPM, a business process is made up of a set of nodes connected by transitions. A process has a single start node and one or more end nodes. A process execution takes place by following the transitions from the start node, through allowed transitions, to other nodes in the graph, until an end node is reached. As each node is reached in the process graph, the node is "executed." What it means to "execute" a node depends on the type of node it is, as you'll see shortly.

A business process can be executing one or more paths through the workflow at the same time. In our article editing example in Figure 7-1, we start at the "start-state" node, and then hit the "write article" node. Once this node executes and completes, we enter a fork node, and execution splits into two concurrent paths: one through the "tech edit" node, and the other through the "copy edit" node. Each of these execution paths will run independently, and jBPM will manage a token for each that points to the current node being executed in that path.

Transitions link nodes together, defining the allowed execution paths through the process. Process events, such as the completion of a task, cause transitions to be taken from the current node in the execution to another. If there are multiple transitions that can be taken from a node, the transition(s) to take will be indicated in the event that triggers the transition. In the article editing example, there are two possible transitions from the "revise article" node, named "complete" and "resubmit". The transition that will be taken is determined by the outcome of the "revise article" task, in this case.

The jBPM process model supports the following types of nodes:

- *State node*: A state node represents a simple state in the process. When the state node is entered in an execution path, it causes the execution path to wait in this state until some event signals a transition to be followed. The event will have to be raised by some external system.

- *Task node*: A task node defines a piece of work that has to be performed in order to push the process forward. The execution path will transition off of the node once the task is complete, and the transition to take will be determined by the outcome of the task.

- *Decision node*: A decision node specifies criteria that should be used to determine the path to be taken by the execution. Each possible transition has its own criteria, and the first one that evaluates to `true` is the one that's followed.

- *Fork node*: A fork node causes the execution to split into multiple, concurrent execution paths. In the article editing example, the "write article" node leads to a fork that causes the execution to split into two concurrent paths. Each path transitions immediately to the next node of the graph: one transitions to "tech edit", the other to "copy edit".

- *Join node*: A join node executes only when all of the inbound transitions to the node are followed, and then execution follows a single path out of the node. In the article editing example, the "tech edit" and "copy edit" nodes have transitions that lead to a join node. Once the execution paths through each of these nodes transition to the join, the execution is merged into a single path, and the execution transitions to the "revise article" node.

- *Custom nodes*: jBPM allows you to also define your own custom nodes. These custom nodes allow you to specify your own behavior in terms of what happens when execution arrives at the node. Custom nodes are rarely used, but can be useful in cases where there's some automatic task that needs to be performed during a process.

In addition to nodes and transitions, a jBPM process can also be annotated with *actions*. An action is performed when execution events, such as entering a node, leaving a node, or following a transition, occur. An action does not drive the execution forward, like a task on a task node. An action is just code that's run when the execution moves forward in the process.

jBPM Process Definitions

BPM suites typically make use of some kind of process definition language. These allow you to configure a workflow in an external configuration file of some sort, separate from the code that implements the various tasks and rules in the process. jBPM primarily[1] makes use of an XML format called the jBPM Process Definition Language (jPDL) for process definitions. You saw a specific flavor of jPDL in Chapter 5 when you saw how Seam uses jBPM for pageflow.

Listing 7-1 shows a jPDL definition that corresponds to the article editing workflow shown in Figure 7-1. The states, forks, and joins depicted in the graphic are represented here using `start-state`, `state`, `end-state`, `fork`, and `join` XML elements from jPDL. The transitions between states are modeled using `transition` elements within the various nodes.

---

1. jBPM can actually be used with various process definition languages, using a plug-in scheme provided with the framework. The industry-standard BPEL definition language has been integrated into jBPM as an add-on, for example. But for the purposes of this chapter, you can assume that process definitions are described using jPDL.

Listing 7-1. *jPDL for Article Editing Process*

```
<process-definition>
    <start-state>
        <transition to="write article" />
    </start-state>
    <state name="write article">
        <transition name="submit" to="edit fork" />
        <transition name="cancel" to="end" />
    </state>
    <fork name="edit fork">
        <transition name="tech-edit" to="technical edit" />
        <transition name="copy-edit" to="copy edit" />
    </fork>
    <state name="technical edit">
        <transition to="edit join" />
    </state>
    <state name="copy edit">
        <transition to="edit join" />
    </state>
    <join name="edit join">
        <transition to="revise article" />
    </join>
    <state name="revise article">
        <transition name="resubmit" to="edit fork" />
        <transition name="complete" to="end" />
    </state>
    <end-state name="end" />
</process-definition>
```

We'll explore more of the format and options in jPDL process definitions in our Gadget Catalog example. This representation of the article editing process, however, shows you how direct the mapping is between a flow diagram like Figure 7-1 and a jPDL representation like Listing 7-1.

Integration of jBPM and Seam

jBPM brings business process modeling to Java environments in general, but if we're developing applications using the Seam environment, we'd prefer to have jBPM integrated into the component and conversation model that is the basis of Seam. And that's precisely what the Seam developers have done for you. Rather than just using the jBPM API to manage process details, Seam allows you to use the same annotation and configuration methods that you use for other aspects of Seam services.

In Seam, a jBPM process operates within a business process context, as I mentioned in Chapter 4 when I discussed Seam's various runtime contexts (refer back to Figure 4-2). A process instance (and its business process context) begins when you execute an action method annotated with the @CreateProcess annotation. Every task in a jPBM process runs within a conversation context. Tasks can be initiated using other code annotations, such as @BeginTask or @StartTask, on action methods. Tasks are complete when an @EndTask method is invoked during the conversation. This also ends the task conversation.

When utilizing jBPM within Seam, a process task can be tied to an action method on a Seam component, a series of interactions with a user, or an entire pageflow running within a conversation and modeled using jPDL.

Figure 7-2 depicts a sample instance of the article editing process running within a Seam application. The figure shows three separate users interacting with a Seam application. At some point during the first user's initial conversation, he or she triggers the start of the article editing process by executing an action method with an @CreateProcess annotation. Later in this same session, the same user starts the "write article" task by invoking an action method annotated with an @StartTask annotation. The conversation and task are ended by an action method with an @EndTask annotation. The business process execution moves along to the editing fork and waits for the "copy edit" and "tech edit" tasks to execute. Two other users perform these tasks by executing @StartTask methods and finish them with @EndTask methods. When both tasks complete, the process execution moves to the join node, and then to the "revise article" task node. The first user comes back to the application and performs this task, and then the process completes.

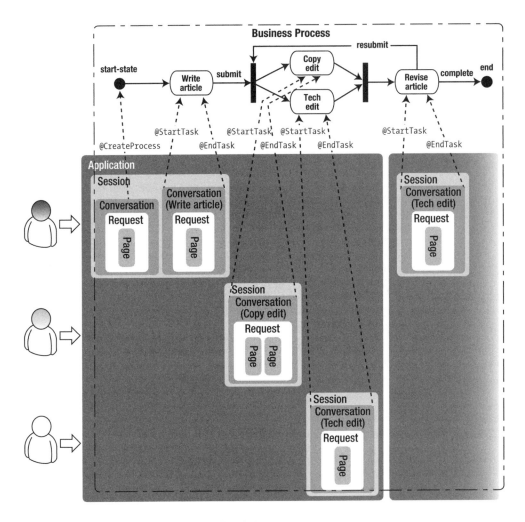

Figure 7-2. *Seam execution of the article editing process*

There are a few details to note in the way jBPM processes map into a Seam application. First, the entire business process executes within a business process context, and this context extends across one or more user sessions, and can even span one or more application contexts. This means that the process state has to be maintained across application restarts (e.g., the application server is bounced, or the application archive is redeployed). This, in turn, means that jBPM has to be persisting the process state someplace, ideally in a database. And that's exactly what jBPM will do for you. This requires some configuration of the jBPM persistence operations, however, as you'll see in a later section on configuring jBPM in Seam.

Gadget Catalog: Verifying New Gadgets

In Chapter 6, to demonstrate the authentication and authorization features provided by Seam's security capabilities, we added support for general users of the Gadget Catalog, allowing them to directly enter new entries for the catalog. This extension of the system is a double-edged sword, though. True, allowing public users to enter new gadgets will increase the amount of information in the Gadget Catalog, and that could increase its value as well. But the value of the catalog is also measured in terms of the quality of the information it contains. If inaccurate information on devices starts to creep (or flood) into the Gadget Catalog, the value of the system to users will drop, and fast.

One way to fix this problem is to introduce a review process. Appointed administrators will be given the responsibility for verifying all new entries put into the Gadget Catalog by public users. They'll ensure that new entries (gadgets, types, or features) aren't duplicates of existing entries, and that the information about the devices is accurate and complete.

In order to distinguish between reviewed and unreviewed gadgets, types, and features, we'll need to introduce the concept of a "status code" to our object model and data model. New entries provided by public users will be given an unreviewed status, and once a Gadget Catalog administrator has reviewed the details of the entries and made any adjustments, the entries will have their status changed to a reviewed status. In addition, we want to notify the original submitter of an entry about the status of those entries. This will allow him or her to examine any changes made by the administrators and raise any concerns he or she might have (everyone makes mistakes, even administrators). This requires that we keep track of who originally submitted a gadget, type, or feature entry, so that we can notify them when the status changes and prompt them to check the final version of these entries.

Figure 7-3 shows the updated object model for the expanded Gadget Catalog. We've introduced a new Status object, which will hold the code and description for the status of Gadget, GadgetType, and GadgetFeature objects. We've also added new submitter properties to Gadget, GadgetFeature, and GadgetType objects. These properties reference User objects that represent the user who originally entered the entries.

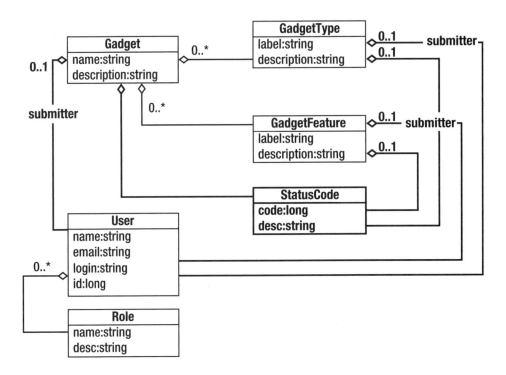

Figure 7-3. *Updated Gadget Catalog object model*

Figure 7-4 depicts the updated data model we'll need to support our new object model. We've introduced a new STATUS_CODE table to store the allowed values for the status codes on gadgets, types, and features. The GADGET, GADGET_TYPE, and GADGET_FEATURE tables have all had STATUS columns added, as foreign keys to the STATUS column on STATUS_CODE. Finally, we added SUBMITTER columns to the GADGET, GADGET_TYPE, and GADGET_FEATURE tables, with foreign keys over to the USER_ID column in the USER table.

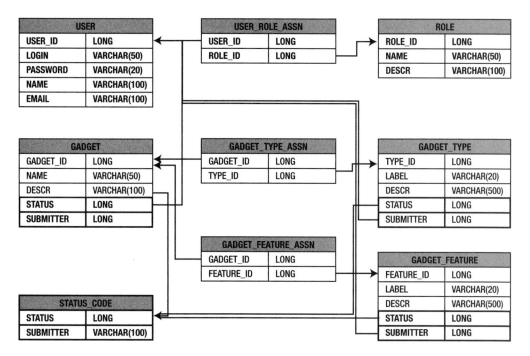

Figure 7-4. *Updated Gadget Catalog data model*

These changes to the data model have been reflected in the EJB 3.0 annotations on the Gadget, GadgetType, and GadgetFeature classes in our application code, and a new StatusCode EJB 3.0 entity bean has been created to represent the data in the new STATUS_CODE table. We won't examine the details of these changes here, since they aren't salient to the current discussion, and you've already seen EJB 3.0 entity beans used within our Seam application in earlier chapters.

In addition to these additions to the data model, we're also going to introduce a new component, a GadgetReviewBean, which we'll use for all the action methods required for implementing the tasks in the gadget review process. The GadgetAdminBean will continue to be used for general administrative tasks, but the details of the jBPM gadget review process will live in the review bean.

As I discuss the details of implementing the gadget review process in the Gadget Catalog, you can follow along in the example code that is provided with this book. The code for this version of the Gadget Catalog can be found in the bpm directory of the source code bundle.

Configuring jBPM in Seam

In order to make use of jBPM services within Seam, you need to configure the jBPM engine. The first step in doing this is to install the `org.jboss.seam.core.Jbpm` component in the Seam `components.xml` configuration file. You saw this same component in Chapter 5 when I discussed jBPM pageflow in Seam, because the same component is used to drive both pageflow and business process management. The difference here is that, instead of referencing some jPDL pageflow definitions using the `pageflowDefinitions` property, we reference jPDL business process definitions using the `processDefinitions` property:

```
<components>
    . . .
    <!-- Install jPBM support -->
    <component class="org.jboss.seam.core.Jbpm">
        <property name="processDefinitions">
            <value>editArticle.jpdl.xml</value>
        </property>
    </component>
    . . .
</components>
```

The Seam jBPM component distinguishes between pageflow definitions and process definitions because their descriptions use different variations on the jPDL format, and their handling at runtime requires different services.

Once this element is added to our `components.xml`, the jBPM engine will be initialized when the application starts, and the referenced jPDL process definition file, `editArticle.jpdl.xml`, will be looked up on the application classpath, parsed, and made available as a business process. We can then start an instance of this process using an `@CreateProcess` method, and perform tasks in the process using `@StartTask`, `@BeginTask`, and `@EndTask` methods.

Well, almost. There are two other configuration files that you might need to worry about, depending on the situation. One is the jBPM base configuration file, `jbpm.cfg.xml`. This file is loaded by jBPM from the classpath and can be used to configure the various services used by jBPM at runtime. The other configuration file is the Hibernate configuration, `hibernate.cfg.xml`, which sets up the Hibernate persistence services.

As mentioned in the section "Integration of jBPM and Seam," a jBPM business process can live across application contexts, which means that the process state needs to be saved in a database or similar persistent store. jBPM uses its own database schema to store the process definitions, process and task instances, and execution paths that are active at any given point in a business process. So jBPM needs to have a way to connect to a database that has this schema available.

By default, jBPM makes use of Hibernate for its persistence operations. It doesn't, however, use EJB 3.0/JPA persistence like Seam and other Java EE environments. As already mentioned, jBPM is intended for use in a broad range of Java environments, including non-Java EE ones. So jBPM uses direct Hibernate calls to persist all of its process state information. This means that the Hibernate services used by jBPM need to be configured separately from the internal JPA configuration used by Seam, even if the JPA engine is using Hibernate for its persistence operations.

I won't enumerate all the configuration options available in the jBPM and Hibernate configuration files. But I will mention a few common situations where you might need to adjust these, and how.

Avoiding Conflicts with JBoss Transaction Management

Seam is used most commonly with the JBoss application server and its EJB 3.0/JPA engine. By default, the JBoss JPA implementation is set up to manage transactions at runtime. By default, the jBPM Hibernate configuration is also configured to manage transactions at runtime. This will cause problems, as you can imagine, so you need to disable one or the other in order to restore harmony. Since there are likely other services in your JBoss environment that depend on its internal transaction management (like the JPA engine, for example), it's likely that you will want to disable the jBPM transaction management.

Doing this is simple enough. You just need to set the isTransactionEnabled property on the persistence services in jBPM. These services are configured in the jbpm.cfg.xml file. The following shows a jbpm.cfg.xml file that disables the persistent transaction management:

```
<jbpm-configuration>
  <jbpm-context>
    <service name="persistence">
      <factory>
        <bean class="org.jbpm.persistence.db.DbPersistenceServiceFactory">
          <field name="isTransactionEnabled">
              <false/>
          </field>
        </bean>
      </factory>
    </service>
    <service name="message" factory="org.jbpm.msg.db.DbMessageServiceFactory" />
    <service name="scheduler"
             factory="org.jbpm.scheduler.db.DbSchedulerServiceFactory" />
    <service name="logging" factory="org.jbpm.logging.db.DbLoggingServiceFactory" />
    <service name="authentication"
        factory="org.jbpm.security.authentication.
        DefaultAuthenticationServiceFactory" />
  </jbpm-context>
</jbpm-configuration>
```

Notice that we've also included entries for the other jBPM required services, such as the scheduler and logging services. That's because when we put this configuration file on the classpath of the application, it will override the default settings in jBPM. If we didn't include these default service implementations here, these services wouldn't work, and jBPM would be crippled.

You can find these default settings in the default `jbpm.cfg.xml` file provided with the jBPM download. There are also versions provided with a few of the Seam example applications. It's a good idea to make sure you're using the services that are required for the version of jBPM being used by your Seam version, so starting with the files from the Seam example applications is a good idea.

This configuration file needs to be available on the classpath of the application. Our Gadget Catalog is packaged as an EAR file, with a web archive and EJB archive included. To make the jBPM configuration file globally accessible in the application, we put it in the root of our EAR file, as shown in Figure 7-5. We've also highlighted the location of our customized `hibernate.cfg.xml` file, discussed in the next section.

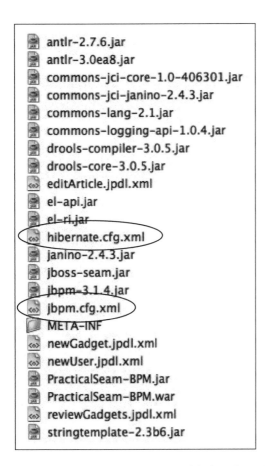

Figure 7-5. *Contents of jBPM-enabled Gadget Catalog EAR file*

Setting the Hibernate DataSource

Most applications (including our Gadget Catalog) make use of a database for persistent storage. In some cases, it might be preferable to have jBPM use the same database to store all of its process state information. Maintaining multiple databases means more complexity in the environment, and unless there are naming conflicts between the jBPM internal schema and your application schema, putting them together in the same place can simplify things. The jBPM package includes the ability to generate its internal database schema for a variety of database engines. If you do integrate the jBPM tables with your application database, you'll want to review the design of the tables to be sure there aren't any potential performance issues.

The database used by Hibernate is configured in its configuration file, so in order to change the database to be the same as the application database, we will need to put a hibernate.cfg.xml file of our own on the application's classpath. But again, jBPM depends on a number of default settings that it includes in its own internal hibernate.cfg.xml file. These include all of the object-relational mappings for its internal data objects, which are critical to making jBPM work properly.

The same approach can be taken here—take a sample hibernate.cfg.xml file from either the jBPM distribution or the Seam example applications, and adjust it to suit your application. The "dvdstore" example in Seam includes a hibernate.cfg.xml file that provides a good starting point, since it includes all of the jBPM data object mappings, and it's already set up to use a JNDI DataSource reference, which is typically how your application's database will be configured in your application.

For our Gadget Catalog application, we've configured our database to be accessible through a DataSource referenced under the JNDI name "java:/PracticalSeam-BPM-db". The following section of the hibernate.cfg.xml file shows how we configured Hibernate to use this same DataSource for its persistence operations:

```
<hibernate-configuration>
  <session-factory>
    <property name="hibernate.dialect">org.hibernate.dialect.HSQLDialect</property>
    <property name="connection.datasource">java:/PracticalSeam-BPM-db</property>
    <property name="transaction.factory_class">
        org.hibernate.transaction.JTATransactionFactory
    </property>
    <property name="transaction.manager_lookup_class">
        org.hibernate.transaction.JBossTransactionManagerLookup
    </property>
    <property name="cache.provider_class">
        org.hibernate.cache.HashtableCacheProvider
    </property>
```

```
    <property name="hbm2ddl.auto">create-drop</property>
    <!-- hql queries and type defs -->
    <mapping resource="org/jbpm/db/hibernate.queries.hbm.xml" />
    <!-- graph.def mapping files -->
    <mapping resource="org/jbpm/graph/def/ProcessDefinition.hbm.xml"/>
    <mapping resource="org/jbpm/graph/def/Node.hbm.xml"/>
    . . .
  </session-factory>
</hibernate-configuration>
```

You'll notice several other settings here that plug Hibernate into the JBoss environment. Again, unless you need to get into these details, it is easiest to start with a sample configuration file and edit the bits that you require.

Another setting here that's worth noting is the `hbm2ddl.auto` property. We've set it here to the value `create-drop`. This setting tells Hibernate to automatically drop and then (re-)create the tables defined in the Hibernate mappings when the application starts. This setting is useful in a development environment, where keeping the mapped data (jBPM process data, in this case) across application restarts isn't necessary, and clearing out the database is actually useful. In a production environment, you'd want to remove this setting and create the jBPM database tables through a separate process when deploying the application for the first time.

We placed the `hibernate.cfg.xml` file in the root of our EAR file, as shown in Figure 7-5. As long as Hibernate can read the configuration file from the runtime classpath, it should take effect.

Defining Process Flows

Now that you've seen how to enable the basic jBPM services in our Seam application, we can turn to the task of actually describing the business processes that we want jBPM to manage for us.

It's often useful to start with a graphical model of a process flow, such as the example shown in Figure 7-1, since these type of flow charts clearly show the paths and decision points that lead the process through the various tasks involved in the process. But the process flow must eventually be turned into a machine-readable format, such as the jPDL format shown in Listing 7-1, in order for the process to be managed and executed in code.

In our case, we want to implement a business flow that starts when a new gadget is entered into the catalog, and requires that the core gadget data, its assigned types, and features are reviewed by one or more administrators. Once the review tasks are complete, we want the original submitter of the gadget to either accept or reject the changes made by the reviewers. If the changes are accepted, the gadget is officially confirmed, and the business process ends. If the submitter disputes the changes made by the reviewers, the review process is repeated from the start. Figure 7-6 shows a flow chart for the gadget review process.

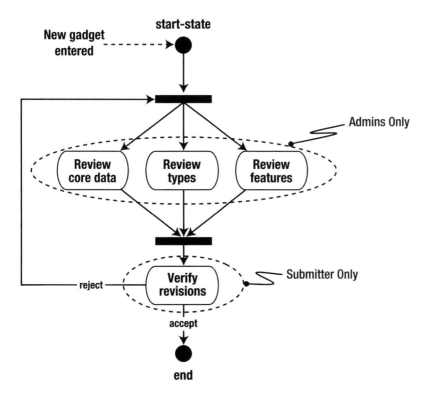

Figure 7-6. *Gadget review process diagram*

Notice that the process allows the three review tasks (core data, types, and features) to happen in parallel. All three of these execution paths lead into a single join node, however, so all three must arrive at this node (i.e., all three of the review tasks must be complete) before the overall process execution can continue. Once this happens, the "verify revisions" task node is entered, causing the submitter of the gadget to be asked to review the final form of the gadget.

Now we need to map this graphical model into jPDL so that jBPM can manage it for us. Listing 7-2 shows a jPDL description of the gadget review process.

Listing 7-2. *jPDL Configuration of Gadget Review Process*

```xml
<!-- jPDL for the gadget review business process. -->
<process-definition name="review-gadget">
    <start-state>
        <transition to="review-fork" />
    </start-state>
    <fork name="review-fork">
        <transition name="core-review" to="review-core" />
        <transition name="types-review" to="review-types" />
        <transition name="features-review" to="review-features" />
    </fork>
    <task-node name="review-core">
        <task name="review-core"
              description="Review the core data for #{gadget.name}">
            <assignment pooled-actors="ADMIN"/>
        </task>
        <transition to="review-join" />
    </task-node>
    <task-node name="review-types">
        <task name="review-types"
              description="Review the types assigned to #{gadget.name}">
            <assignment pooled-actors="ADMIN"/>
        </task>
        <transition to="review-join" />
    </task-node>
    <task-node name="review-features">
        <task name="review-features"
              description="Review the features assigned to #{gadget.name}">
            <assignment pooled-actors="ADMIN"/>
        </task>
        <transition to="review-join" />
    </task-node>
    <join name="review-join">
        <transition to="verify-revisions" />
    </join>
    <task-node name="verify-revisions">
        <task name="verify-revisions" description="Verify revisions made by admins">
            <assignment actor-id="#{gadget.submitter.idStr}"/>
        </task>
        <transition name="reject" to="review-core"/>
        <transition name="complete" to="end" />
    </task-node>
    <end-state name="end" />
</process-definition>
```

You can directly trace the execution of the process flow in Figure 7-6 in this jPDL definition. The start node is represented with a start-state element. A start-state contains a single transition, indicating where the process execution should go when the process instance is created. In this case, our start node has a transition to the "review-fork" node. The "review-fork" node is a fork, represented using a fork element. When a fork node is encountered, each transition found in the node is triggered concurrently, creating a separate execution path for each. In our case, we have three transitions in our fork, one to the "review-core" node, one to the "review-types" node, and one to the "review-features" node.

Each of these review nodes is a task node, represented using a task-node element. When a task node is encountered in an execution path, the execution path waits until the indicated task has been completed. When the task completes, one of the transitions in the task node will be taken, depending on the outcome of the task. In our case, each of our review tasks has a single, unnamed transition. This is a default transition that will be taken regardless of the outcome of the task. In the next few sections, we'll discuss the details of how specifically a named task in a process is assigned to a user and then executed by a user.

All of our review tasks transition to the "review-join" node, which is a join node represented with a join element. A join element waits until all transitions that lead to it are followed. Once this happens, all of the inbound execution paths are joined into a single execution path, and then the transition defined on the join node is followed. In our case, the "review-join" node transitions to the "verify-revisions" node, which is another task node. This task node has two possible transitions defined. If the "reject" transition is taken, the execution goes back to the "review-fork" node, causing the three review tasks to be activated again. If the "confirm" transition is taken, the process execution moves to the "end" node, which is an end node represented by an end-state element. Once an end node is entered by a process execution, the execution halts and the process instance ends.

Starting a Business Process

As mentioned earlier in this chapter, Seam provides you with the @CreateProcess annotation to make it easy to start jBPM processes at runtime. The @CreateProcess annotation has a single attribute, "definition", that you use to specify the name of the business process you want to start. This name comes from the name attribute on the root process-definition element in the jPDL file that describes the process.

In the Gadget Catalog, we want to kick off the gadget review process as soon as a user saves a new gadget in the database. This operation is handled by the GadgetAdminBean. saveGadget() action method, so all we need to do to start our process is add the @CreateProcess annotation there:

```
@End // End the pageflow/conversation when this completes
@CreateProcess(definition="review-gadget") // Start the review process
public String saveGadget() {
    // The submitter is whoever is logged in when saving
    // Our security configuration ensures the user had to be
    // authenticated to save a gadget
    getActiveGadget().setSubmitter(getUser());
    saveGadget(getActiveGadget());
    // Outject the new gadget into the business process
    // about to be created, so the BPM tasks can pull it from the
    // catalog
    setReviewGadget(getActiveGadget());
    return "success";
}
```

When this method completes successfully (no exceptions thrown, nonnull return value), Seam will create a new business process context and ask jBPM to look up the business process definition named "review-gadget" and create a new instance of it. The "review-gadget" process is defined by the jPDL in Listing 7-2, which we included on the classpath of our deployed application. At startup, jBPM loaded and parsed the jPDL into an internal representation of the process. It now uses that to create a process instance and takes the execution path to the start node. The start node has a single default transition to the "review-fork" node, which is our fork to start the three concurrent review tasks. An execution path is created for each of the transitions in the "review-fork" node, and each one hits a task node and then waits for that task to be done.

Business Process Data

As discussed at the start of this chapter and as depicted in Figure 7-2, jBPM manages the overall business process execution for you, and Seam exposes the business process execution in the form of a special context called the "business process context." You can use all the Seam bijection facilities we've been using to manage data in the other Seam contexts (session, conversation, etc.). You simply need to specify the appropriate scope for the data using ScopeType.BUSINESS_PROCESS. So if we wanted to inject a String value from the business process context, we'd just do something like this:

```
@In(scope=ScopeType.BUSINESS_PROCESS)
private String myString;
```

This will examine the business process context for an object named "myString" and set the myString variable to its string value.

The key difference with the business process context, which will affect when and how you put data into it, is the long-lived nature of business processes. As depicted in Figure 7-2, a business process context can live across application boundaries. Some business processes can take days, weeks, or months to complete, and your average application server will probably need to be restarted during time intervals this long. That means that a business process engine, like jBPM, needs to persist process-specific data so that it can be restored when the application is revisited.

In order to persist process data, jBPM needs to know how the data is structured and how to map it to database tables in the database that it's configured to use. By default, jBPM knows how to persist basic Java types, like `Integer`, `Long`, `String`, etc. But if we want jBPM to persist some custom JavaBean that we've created, we need to tell jBPM how to do that. As discussed in the section "Configuring jBPM in Seam," jBPM uses Hibernate as its default persistence service, so we would need to set up a Hibernate object-relational mapping for our JavaBean and add it to the `hibernate.cfg.xml` configuration file for jBPM.

This in itself isn't a terrible burden, but it does present a problem for a typical Seam application that's using EJB 3.0 to manage the persistence of its data. In our Gadget Catalog, for example, all of our persistent data is represented using EJB 3.0 entity beans. Suppose we wanted to inject a `Gadget` object into the business process context and have it persisted by jBPM. Well, as I just mentioned, we'd need to create a Hibernate mapping for our `Gadget` bean and provide it to jBPM. But our `Gadget` bean is an EJB 3.0 entity bean, and the EJB 3.0 engine in our Java EE server is managing its persistence. We could try to cobble together a way for jBPM to persist our `Gadget` objects (and any other entity beans we want to put into the process context), but this could be fairly risky, because we're concurrently running two persistence engines (our EJB 3.0 container and the Hibernate runtime) against the same database tables, using the same Java objects. And even if we could get this to work safely and reliably, we would be losing a lot of the ease-of-use advantages of EJB 3.0. We're now forced to manually create object-relational mappings for our data objects, in addition to defining the persistence annotations on the entity bean, among other things.

There are some other options for persisting custom data structures in jBPM. We could create shadow JavaBeans that mirror the data in our entity beans, for example. This avoids the risk of mixing two persistence engines with the same data, but we're still left with doing redundant object-relational mappings, and we have to translate between the data objects at runtime. Another option is to restrict ourselves to using basic Java types for persistent process data, which can be messy if there are lots of key data elements that need to be carried along with the process instance.

In the case of the Gadget Catalog, using basic Java types for persistent process data seems to be the right approach. We need to know, at each stage of the process, the particular gadget that is being reviewed. A `Gadget` is uniquely identified in our database by its identifier, so we can simply put the gadget identifier in the business process context as a `Long` object. Whenever we need the full gadget, we can load it from the database using the identifier.

We still want the convenience of having the Gadget object itself as a contextual component, however, so that we can reference its various properties. In the jPDL for the "review-gadget" process, for example, we use the gadget's name and the identifier of the submitter, using a "reviewGadget" component (see Listing 7-2). This seems pretty easy to accomplish—we can use the gadget identifier from the process context to initialize a Gadget, and then use bijection to put it into the current conversation context.

We still have one small hurdle, though. How do we transfer the gadget to be reviewed into the business process in the first place? At first this seems simple enough: just outject it from the gadgetAdmin component into the business process scope, and the gadgetReview component can inject it and use it in its task conversations. We might set this up in the GadgetAdminBean by creating an outjected variable:

```
@Out(value="reviewGadget", scope=ScopeType.BUSINESS_PROCESS, required=false)
private Gadget mReviewGadget;
```

Then, in the saveGadget() action method, we simply set this variable to the value of the active gadget:

```
@End // End the pageflow/conversation when this completes
@CreateProcess(definition="review-gadget") // Start the review BPM
public String saveGadget() {
    getActiveGadget().setSubmitter(getUser());
    saveGadget(getActiveGadget());
    mReviewGadget = getActiveGadget();
    return "success";
}
```

There's a problem with this, though. The gadgetAdmin component is used in several different pages and user conversations, and every time it is invoked, the outjection we just set up will take place. The mReviewGadget variable will be null most of the time, and the outjection will be putting an invalid value into the business process context. For these reasons, instead of using outjection, we simply make direct access to the business process context from the saveGadget() method, placing the gadget to be reviewed into the business process that is started by the @CreateProcess annotation:

```
@End // End the pageflow/conversation when this completes
@CreateProcess(definition="review-gadget") // Start the review BPM
public String saveGadget() {
    getActiveGadget().setSubmitter(getUser());
    saveGadget(getActiveGadget());
    Contexts.getBusinessProcessContext().set("reviewGadget", getActiveGadget());
    return "success";
}
```

This is somewhat un-Seam-ly[2] in that we are programmatically manipulating the context data. But in this case, it's an effective way to make a bridge between the conversational context and the persistent process context.

As I mentioned when I provided an overview of the object model changes in the Gadget Catalog, the actions and data needed to implement the review process will be the responsibility of a new component, implemented by the GadgetReviewBean class. In the GadgetReviewBean, we need to initialize our gadget identifier as a process identifier, and keep the gadget being reviewed as a conversational variable. First we create two bijected variables on the GadgetReviewBean:

```
@In(value="reviewGadget",
    required=false)
@Out(value="reviewGadget",
     required=false)
private Gadget mReviewGadget;

@In(value="reviewGadgetID",
    scope=ScopeType.BUSINESS_PROCESS,
    required=false)
@Out(value="reviewGadgetID",
     scope=ScopeType.BUSINESS_PROCESS,
     required=false)
private Long mReviewGadgetID;
```

The reviewGadget component represents our gadget being reviewed, and the reviewGadgetID is its identifier, kept in the process context. Notice that we've left the scope unspecified on the @In and @Out annotations for the reviewGadget. When we inject the value for the first time, it will be pulled from the process context where the gadgetAdmin component placed it in saveGadget(). We've left the gadgetReview component as a conversational component, so the outjection will be to the conversation context by default.

The final piece of the puzzle is to put some code in place to initialize the reviewGadget component and/or the gadget identifier, depending on the situation. When the first task is performed in a process instance, there will be a reviewGadget component initialized by the gadgetAdmin.saveGadget() action. But there won't be a gadget identifier, because we haven't injected it into the process context yet. In other cases (e.g., across application restarts), we'll have the gadget identifier in persistent process scope, but no reviewGadget. So we check for both situations in our task method(s):

```
@StartTask
public String startReviewTask() {
    // If the review gadget ID is unset, we must be starting the process,
    // so pull the review gadget placed in the process context by the
```

---

2. Please, please pardon the pun, but I had to use it at least once.

```
            // gadgetAdmin component, and initialize the id
            if (mReviewGadgetID == null) {
                if (getReviewGadget() == null) {
                    facesMessages.add(
                        new FacesMessage(FacesMessage.SEVERITY_ERROR,
                            "Invalid process data",
                            "There is no active review gadget or gadget ID"));
                    return null;
                }
                else {
                    mReviewGadgetID = getReviewGadget().getId();
                }
            }
            // If necessary, load the gadget being reviewed from the catalog DB,
            // and place it into conversation scope
            if (getReviewGadget() == null) {
                String queryStr = "from Gadget g where g.id = " +
                                  mReviewGadgetID;
                Gadget rg =
                    (Gadget)gadgetDatabase.createQuery(queryStr).getSingleResult();
                setReviewGadget(rg);
            }

            return getTask().getName();
    }
```

This can all get confusing very easily, so let's review the steps in the process from the start:

1. A user saves a new gadget using the gadgetAdmin.saveGadget() action method.

2. A new process instance is created because of the @CreateProcess annotation on the method.

3. The saved Gadget object is programmatically placed into the process context under the component name "reviewGadget", and saveGadget() returns successfully.

4. Later, a user decides to perform one of the review tasks (how this happens is the topic of the next section). The appropriate action method on GadgetReviewBean is invoked. The reviewGadget component is injected from the process context, and the action method initializes the gadget ID variable from the reviewGadget.id property. The identifier is outjected into the process context.

5. As future tasks are executed in the business process, the same check is performed each time. The gadget ID is always available, since it resides in the persistent process scope, so the `reviewGadget` can always be reloaded from the database using that.

Executing Tasks

During the execution of a process, if a `task-node` is encountered (such as the "review-core" node in our gadget review process), jBPM will create an instance of the `task` configured in the node, and then the execution path will wait for that task to be completed. Every task instance has a task ID associated with it. A task is completed when the task instance with that ID is marked as complete.

I'll focus here on executing process tasks through the Seam framework, using Seam annotations and built-in components. If you are writing a Seam application, you want to handle business processes the same way you handle other concerns. If you'd prefer, you can directly access the current process and task instances being managed by jBPM, using the jBPM API, but we won't explore this approach here. For full details on programmatic business process management using jBPM's direct APIs, refer to the jBPM documentation.

Assigning Tasks to Users

A user can only execute a task once it has been assigned to him or her. Tasks can be assigned to users in two ways: a task can be assigned directly to an individual user, or it can be assigned to a role held by the user.

Tasks are initially assigned to users (either individually or by role) in the process definition. Looking back to Listing 7-2, you can see that each `task` element in each task node has an assignment element that specifies who is supposed to perform the task. Here's the task node for the "review-core" task, for example:

```
<task-node name="review-core">
    <task name="review-core"
        description="Review the core data for #{reviewTaskGadget.name}">
        <assignment pooled-actors="ADMIN"/>
    </task>
    <transition to="review-join" />
</task-node>
```

Here we're saying that any user with the role of "ADMIN" can perform this task. The attribute we're using on the assignment is called "pooled-actors" because this type of task assignment puts the task into a pooled list of tasks, assigned to anyone with the "ADMIN" role.

You can also assign a task to an individual user. In the "verify-revisions" task, for example, we're assigning the task to the user who submitted the original gadget to the catalog.

```
<task-node name="verify-revisions">
    <task name="verify-revisions" description="Verify revisions made by admins">
        <assignment actor-id="#{submitterID}"/>
    </task>
    <transition name="reject" to="review-core"/>
    <transition name="confirm" to="end" />
</task-node>
```

We use the actor-id attribute on the assignment in this case. We're using a context variable called submitterID as the actor-id value—the initialization of this context variable was discussed in the section "Business Process Data" earlier in this chapter.

How does jBPM identify users and their roles? Every user participating in a jBPM process is associated with an actor ID, and with one or more named roles. Seam provides a built-in component called actor, implemented by the Actor class, that wraps these user attributes into a Seam context variable and makes them available to the jBPM runtime when needed. In Chapter 6, we integrated Seam's security services into the Gadget Catalog to authenticate users and associate their roles with them. We keep the user's authenticated identity and roles in our User object, and that object is created during authentication when the Login.login() action method is invoked. All we need to do in order to plug these two things together is to ensure that, whenever a user's User object is created, the information is also used to populate their actor component. This is very simple to implement: we just need to inject the actor component into the Login bean, and when the user authenticates and invokes the Login.login() method, we map over the user's identifier and roles to the appropriate properties on the actor component. Listing 7-3 shows the modified Login bean, with the relevant changes highlighted.

Listing 7-3. *Login Bean, Modified to Initialize the jBPM Actor*

```
@Stateful
@Name("login")
public class Login implements ILogin, Serializable {
    @In(value="user", required=false)
    @Out(value="user", required=false)
    private User mUser;

    @In(create=true)
    private EntityManager gadgetDatabase;

    // Inject the jBPM Actor component
    @In(value="actor")
```

```
    private Actor actor;

public boolean login() {
    boolean result = false;
    if (getUser() == null) {
        try {
            Identity identity = Identity.instance();
            String queryStr =  "from User " +
                                "where login = :userName " +
                                "and password = :password"
            Query q =
                gadgetDatabase.createQuery(queryStr)
                    .setParameter("userName", identity.getUsername())
                    .setParameter("password", identity.getPassword());
            setUser((User) q.getSingleResult());
            if (getUser() != null) {
                // Map the user over to the jBPM actor
                actor.setId(Long.toString(getUser().getId()));

                // Register the user's roles with the Seam security system,
                // and with the jBPM actor
                for (Role r : getUser().getRoles()) {
                    identity.addRole(r.getName());
                    actor.getGroupActorIds().add(r.getName());
                }
            }
        }
        catch (NoResultException nre) {
            FacesMessages.instance().add("Username/password do not match");
        }
    }
    result = (getUser() == null ? false : true);
    return result;
}

@Destroy @Remove
public void destroy() {}

public User getUser() {
    return mUser;
}

public void setUser(User user) {
    mUser = user;
}
}
```

Once jBPM knows who the user is and what groups he or she is in (which is accomplished by initializing the user's `actor` component), it keeps track of all the pending tasks that are waiting for that user, in any active business process instances. jBPM keeps an internal record of these task assignments, and Seam exposes them as the following components:

- `taskInstanceList`: This is a list of all pending tasks that have been directly assigned to the current user. In other words, this list has all the tasks whose actor ID matches the actor ID in the current user's `actor` component.

- `pooledTaskInstanceList`: This is a list of all pending tasks that have been assigned to one or more of the current user's groups. If a task is assigned to a particular group, all users with that group in their `actor.groupActorIds` list will see that task appear in their `pooledTaskInstanceList` context variable.

- `taskInstanceListForType`: This context variable allows you to select tasks from the user's current list, based on type (i.e., the name of the task, as specified in the `name` attribute in the `task` element in the jPDL process definition).

To demonstrate the use of these components, let's enhance the Gadget Catalog to allow administrators to pick review tasks to perform when new gadgets are entered into the catalog. As you already saw in the section "Starting a Business Process," the `gadgetAdmin.saveGadget()` action method has been enhanced with an `@CreateProcess` annotation, causing an instance of the "review-gadget" process to start when a gadget is saved. As you can see in Figure 7-6 and Listing 7-2, the start node in the process immediately transitions to the "review-fork" node, and that in turn branches to the three review tasks. These tasks are each assigned to any actor in the "ADMIN" group. Our enhancements to the `Login` component have ensured that all Gadget Catalog administrators will also fall into this jBPM group, so once these task nodes are entered, the three review tasks will be placed into the `pooledTaskInstanceList` for any administrator.

Making available tasks visible to our administrators (or any users, for that matter) is simply a matter of referencing these components in a page. These lists all contain `TaskInstance` objects, which is how jBPM represents a task instance during the execution of a process. A `TaskInstance` has many properties available, but a few of the more commonly used ones are listed here:

- `name`: The task name, as specified in the `name` attribute of the `task` element in the jPDL

- `description`: The task description, as specified in the `description` attribute of the `task` element

- id: The unique task ID assigned to this task instance by the jBPM runtime

- actorId: The ID of the actor currently assigned to this task (if any)

It's a simple matter to add a JSF dataTable to the adminHome.jsp page, listing out any pooled tasks that the administrator can choose to perform:

```
<h:dataTable rendered="#{not empty pooledTaskInstanceList}"
            value="#{pooledTaskInstanceList}" var="task">
    <h:column>
        <f:facet name="header">Description</f:facet>
        <h:outputText value="#{task.description}"/>
    </h:column>
    <h:column>
        <s:link action="#{pooledTask.assignToCurrentActor}"
                value="Accept" taskInstance="#{task}"/>
    </h:column>
</h:dataTable>
```

The only new details we've introduced here are the use of the pooledTask component and the use of the taskInstance attribute on the Seam s:link control. The pooledTask component is another built-in Seam component that is enabled when you enable jBPM support in your application. This component is used to assign tasks to users. When you invoke the assignToCurrentActor action method, it assigns the task to the current actor. The actor ID is accessed from the currently active actor component. The task is referenced on the link using its task ID. In this case, we're using the taskInstance attribute on s:link, which is a shortcut to adding the task ID to the request. If you were using a regular JSF commandLink control instead, you would have to pass in a taskId parameter using the id property of the task:

```
<h:commandLink action="#{pooledTask.assignToCurrentActor}" value="Accept">
    <f:param name="taskId" value="#{task.id}"/>
</h:commandLink>
```

Now, when any user saves a gadget to the catalog (using the newly annotated saveGadget() action method), the "review-gadget" process kicks off, and the execution paths land eventually on the three review tasks. Each of these is assigned to the "ADMIN" group and will appear in any administrator's list of pooled tasks. So when an administrator goes to the administration home page, he or she will now see the screen in Figure 7-7, assuming that the new gadget was named "Solar Plexus 2000".

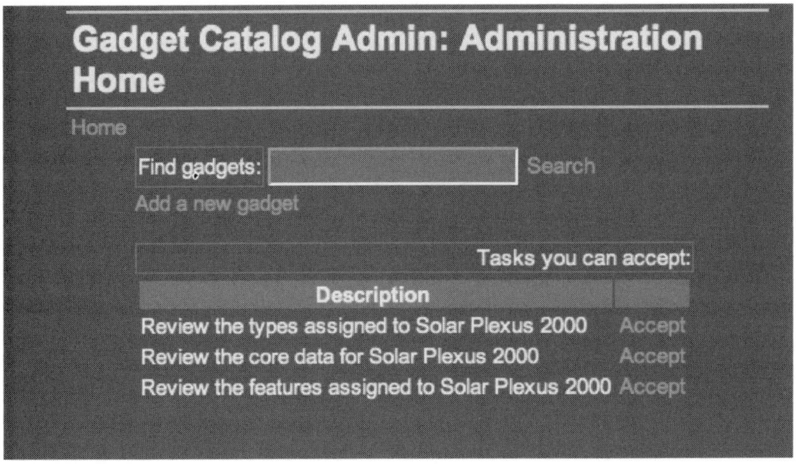

Figure 7-7. *Admin home page showing available tasks*

When an administrator clicks one of the "Accept" links, the task is put into his or her list of assigned tasks, and it will then appear in his or her `taskInstanceList`.

Starting and Ending Tasks

You've seen how tasks can be assigned to a user, now let's see how a user actually performs a task. In Seam, a task is started when the user executes an action with an `@StartTask` annotation, with the task ID included as a request parameter. So we can easily create a link to start a task in essentially the same way that we created the table of pooled tasks in the previous section.

Once a user has been assigned to a task, the task will appear in that user's `taskInstanceList` component. We can place a table of task links on the Gadget Catalog home page by adding the following `dataTable` control to the `index.jsp` file:

```
<h:dataTable rendered="#{identity.loggedIn and not empty taskInstanceList}"
          value="#{taskInstanceList}"
          var="task">
    <h:column>
        <f:facet name="header">Description</f:facet>
        <h:outputText value="#{task.description}"/>
    </h:column>
    <h:column>
        <s:link action="#{gadgetReview.startReviewTask}"
                value="Begin" taskInstance="#{task}"/>
    </h:column>
</h:dataTable>
```

Except for the fact that we're using the `taskInstanceList` instead of the `pooled TaskInstanceList`, there's very little different between this table and the one you saw earlier. One difference is that, since we're placing this table on the main home page, and since that page does not require authentication, we need to check to see whether the user is logged in before we render the table. If a user is not authenticated, checking his or her `taskInstanceList` isn't possible, because we don't know who that user is.

The other difference in the links is that, instead of using the `pooledTask` component to assign tasks to users, we're pointing the links to an action method, `startReviewTask()`, on our `gadgetReview` component. This task is annotated with an `@StartTask` annotation, so when the user follows this link, a new conversation will be started, and the task whose `taskId` is passed in the request will be started in the corresponding business process instance:

```
@StartTask
public String startReviewTask() {
    // Details of initializing process data omitted here
    return getTask().getName();
}
```

We looked at this action method earlier in the section "Business Process Data," where we looked at the handling of business process variables. I've omitted the data initialization details here for brevity. But there is another interesting practical detail to mention here. You may have noticed that all of the links we generate in the home page point to the same action method, regardless of the type of task the user is executing. This seems odd, since we obviously need to perform different actions depending on what task is being performed, right? Well, we're using JSF navigation rules to route the user to the page that's relevant to the task being performed. You'll notice in the method implementation that the outcome of the method is the name of the task being performed. We injected the current task into the `gadgetReview` bean as the value of its `task` property:

```
@In(value="taskInstance")
private TaskInstance mTask;
public TaskInstance getTask() {
    return mTask;
}
public void setTask(TaskInstance task) {
    mTask = task;
}
```

In the `@In` annotation, we're referencing the built-in `taskInstance` component provided by Seam. This represents the current task being performed by the user, if he or she is running within a conversation with an active task.

In order to route the user to the right page, we then added the following navigation rules to the `faces-config.xml`:

```
<navigation-rule>
    <navigation-case>
        <from-outcome>review-core</from-outcome>
        <to-view-id>/admin/reviewGadgetCore.jsp</to-view-id>
    </navigation-case>
    <navigation-case>
        <from-outcome>review-types</from-outcome>
        <to-view-id>/admin/reviewGadgetTypes.jsp</to-view-id>
    </navigation-case>
    <navigation-case>
        <from-outcome>review-features</from-outcome>
        <to-view-id>/admin/reviewGadgetFeatures.jsp</to-view-id>
    </navigation-case>
</navigation-rule>
```

This creates a handy little task-routing entry point—a single action method, startReviewTask(), can be used for starting all tasks in the "review-gadget" process, and we just make the appropriate entry in faces-config.xml to associate the appropriate page with the task to be performed.

So far, so good—we've started the process, assigned tasks to users, and users can start these tasks. But we still need to make sure that jBPM knows when these tasks are complete. Seam has made this a simple matter as well. As an example, let's look at the "review-core" task. In the navigation rules earlier, note that the user will be routed to the /admin/reviewGadgetCore.jsp page when he or she starts this task. That page displays a form that allows the administrator to review/change the core metadata for the gadget, and also to set the status for the gadget as a whole (e.g., from "UNCONFIRMED" to "CONFIRMED", etc.), as shown in Figure 7-8.

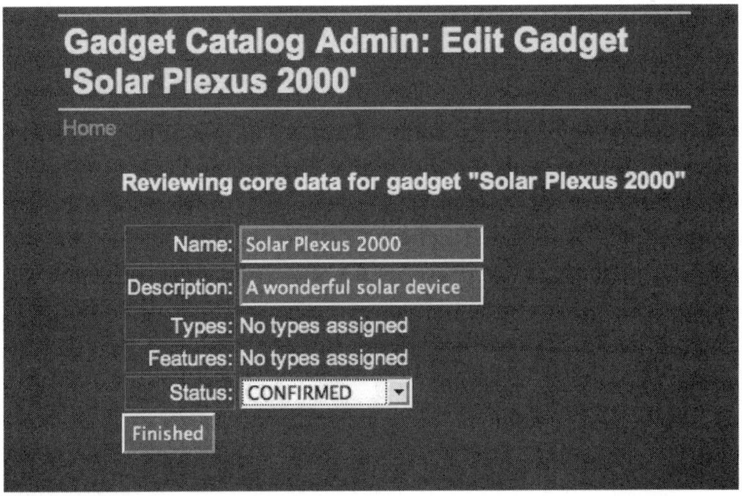

Figure 7-8. *Core gadget data review form*

This form submits to the gadgetReview.saveCoreReviewData() action method:

```
<h:commandButton type="submit" value="Finished"
                 action="#{gadgetReview.saveCoreReviewData}"/>
```

This action method has an @EndTask annotation, ensuring that, if it completes successfully, the currently active task (associated with the current conversation context) will be ended:

```
@EndTask
public String saveCoreReviewData() {
    saveGadget(getReviewGadget());
    return "success";
}
```

The ending of the task triggers jBPM to update the process execution path that is waiting on this task, advancing it to the "review-join" node (as specified in our jPDL in Listing 7-2). Once all of the review tasks that transition to this join node are complete, the join will execute, and the transition to the "verify-revisions" task node will occur. Since this task is assigned directly to the user who submitted the new gadget, it will immediately be placed in that user's taskInstanceList, and the task will appear as a link in the home page the next time he or she visits it. Once the user completes that task, the process will either end or loop back to the review fork, depending on the outcome of the verification task.

Summary

In this chapter, we've explored Seam's support for business process management, using the jBPM framework. Seam's integrated jBPM support simplifies the use of business processes in your applications. Processes and their tasks can be started and ended using annotations on action methods, and Seam exposes the process runtime as a Seam component context, allowing you to use all the contextual component facilities of Seam in your process.

I also discussed some of the special issues involved in managing business processes, since they are very long-lived contexts that can span multiple user sessions and multiple application lifetimes. This long-lived characteristic of business processes requires persistence of key process variables, and this persistence must be considered when using components in the process context. You saw some how these persistence needs impacted our use of business processes in the Gadget Catalog. We needed to implement some special handling of context components, depending on whether they could be persisted by jBPM or not.

CHAPTER 8

Rich Web Clients

The term "rich web clients" is typically interspersed with the terms "Web 2.0" and "AJAX." It refers to web interfaces that provide a relatively high level of interactivity compared to traditional click-and-reload web interfaces. These rich web interfaces are thought of as the next generation of user experience on the Web (hence the association with Web 2.0), and the technology most often brought to bear to create them is JavaScript (hence the association with Asynchronous JavaScript and XML, or AJAX).

In this chapter, we will explore Seam's support for integrating rich web clients with your Seam components, using these components to provide the server-side data and functionality needed for the web interface. The key factor here is that the data and functionality is accessed directly from the web client (the browser) rather than through the standard JSF web request processing life cycle. This enables more immediate and interactive user experiences in the web interface, among other things.

Much of the discussion in this chapter involves JavaScript and dynamic DOM manipulation, which are typical parts of any AJAX interface. I am not going to provide a tutorial on JavaScript here. If you are not already familiar with the basics of JavaScript and accessing the page DOM at runtime, you might want to defer reading this chapter and instead get familiar with these foundations first.

What Is a Rich Web Client?

Typical web interfaces are like the ones you've seen so far in this book. The user navigates through a series of pages to accomplish tasks, like creating entries in catalogs, searching for information, and so on. The interaction paradigm is very simple: a page is presented to the user, the user edits fields and/or clicks a link or a button on the page, and he or she is taken to another page. In between the two page views, the client browser sends an HTTP request to the site, and this request can cause information to be updated, data to be retrieved, and so forth. This sequence (view a page, perform an action on that page, and be redirected to another page) continues until the user is done with whatever he or she is doing.

This mode of interaction leaves a lot of room for improvement. It doesn't feel very interactive to users, for obvious reasons. User interactions are broken down into relatively coarse transactions, delimited by pages and browser redirects. Users experience a "read/edit/wait" sequence, where they are presented with a page, they have to visually parse what's on the page and what's being asked of them, decide what action they want to take, take it, and then wait for the browser to load up the next page.

A rich web client implements a more interactive experience for the user. Transactions with the system are broken down into smaller units of work, and users see more immediate feedback from their actions (more immediate than a full browser page load, at least). A rich web client allows a user to push a button and see the impact immediately in the page that he or she is viewing. There's no disorienting context switch to a new page, and the user feels more effective and more efficient.

The most commonly used technology currently for implementing rich web clients is AJAX. AJAX is more of a technique than a specific API or tool. It involves the use of JavaScript to make "intrapage" requests back to a web server to perform actions on the user's behalf. The JavaScript is loaded in the page along with the HTML used to display the contents, and as the user interacts with the HTML elements (clicks buttons, types into text fields, etc.), JavaScript calls are made in response to the user's actions in the page. These calls can, among other things, exchange XML information with some server-side component, such as a CGI script, a Java servlet, or any active code. This exchange might bring additional information into the page, update server-side data, or just about anything else that's needed to accomplish what the user is trying to do. Again, the difference is that these server calls are made without a full page request being made by the web browser, so a user sees more immediate feedback to his or her actions in the page.

Seam's Remoting Services

Seam's primary support for rich web clients is provided in its component remoting services. These services will dynamically (and automatically) generate JavaScript client stubs for your Seam components and use them from a web browser client to interact directly with your server-side Seam components.

Figure 8-1 shows the runtime model used by the Seam remoting services, and the interaction that they enable between your Seam components and client-side JavaScript code.

At the bottom of the figure is your Seam application running in an application server. At the top is the client browser. The Seam remoting services consist of a set of Java code running on the server and another set of JavaScript code running in the browser. The server-side code generates a JavaScript binding for any Seam components that you choose to export. This JavaScript code runs in the browser and can be used to make direct calls back to the Seam components. Seam's remoting services handle all of the communication between the browser and the Seam components. This support code converts JavaScript calls made in the browser to XML and back again. Similarly, the Seam remoting services running on the server convert the XML coming from the browser into appropriate calls to your Seam components, and the results are converted into XML and streamed back to the browser. On the server, you write Seam components in Java as usual, and on the client, you invoke those components using regular JavaScript calls. All the ugly details of the XML communications and the creation of JavaScript interfaces for the components are done for you by Seam's remoting services.

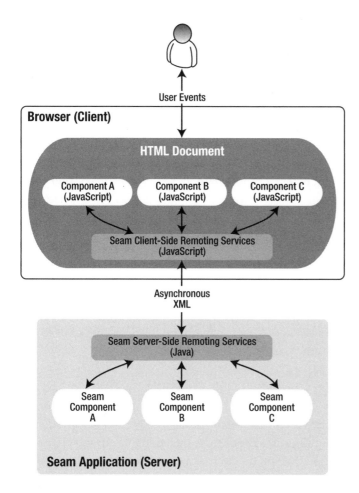

Figure 8-1. *Seam remoting runtime*

The Seam remoting services are ideally suited to help with creating rich web clients using AJAX. The JavaScript interfaces for your Seam components allow you to call them directly from the browser, triggered by user events within the HTML page. Information provided by the Seam components can be displayed immediately to the user within the page, without requiring a page reload.

Gadget Catalog: Improving the User Experience

The user experience in the Gadget Catalog has been improving slightly as we've progressed. The use of Seam's pageflow capabilities in Chapter 5 allowed us to provide wizards to simplify the creation of new gadget entries, for example. But now that we've opened up the application for general users, we need to consider ways to integrate rich client technology into the interface to make it more interactive and appealing to users.

One way we could improve things is to streamline the search features of the catalog. Currently, a user (either a general public user using the main home page or an administrator using the administrator home page) has to type in some search text and browse through the list of results to find the gadget he or she is seeking. It would be much more efficient to show candidate matches to the user while he or she types, allowing that user to pick the one he or she is after directly from the search page. In the world of AJAX this is commonly referred to as an *auto-complete feature*, and many AJAX JavaScript libraries provide auto-complete tools.

There are many other rich client extensions we could make to the Gadget Catalog interface as well, but this simple enhancement to the search function will allow us to demonstrate the key features of Seam remoting.

Configuring Seam Remoting

As with all the other Seam services, you need to configure the remoting services before you can use them. Since Seam remoting involves both server-side and client-side elements, you need to do server-side and client-side configuration. Luckily, both ends of the configuration are very straightforward.

Server-Side Configuration

The implementation and support classes for the Seam remoting services are in the `jboss-seam-remoting.jar` library, so this jar file needs to be included in your application archive. You can add it to the `WEB-INF/lib` directory of your web archive, or put it into your application archive (the EAR) and load it as a jar module in the `application.xml`. As with any other libraries, make sure you only load it in one place in your overall application archive, to avoid classloader issues.

If you want to configure any of the behavior of the remoting services, you can add an entry to your `components.xml` file:

```
<components>
    . . .
    <component name="org.jboss.seam.remoting.remoting">
        <property name="debug">true</property>
    </component>
    . . .
</components>
```

In the current version of Seam, the only property you can configure on the remoting service is the debug option.[1] I'll describe this option a little later when I discuss the client-side JavaScript code in the section "Debugging Remote Calls."

The last piece of server-side configuration is the most important. The heart of the server-side remoting services is the Resource Servlet. This is a general-purpose servlet provided with Seam that you can include in your web application. It provides HTTP access to various runtime resources that might be needed by Seam components, client-side code, and so on. The Seam `GraphicImage` JSF control, for example, uses the Resource Servlet to pull a dynamic image resource to display in the page.

Seam's remoting services make use of the Resource Servlet in several ways. First, it provides access to all the JavaScript needed within the web page, including both the base JavaScript library needed to communicate with the Seam application and the automatically generated JavaScript interfaces to your Seam components. The Resource Servlet also provides the JavaScript code with runtime access to the Seam components. The JavaScript client stubs pass their XML messages to the Seam remoting services through the Resource Servlet.

Configuring the Resource Servlet is done like any other servlet. You need to add servlet and servlet-mapping entries to your `web.xml` to activate the servlet:

```
<web-app>
    . . .
    <servlet>
        <servlet-name>Seam Resource Servlet</servlet-name>
        <servlet-class>org.jboss.seam.servlet.ResourceServlet</servlet-class>
    </servlet>
    <servlet-mapping>
        <servlet-name>Seam Resource Servlet</servlet-name>
        <url-pattern>/seam/resource/*</url-pattern>
    </servlet-mapping>
    . . .
</web-app>
```

You should use this servlet mapping as-is, because there are elements of the Seam services that depend on this particular URL pattern.

Client-Side Configuration

Once the Seam remoting services are configured in your application, you can configure the client-side of the remoting connection. In each web page where you want to make use of Seam components, you'll need to import the Seam remoting base JavaScript

---

1. The Seam remoting services also include an experimental release of support for accessing JMS message destinations from client-side JavaScript, along with a set of configuration properties for these features. At the time of this writing, these are still only experimental, so I don't discuss them here.

library in the page using an HTML script tag. The JavaScript library is accessed through the Resource Servlet, using the URL `seam/resource/remoting/resource/remote.js` within your application's web context. So if your page sits in the root of your web archive, you would import the remoting JavaScript library like so:

```
<script type="text/javascript"
        src="seam/resource/remoting/resource/remote.js"></script>
```

Like any other JavaScript library, you can import the code in the `head` or the `body` of your page.

If your Seam component is a session EJB, requiring an "executable" stub (see the next section, "Enabling Access to Server Components"), you'll need to load the JavaScript client stubs for the component through the Resource Servlet as well. If you have a session EJB Seam component named "widget", for example, you would import the JavaScript bindings for that component using the following `script` tag:

```
<script type="text/javascript"
        src="seam/resource/remoting/interface.js?widget"></script>
```

Now that you've seen how to configure the server-side and client-side of the remoting link, let's look at how you enable your Seam components to be remotely accessed.

Enabling Access to Server Components

Seam allows you to remotely access any of your components and other Java types from the web client. Native Java types, and some Java collections, are mapped directly into corresponding JavaScript types, as described in the next section, "Basic Java Type Mappings." Any JavaBeans or EJB components that you want to access will be mapped to client-side JavaScript stubs.

There are two types of client stubs that Seam generates for your Java objects: executable stubs and type stubs. *Executable stubs* are used to expose key business functionality to your web client, while *type stubs* are used to represent various data types employed as method arguments and return values.

Basic Java Type Mappings

Table 8-1 lists the mappings that Seam remoting uses for basic Java types, such as native types, built-in classes, and so on. JavaScript is a more loosely typed language than Java, so in some cases it may be possible to force a mapped type into another when needed.

Table 8-1. *JavaScript Mappings for Basic Java Types*

Java Type	JavaScript Mapping
java.lang.Boolean	Boolean
java.util.Date, java.sql.Date, java.sql.Timestamp	Date
enum	Enumerated values will be represented as String values in JavaScript. To pass enum values back to the server, you need to use their names as strings.
java.lang.Number	The number value will be serialized into a string in the XML passed between the client and server, and on the client it will be mapped to an appropriate JavaScript number value.
java.lang.String	String
java.util.Array, List, Set, Queue collections	Any Java collections that fall under these types will be mapped to JavaScript arrays.
java.util.Map	Any Java Map collections will be mapped to Seam.Remoting.Map objects. JavaScript does not contain native support for maps, so Seam's remoting services provide their own implementation of a JavaScript map. The definition of this JavaScript object is part of the base JavaScript code in the remote.js script, loaded through the Resource Servlet.

Executable Stubs

Executable stubs are generated for Seam components that are session EJBs, or JavaBeans that contain methods annotated with @WebRemote. If neither of these conditions apply, the component will have a type stub generated for it instead.

When an executable stub is generated, it will only contain bindings for the methods that have been annotated with the @WebRemote annotation. The @WebRemote annotation can be used without any attributes, or an exclude attribute can be used to filter the data flowing from the component to the client. I'll discuss the exclude attribute later in the section "Restricting the Client-Side Data," when we look at how the XML data flowing to the client can be managed.

Listing 8-1 shows an example JavaBean component, PurchaseOrder, that has several methods used for accessing and updating information about a purchase order.

Listing 8-1. *Example JavaBean Annotated for Remote Access*

```
@Name("purchaseOrder")
public class  PurchaseOrder implements Serializable {
    @WebMethod
    public List<LineItem> getLineItems() { . . . }
    @WebMethod
    public boolean validateOrder() { . . . }
    public Status getOrderStatus() { . . . }
    public boolean addItem(LineItem l) { . . . }
}
```

Two methods have been annotated for remote access: getLineItems() and validateOrder(). When a client imports the JavaScript bindings for this component, the executable stub interface for PurchaseOrder will contain functions corresponding to these two methods.

In the case of our Gadget Catalog enhancements, we want to remotely access the gadget searching functionality from the home page. This will allow us to take the user's text from the search box as he or she is typing, perform a search, and show some suggestions that might help the user get right to the gadget he or she is after. If the user wants, he or she can still do the full search and browse through the results on the gadget list page, but the suggested matches will give the user some immediate feedback and give him or her the option to take a shortcut right to a specific gadget.

The search functionality in the Gadget Catalog is provided by the GadgetAdminBean component. This component is a session EJB, and when annotating methods on a session EJB for remote access, they must be marked in the bean's local interface. This may sound nonintuitive at first, but it actually makes sense when you think about how EJB components are managed and how Seam's remoting services operate. When you deploy a session EJB to the EJB container, it will take any local (annotated with the EJB @Local annotation) or remote (annotated with the EJB @Remote annotation) interfaces and generate internal proxies for them. These proxies interact with the EJB container's internal runtime services to ensure the component is managed properly at runtime. Seam's remoting services operate as a client to these EJB components, so its annotations need to be applied to the EJB's interfaces, not its implementation class. In addition, since the Seam remoting services will be running on the server with the EJB components, the local interfaces for the EJB should be used.

Luckily, GadgetAdminBean already has a local interface defined, the IGadgetAdminBean interface. On examination of the IGadgetAdminBean interface, however, we see that the search method defined there isn't structured in a way that's convenient for our client calls. The search() method is an action method, taking no arguments and returning an outcome as a String. The search text is pulled from the searchField property, and the property value is populated by a JSF form. For our remoting use case, we need a search method that accepts the search text directly and returns the matching Gadget beans. So we'll refactor our search() action method into two search() methods:

```
public String search() {
    mGadgetMatches = search(getSearchField());
    mSelGadget = null;
    if (mGadgetMatches.size() == 1) {
        setActiveGadget(mGadgetMatches.get(0));
        return "editGadget";
    }
    return "listGadgets";
}

public List<Gadget> search(String str) {
    List<Gadget> results = new ArrayList<Gadget>();
    String searchField = "%" + str + "%";
    try {
        String queryStr =
            "select g from Gadget as g " +
            "where UPPER(g.name) like UPPER(:searchField) " +
            "or UPPER(g.description) like UPPER(:searchField) " +
            "order by g.name"
        Query q = gadgetDatabase.createQuery(queryStr)
                        .setParameter("searchField", searchField);
        results = q.getResultList();
    }
    catch (Exception e) {
        e.printStackTrace();
    }
    return results;
}
```

We have to add a declaration for our new search() method in the IGadgetAdminBean interface and annotate it for remote access as well:

```
@Local
public interface IGadgetAdminBean {

    . . .
    @WebRemote
    public List<Gadget> search(String str);

    . . .
}
```

In order to use an executable stub in the browser, you have to explicitly load the executable stub through the Seam Resource Servlet, similar to how we loaded the base

JavaScript code for Seam's remoting services earlier. An HTML `script` tag is used, with the source of the script set to reference the `interface.js` module:

```
<script type="text/javascript"
        src="seam/resource/remoting/interface.js?myComponent"></script>
```

The "myComponent" portion of the reference is the name of the Seam component that you want to access from the web page using its executable stub. In the case of the Gadget Catalog, the component we need to access is named "gadgetAdmin", so our script tag looks like this:

```
<script type="text/javascript"
        src="seam/resource/remoting/interface.js?gadgetAdmin"></script>
```

You only need to do this explicit generation of JavaScript stubs when an executable stub is needed. This import triggers the check for `@WebRemote` annotations in the referenced component. Type stubs, discussed in the next section, are automatically generated by the Seam remoting services when they are needed.

Calling Remote Methods

Figure 8-2 depicts the steps that occur when you invoke a remote component method from your JavaScript code. In the scenario shown in the figure, we've written a JavaScript function, `doGadgetSearch()`, that is remotely invoking our Seam component, `GadgetAdminBean`. The results of the remote method call are being handled by another JavaScript function that we've written, `handleResults()`. All of the back-and-forth with the remote Seam component is handled by the executable JavaScript stub for `GadgetAdminBean` and the Seam remoting services.

Each annotated method in the Seam component will have a corresponding JavaScript method on the executable stub. This method will have the same name as the component method, and the arguments and return values will correspond to those on the component method, mapped according to the overall mapping rules we're covering in this section. There will also be an additional argument added to the JavaScript method, which is a JavaScript callback function that should be invoked when the remote method call returns. Remember that, behind the scenes, the Seam JavaScript code is making an asynchronous XML exchange with the server in order to carry out the remote method call. When the XML response is received from the server and the XML is converted into corresponding JavaScript objects, the callback function that you pass into the method call will be invoked, and the results of the method call will be passed in as function arguments.

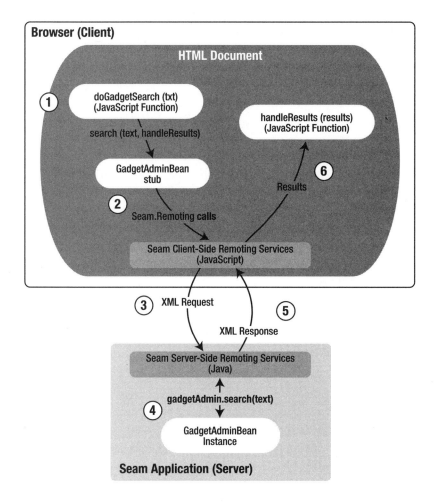

Figure 8-2. *Runtime handling of remote component methods*

Assuming we've used the script tag shown earlier to load the JavaScript client stub for our gadgetAdmin component, we could invoke the search() method with JavaScript code along these lines:

```
function handleResults(gadgetMatches) {
    /* Iterate through the returned gadgets and do something interesting */
}

function doGadgetSearch(txt) {
    var gadgetAdmin = Seam.Component.getInstance("gadgetAdmin");
    gadgetAdmin.search(txt, handleResults);
}
```

Any public method on a session EJB or JavaBean component can be annotated for remote access through an executable stub. You aren't limited to action methods or methods with a particular signature. You do, however, need to consider the data types of the method arguments and return values. These are going to be mapped to client-side type stubs, discussed in the next section.

Debugging Remote Calls

I mentioned in passing that Seam's remoting services can be configured with a debug option. This option allows you to see the XML being passed back and forth from the JavaScript code in the browser to the Seam components on the server. This can be very handy when you need to figure out whether the correct data is being sent to the server component, and whether the expected data is coming back.

The debug option is enabled by setting the debug property when configuring the remoting services in the components.xml:

```
<components>
    . . .
    <component name="org.jboss.seam.remoting.remoting">
        <property name="debug">true</property>
    </component>
    . . .
</components>
```

Enabling this option will cause every remote method call made on the client to be displayed in a pop-up window on the browser. The window shows the full XML for each method call and response.

Restricting the Client-Side Data

Whenever you are passing information across the network, you need to be concerned about the size and nature of the data being transmitted. You need to ask yourself questions like, "What if someone intercepted the information before it reached the browser?", "What information is actually flowing across the connection?", and so on. In our case, we're allowing code running in the browser to make a remote call to our Seam component running on the server, as depicted in Figure 8-2. The search text is being packaged up in an XML message to the server. There's probably no real problem there, unless users get concerned about the contents of their searches being stolen and searches in the Gadget Catalog aren't likely to be very interesting to outside parties. The result of the search is an array of Gadget objects, converted into an XML message back to the browser. At first glance, this might not seem like an issue, either. After all, anyone can get access to the Gadget Catalog for free (so far), and it's much easier to get at the gadget information through our nice web interface than by sniffing HTTP packets on the network. But if we take a look at the XML flowing back to the browser (using the debug option we discussed in the previous section), we might be surprised (at first) to see the following:

```xml
<envelope>
    <body>
            . . .
            <ref id="1">
                <bean type="user">
                    <member name="password">
                        <str>secretpassword</str>
                    </member>
                    <member name="login">
                        <str>jane</str>
                    </member>
                    <member name="email">
                        <str>jane%40gadgetcatalog.com</str>
                    </member>
                    <member name="roles">
                        <bag/>
                    </member>
                    <member name="name">
                        <str>Jane%20the%20Admin</str>
                    </member>
                    <member name="id">
                        <number>4</number>
                    </member>
                </bean>
            </ref>
            . . .
    </body>
</envelope>
```

Yikes! We're passing user's passwords across the network in clear text. If you think for a minute, you'll realize why this happened. Our Gadget bean has a submitter property, which is the User that submitted the gadget to the catalog. This User bean has a password property on it, and its value is persisted in a clear text column in the USER table in the database. When the Gadget is converted to XML, Seam serializes the whole object, including all its properties and their properties, until it hits the end of the object tree. When we originally designed the User object and the USER table, we might have fooled ourselves into thinking that it wasn't a security issue. The database was protected by passwords and the User objects only existed in the application server, and we would never display the user's password in the web UI, so where's the problem? Well, we just created a huge problem by simply remote-enabling our search() method.

The long-term answer to this problem is to stop storing passwords in clear text and to remove the password property from the User object. But we probably don't want to be passing the other user information, like e-mail addresses, over the network either, because our users might have some serious issues with that.

In addition to these security concerns, we may want to restrict the data sent back to the client for performance reasons as well. Our object model might be very complex on the server, while the client only requires a very specific subset of our model data. In this case, sending the entire model object in XML format over an HTTP connection would be both wasteful and slow.

Luckily, Seam thought ahead about this, and provided a way to filter the data that's passed back from the Seam component to the web client. The @WebRemote annotation that's used to mark remote-accessible methods has an exclude attribute that can be used to specify properties and/or data types that should be excluded from the data passed back to the browser. The exclude attribute accepts one or more dot-delimited path expressions that indicate which properties you want to exclude from the XML data. These path expressions can be very simple, pointing to a single property in a specific component type. In our case, if we wanted to remove the password from the XML data, we would change our annotation to the following:

```
@Local
public interface IGadgetAdminBean {

    . . .

    @WebRemote(exclude="submitter.password")
    public List<Gadget> search(String str);

    . . .
}
```

The path expressions used in the exclude attribute refer to properties on the return value of the method being annotated by @WebRemote. In this case, we're saying that we want to exclude the password property of the submitter property of each Gadget returned by the search() method. Consult the Seam documentation for additional options for these exclude path expressions.

Batching Remote Calls

If you want to reduce the number of requests sent back and forth between the server and the client, Seam's remoting services support the batching of remote method calls on executable stubs. Batching requests can improve overall performance, since there is some overhead involved in making a server connection, serializing all of the request data into an XML message, and deserializing the response XML into JavaScript objects. You want the user interface to be as responsive as possible to the user's actions on the page, so the possibility of batching requests is something you should always consider when developing a rich web client, with or without Seam remoting services.

Batching remote calls is fairly simple to do with Seam. Calling the `Seam.Remoting.`
`startBatch()` method will open up a new batch call, and any subsequent calls to executable stub methods will be added to that batch. The batch of method calls will be executed when you call `Seam.Remoting.executeBatch()`. All of the batched commands will be sent to the server in a single HTTP request, and all of the results will be sent back to the client in a single HTTP response. When the response is received, the callbacks registered with each remote call will be executed in the order in which the remote methods were added to the batch.

If, for example, we wanted to save an existing `Gadget` (perhaps using the data pulled from client-side form elements), and then perform a search against the Gadget Catalog, we could execute a batch request like so:

```
. . .
var currGadget = . . .; // The Gadget being edited
var gadgetAdmin = Seam.Component.getInstance("gadgetAdmin");
Seam.Remoting.startBatch();
gadgetAdmin.saveGadget(currGadget, saveCallback);
gadgetAdmin.search(someText, searchCallback);
Seam.Remoting.executeBatch();
. . .
```

Here, we're making a remote call to the `saveGadget()` method on the `gadgetAdmin` component to save the edited `Gadget`, and then we're calling `search()` to perform a search. We registered a callback function called `saveCallback()` on the call to `saveGadget()`, and another callback, `searchCallback()`, on the call to `search()`. We started a batch before making these calls, so the two calls will be sent in one request to the server when the `executeBatch()` is called. When the response is received, the results for the `saveGadget()` call (if any) are assembled, and the `saveCallback()` function is invoked. Once that completes, the results from the `search()` call are passed to the `searchCallback()` function.

Batching requests only has an effect on remote method calls on executable stubs. Method calls on type stubs (described in the next section) are local, so they always execute immediately regardless of whether a batch has been opened or not.

Type Stubs

If the server object being mapped by the remoting services is an entity EJB or a JavaBean with no @WebRemote annotations, the object will be mapped to JavaScript using a type stub. Type stubs contain only local accessors for JavaBean properties found on the class. Any other methods on the component will not be accessible on the client side. In effect, a type stub serves as a local copy of a data type. The data associated with a type stub is only transmitted remotely when the object is passed as an argument to a remote method call on an executable stub, or returned as the result of a remote method call.

Looking back at our `PurchaseOrder` example in Listing 8-1, if we removed the `@WebRemote` annotations, the component would be a regular JavaBean and would be mapped using a type stub. The `getLineItems()` and `getOrderStatus()` methods would be the only ones mapped in the type stub, since they have the format of JavaBean property accessors. If a `PurchaseOrder` is returned as the result of a remote method call, values for the `lineItems` and `orderStatus` properties will be serialized to the client and made accessible through the mapped `getLineItems()` and `getOrderStatus()` methods.

In most cases, type stubs will be dynamically generated as the result of calling methods on executable stubs. You'll typically identify (or write) a session EJB interface with the functionality that you need to expose to the JavaScript client, and that will be exposed to the JavaScript client as an executable stub. When you invoke methods on that stub, the types for the arguments and return values for the method will have type stubs generated for them automatically.

In the case of the Gadget Catalog, our `search()` method accepts a `String` and returns a list of `Gadget` objects. The `Gadget` class is an entity EJB, and it will have a type stub generated for it by Seam remoting when we invoke the `search()` method.

The Seam JavaScript Object

As mentioned earlier, you must import Seam's base JavaScript library in your page in order to make remote calls to any Seam component:

```
<script src="seam/resource/remoting/resource/remote.js"
        type="text/javascript"></script>
```

This JavaScript library includes two JavaScript objects that provide Seam's client-side support for remoting components: `Seam.Component` and `Seam.Remoting`.

Seam.Component

The `Seam.Component` object provides methods for accessing existing Seam server components, as well as creating new ones, from the web client. If you want to access an existing Seam component, you use the `getInstance()` method with the name of the component:

```
var gadget = Seam.Component.getInstance("gadget");
```

This call will request a JavaScript client stub for the component named "gadget" and store it in the `gadget` variable. If the referenced component is a session EJB, or if the component is a JavaBean with `@WebRemote` annotations, and its JavaScript mapping has been preloaded through the Resource Servlet, the stub will be an executable stub. The executable stub that's returned is a singleton instance, within the scope of the page. In other words, if you request the same named component in multiple calls to getInstance() within the same page view, the same JavaScript stub will be returned each time.

If the named component is not suitable for an executable stub (i.e., it's an entity bean or a JavaBean with no @WebRemote methods), the returned stub will be a type stub. Now that we have this stub, we can access the data on the component and use it in the web page. In the case of our Gadget component, it is an entity EJB and will be mapped using a type stub, so we can access the Gadget's name, for example, like so:

```
var name = gadget.getName();
```

In addition to requesting existing named components, you can also request a brand new instance of a given component type. This can be useful when you want to use AJAX calls to add a new object to the server-side persistence, for example. The newInstance() method takes the name of a Seam component, makes a request to the server to create a new instance of the same type of component, generates a JavaScript client stub for the new component, and returns it. If we wanted a new Gadget object, for example, we could make the following JavaScript call in the web page:

```
var newGadget = Seam.Component.newInstance("gadget");
```

If you have a JavaScript reference to a component and need to know its component name, you can use the getComponentName() method:

```
var compName = Seam.Component.getComponentName(gadget);
```

This method is useful when you are passing JavaScript references between functions in the page and need to know whether a reference is a component reference or not. If the getComponentName() method returns null, the reference does not refer to a Seam component.

Seam.Remoting

The Seam.Remoting object provides lower-level remoting functions. Typically, you'll be using methods from the Seam.Component object in your JavaScript code, and these methods will in turn use the Seam.Remoting functions to implement the component-level functionality. But Seam.Remoting methods are available for you to use if needed.

The Seam.Remoting.createType() method can be used to create references to regular Java objects. While Seam.Component.newInstance() is used to create a new instance of a Seam component, Seam.Remoting.createType() is used to create noncomponent Java objects. The argument to createType() is the full classname of the object you want created. Seam will instantiate the object on the server, and then generate a JavaScript type stub for it on the client. In the Gadget Catalog object model, for example, the StatusCode class is an entity bean that is not marked as a Seam component. If we wanted to create a new `StatusCode` object and get a reference to it from the web client, we would do the following:

```
var statCode = Seam.Remoting.createType("org.jimfarley.gadgets.StatusCode");
```

If the call is successful, the `statCode` JavaScript variable will be a type stub for a new `StatusCode` entity bean created on the server. This can then be updated on the client and/or passed into component method calls through execution stubs.

The other useful method in `Seam.Remoting` is the `getTypeName()` method. This method will return the fully qualified classname for the server-side object reference passed into the method.

Implementing the Auto-Complete Search Box

After all that background on Seam remoting services, we can finally turn to implementing the auto-complete search box in the Gadget Catalog home page. For now, we are going to limit ourselves to using just the Seam JavaScript library and native browser JavaScript to implement a simple auto-complete function on the main home page in the Gadget Catalog. In the next section, we'll look at how Seam's remoting functions can be integrated with another AJAX library to implement more complex and interesting rich client elements.

In order to implement the auto-complete function, we need to do the following:

1. Capture the characters that the user types into the search input field as they are being typed.

2. Make a remote call to the `search()` method on the `gadgetAdmin` component, passing it the text the user has typed so far in the search box.

3. Take the returned list of matching `Gadget` objects and give the user the appropriate feedback in the page.

The first step is to add a JavaScript callback to the input field in the page that will be triggered whenever the user types text into the field. Our input field is just a JSF `inputText` control, so we can accomplish this by adding an `onkeyup` callback to the control:

```
<h:inputText id="gadgetSearch"
             value="#{gadgetAdmin.searchField}"
             onkeyup="searchGadgets();"/>
```

With this change, the `searchGadgets()` JavaScript function will be invoked whenever a key is released inside the input field. In the `searchGadgets()` JavaScript function, we'll need to pull the characters from the input field. This is typically done in AJAX contexts by pulling the `input` element from the DOM for the page and querying its `value` property. The simplest way to accomplish this is to put a unique ID value on the `input` element:

```
<html>
    . . .
    <input id="searchField" . . ./>
    . . .
</html>
```

Then in your JavaScript you can use the `getElementById()` method on the DOM to get the `input` element directly:

```
function searchGadgets() {
    var inputElement = document.getElementById("searchField");
    var txt = inputElement.value;
}
```

We can't use this approach directly, however, because we are using JSF controls, and JSF assigns its own internal unique ID to the HTML `input` element that it generates. We won't know what that ID will be at runtime, so we need to look up the input field some other way.

One trick that we can use is to wrap the JSF input control with a `div` tag with a unique ID that we assign:

```
<html>
    . . .
    <div id="searchFieldWrapper">
        <h:inputText id="gadgetSearch"
                     value="#{gadgetAdmin.searchField}"
                     onkeyup="searchGadgets();"/>
    </div>
    . . .
</html>
```

This allows us to easily "locate" the generated `input` element in the DOM by first looking up the `div` tag by ID, and then getting its child, which will be the input field:

```
function searchGadgets() {
    var divElement = document.getElementId("searchFieldWrapper");
    var inputElement = divElement.getElementsByTagName("input")[0];
    var txt = inputElement.value;
}
```

Once we have the user's text, we can then make our call to the gadgetAdmin
component to perform the search:

```
function searchGadgets() {
    var divElement = document.getElementId("searchFieldWrapper");
    var inputElement = divElement.getElementsByTagName("input")[0];
    var searchText = inputElement.value;
    var gadgetAdmin = Seam.Component.getInstance("gadgetAdmin");
    gadgetAdmin.search(searchText, searchGadgetsCallback);
}
```

The last argument to the search() method is our callback function, to be invoked
when the response is received. For our purposes, the callback function will take the list
of Gadget objects and provide feedback to the user. To keep things simple to start, we'll
just check the list, and if there is a single match in the list (i.e., the user has typed enough
text to target a single gadget in the catalog), we'll change the text in the input field to the
full name of the gadget. If there are multiple matches, we'll simply ignore them and not
do anything. Listing 8-2 shows our final pair of JavaScript functions—the searchGadgets()
function that receives the onkeyup events from the input field and the
searchGadgetsCallback() function that is called when the remote search() method
call gets a response.

Listing 8-2. *JavaScript for Basic Auto-Complete Enhancement*

```
<script type="text/javascript">
//<![CDATA[
function searchGadgets() {
    var divElement = document.getElementId("searchFieldWrapper");
    var inputElement = divElement.getElementsByTagName("input")[0];
    var searchText = inputElement.value;
    var gadgetAdmin = Seam.Component.getInstance("gadgetAdmin");
    gadgetAdmin.search(searchText, searchGadgetsCallback);
}

function searchGadgetsCallback(result) {
    var divElement = document.getElementId("searchFieldWrapper");
    var inputElement = divElement.getElementsByTagName("input")[0];
    if (result.length == 1) {
        searchField.value = result[0].getName();
    }
}
// ]]>
</script>
```

Notice that our `searchGadgetsCallback` function accepts a single argument, `results`. As mentioned in the section "Calling Remote Methods" earlier, Seam will map the return value from the remote method call into the appropriate JavaScript entities and pass them into the callback that was provided when the method call was requested. In this case, `GadgetAdminBean.search()` returns a list of `Gadget` objects, so this will be converted to a JavaScript array of objects mapped from the `Gadget` bean. In our `searchGadgetsCallback` earlier, we check the length of this array, and if it's a single gadget only, we take the name from the gadget and assign it as the value of the search input field.

Now, if the user types in enough text to match a single gadget in the catalog, our AJAX code will auto-complete the full gadget name, as shown in Figure 8-3.

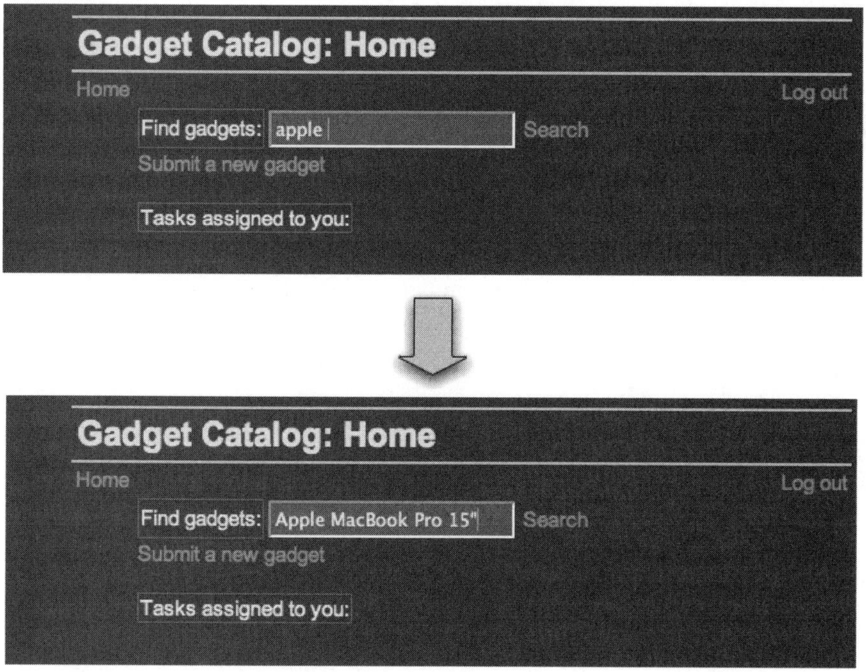

Figure 8-3. *Simple auto-complete enhancement*

Since the auto-complete function has ensured that the search matches a single gadget, the user can now hit the Search button and see a results page with just the gadget he or she wants. To make the experience a bit better, we can adjust the navigation rules to take the user directly to the gadget edit page if the search results contain a single gadget. I won't show those details here since it's just basic JSF manipulation, but you can see the changes to the `faces-config.xml` and `GadgetAdminBean.search()` action method in the downloadable code examples that accompany this book.

Integration with AJAX Libraries

Our simple auto-complete function is a good start, but there are a number of ways we could improve it. For one, it would be nice to show users multiple matches to the text they are typing in the search field, so that they can dynamically see their options narrowing as they type, and can pick the gadget they want as soon as it appears rather than typing more characters to try to get a single match. We'd like to show the matches in a dynamic drop-down menu as well.

We could go ahead and write our own DOM manipulation code in JavaScript to make these enhancements, but there are many, many AJAX libraries available (Script.aculo.us, Yahoo! UI, Google, etc.) that provide this functionality and much, much more. Why should we reinvent something that's already been done?

The complication we face is that we want to use Seam's remote services to make calls back to our Seam components, but we want to use an AJAX library to do the event handling and DOM manipulation. AJAX libraries provide their own client/server request handling (after all, asynchronous XML requests are a core part of AJAX), so we need to be able to unplug the AJAX communications from the library and plug in our remote component calls.

In some cases, this will be easy; in other cases, it will be difficult or even impossible, depending on how the library is designed. To demonstrate how this would be done in cases where the library supports it, we'll use the Yahoo! UI[2] AJAX library to enhance our search auto-complete feature. I won't go into deep details about how the Yahoo! UI library works. Instead, I'll just highlight the details relevant to our integration with Seam's remoting capabilities.

First of all, the auto-complete library in Yahoo! UI needs to know the field that is the source of the text for the auto-complete matching, and it needs a div tag that will be used to display the contents of the matches. We already devised a way to get the id attribute of our JSF-generated input field, so we're set on that front. We just need to insert a new, empty div tag as the target of the auto-complete match display:

```
<html>
    . . .
    <div id="searchFieldWrapper">
        <h:inputText value="#{gadgetAdmin.searchField}"/>
    </div>
    <div id="gadgetMatches"></div>
    . . .
</html>
```

---

2. The code in this section was written using version 2.2.2 of the Yahoo! UI AJAX library.

Notice that we've also removed the onkeyup JavaScript callback—the Yahoo! UI library is going to take care of all the event handling and display for us, so it's no longer needed.

Configuring the Yahoo! UI auto-complete feature involves two basic steps. First, you need to configure a data source that will be used to do the matching. Yahoo! UI comes bundled with several data source implementations, including ones that support client-side data arrays embedded in the page, AJAX calls over an HTTP connection, and so forth. For our purposes, we want to use a custom data source, one that uses Seam remoting to acquire the match data from our server-side Seam component.

The key method that we need to override on the Yahoo! UI DataSource object is doQuery(). This method performs the query against whatever data source is being used, and then invokes internal Yahoo! UI code to render the results in the page dynamically. We want doQuery() to make a Seam remoting call to our gadgetAdmin component rather than use one of the bundled query approaches, so we implement our version like so:

```
DS_SeamRemoting.prototype.doQuery = function(callback, query, parent) {
    var origCallback = callback;
    var instance = this;
    var callbackWrapper = function(results) {
        /* Put the results into the internal results cache */
        var resultObj = {};
        resultObj.results = results;
        instance._addCacheElem(resultObj);
        /* Fire an event to signal the arrival of new results */
        instance.getResultsEvent.fire(instance, parent, query, results);
        /* Invoke the callback passed in by the auto-complete library, to
            cause the auto-complete magic to happen */
        origCallback(query, results, parent);
    }
    var gadgetAdmin = Seam.Component.getInstance("gadgetAdmin");
    gadgetAdmin.seamComponent.search(query, callbackWrapper);
    return;
};
```

The bulk of the doQuery() method is setting up a wrapper callback that is a simplified version of the one used by the bundled DataSource versions in Yahoo! UI. Then we simply call our Seam remote method, using our wrapper callback as the callback for the remote call. Seam makes the remote call, and when the response is received, our callbackWrapper() function is called. In the function, we do some required Yahoo! UI housekeeping, and then we call the callback passed into the doQuery() method. This callback is provided by the auto-complete library and performs all the DOM manipulation needed to render the results to the user.

Finally, we need to configure an auto-complete object from the Yahoo! UI library, telling it to use our specialized DataSource, and also attaching it to the search field and the div tag to be used for the results display.

```
var divElement = document.getElementId("searchFieldWrapper");
var inputElement = divElement.getElementsByTagName("input")[0];
gadgetDS = new DS_SeamRemoting();
gadgetAC =
    new YAHOO.widget.AutoComplete(inputElement.id, 'gadgetMatches', gadgetDS);
gadgetAC.formatResult =
    function(oResultItem, sQuery) {
        var sMarkup = oResultItem.getName();
        return (sMarkup);
    };
```

The AutoComplete constructor takes three arguments: the ID of the input text field to use for the matching, the ID of a div tag to be used to display the auto-complete matches, and the DataSource to be used for the matching itself. We use the same trick we used earlier to find the ID of our input element, and we pass it in as the ID of the input element. We know the ID of the div tag since we inserted it directly into the HTML, so we just pass that in as a literal value. The DataSource is an instance of our custom subclass. The only other piece of integration work we need to do is specialize the formatResult() method on the AutoComplete object. The results coming back from our custom DataSource will be an array of mapped Gadget objects, so we need to adjust this method to call the appropriate method on the result items in order to get the text to display in the drop-down menu generated in the web page.

With all of this in place in our home page, the user will now see a nice drop-down list of possible matches as he or she types text into the search field, as shown in Figure 8-4.

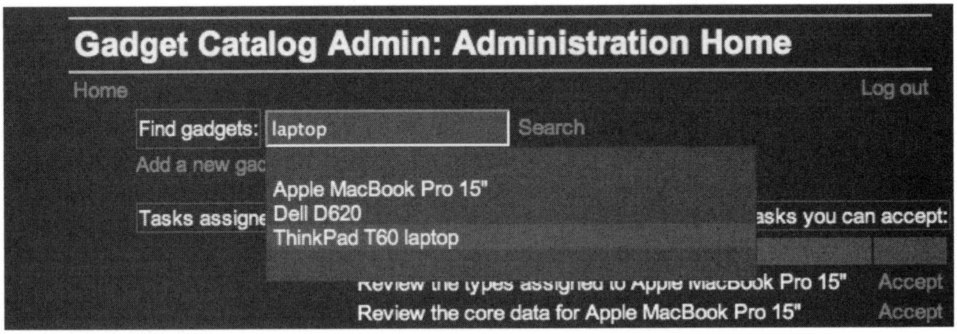

Figure 8-4. *Auto-complete using Seam remoting and Yahoo! UI*

There are any number of other rich client enhancements we could make to the Gadget Catalog interface using Seam remoting. We could, for example, create in-place editing of gadgets right from the search results page. The user could hover over a gadget in the list until an edit pane appeared, and changes he or she makes in the edit pane could be transferred back to the server using a Seam remote call to the `gadgetAdmin` component. The principles in these enhancements would be the same as what you've already seen, though.

Summary

In this chapter, we've explored the Seam remoting services and the ways that they enable you to integrate rich web features into your Seam applications.

Seam remoting services are a general-purpose tool for generating JavaScript stubs for your Seam components and other Java objects. But their most useful application is in AJAX contexts, where you want to incorporate more interactive UI elements and improve the user experience in your application. The exciting aspect of this is that Seam automatically creates a direct bridge between JavaScript in the browser and EJBs and JavaBeans running in the Seam application on the server. All the AJAX details are hidden from you by the Seam JavaScript library on the client and by the remoting services running in your application. You don't have to generate or consume any XML or JSON data directly (unless you really want to). Everything on the server side is Java; everything on the client is JavaScript objects and functions.

We examined the general model behind the Seam remoting services, and you saw how to configure the server to run the remoting services. You also saw how to load the required JavaScript in the browser using the Seam Resource Servlet. Then we used the Seam remoting services to add auto-complete features on the search fields in the Gadget Catalog. We did this in two ways: first we did a simple version using just the JavaScript generated by Seam, and then we implemented a richer version by integrating the Seam JavaScript code with the Yahoo! UI library and its auto-complete objects.

Index

You Need the Companion eBook

Your purchase of this book entitles you to buy the companion PDF-version eBook for only $10. Take the weightless companion with you anywhere.

We believe this Apress title will prove so indispensable that you'll want to carry it with you everywhere, which is why we are offering the companion eBook (in PDF format) for $10 to customers who purchase this book now. Convenient and fully searchable, the PDF version of any content-rich, page-heavy Apress book makes a valuable addition to your programming library. You can easily find and copy code—or perform examples by quickly toggling between instructions and the application. Even simultaneously tackling a donut, diet soda, and complex code becomes simplified with hands-free eBooks!

Once you purchase your book, getting the $10 companion eBook is simple:

❶ Visit **www.apress.com/promo/tendollars/**.

❷ Complete a basic registration form to receive a randomly generated question about this title.

❸ Answer the question correctly in 60 seconds, and you will receive a promotional code to redeem for the $10.00 eBook.

THE EXPERT'S VOICE™

2855 TELEGRAPH AVENUE | SUITE 600 | BERKELEY, CA 94705

Offer valid through 1/08.